Math *Can* Be Easy!

Tackle common math problems:
• Determine the gas mileage of your car • Calculate your caloric intake from FDA food labels • Convert a recipe from eight servings to ten • Compute the *true* interest rate of your credit card • Demystify the prime rate and consumer price index.

Do mental math on the spot:
• Calculate discounts, markups, and sales tax • Multiply and divide with numbers in the millions, billions, and trillions • Convert from centigrade to Fahrenheit • Round off the right restaurant tip.

Master probability, odds, and statistics:
• What are the odds that your next two children will both be boys? • Which games should you play when you go to a casino? • What is the significance of polls and their margin of error? • What is the bell curve and what does its standard deviation tell you? • Do men or women have more sex partners? The answers may surprise you!

everyday
MATH
for
everyday
Life

everyday

MATH

for

everyday

Life

A Handbook for
When It Just Doesn't Add Up

MARK RYAN

WARNER BOOKS

An AOL Time Warner Company

Copyright © 2002 by The Math Center, Inc.
All rights reserved.

Warner Books, Inc., 1271 Avenue of the Americas, New York, NY 10020

Visit our Web site at www.twbookmark.com.

 An AOL Time Warner Company

Printed in the United States of America

First Printing: December 2002

10 9 8 7 6 5 4 3 2 1

Library of Congress Cataloging-in-Publication Data

Ryan, Mark.
    Everyday math for everyday life : a handbook for when it just doesn't add up / Mark Ryan.
        p. cm
    Includes index.
    ISBN 0-446-67726-4
      1. Mathematics—Popular works. I. Title.

    QA93 .R93 2002
    510—dc21   2002069027

Book design and text composition by H. Roberts Design
Cover design by Brigid Pearson.

For my mother and in memory of my father.
They taught me by word and example
the love of learning.

Acknowledgments

This book would not exist if it wasn't for the efforts of my agent, Sheree Bykofsky—many thanks. My editors at Warner Books, Katharine Rapkin and Karen Melnyk, made many needed improvements to the book; editor Jessica Papin gave the project the right direction in its early stages; Brigid Pearson created a beautiful cover; I'm grateful to production editor Mari Okuda for her professionalism and good humor; production manager Anna Maria Piluso did excellent work, as did managing editor Bob Castillo; and Roland Ottewell's copyediting was virtually flawless. Everyone at Warner Books has obvious high standards. And H. Roberts Design created a handsome book.

My typist, Jerilyn Schumacher (1946–2001), did meticulous work. The intelligence and thoroughness of my research assistant, Elizabeth Dickey, made my work much easier. Former students of mine, Claire Adams, Shana Franklin, and Justin Platt, have been valuable assistants. I'm also grateful to Sharon Blue Spruce, Charles Downing, Alison Drumm, Ben Leech, Josh Lowitz, Mike Lukasiewiez, John Nilson, Josh Radinsky, and Aaron Retica.

Attorney Robert Stein made critical improvements to my author-publisher contract.

The book is markedly better because of the suggestions of many friends who read portions of my manuscript. Many thanks to Roland Dieter (for his help with chapters 11 and 12), Henry Fetta, Cory Franklin, Tom Frederick, Warren Hawley, Jake Jacobs, Art Kupferman, Richard and Virgina Lombardi, Barry Sullivan, and John Wick.

My sister, Ellen Ryan Mardiks, and my brother-in-law, Steve Mardiks, have been a great help with this and all of my writing projects. Their writing talents and sound judgment make them invaluable sounding boards. I consult with my friend Ted Lowitz on all of my projects. Whether it's a writing question, an aesthetic choice, or a business decision, it's difficult for me to sign off on anything before I run it by him.

Lastly, a special thanks to Leah Radinsky. She read my entire manuscript twice, and made countless significant improvements to the book. She has a great eye for detail and a great sense of the big picture. Her support has increased my productivity and enhanced my creativity.

Contents

Introduction

Like it or not, math is here to stay. We live in a world of percentages, statistics, interest rates, and taxes. The Dow goes up 3 percent, the NASDAQ drops 5 percent. The inflation rate is such-and-such a percent, the trade deficit is so many billions, and the national debt is so many trillions. And how big of a tip should you leave? You just can't get away from numbers.

My aim in writing this book is to give you an easy-to-follow guide to the math you encounter in your everyday life. I hope this single volume will become the first resource you turn to for all your mathematical or numerical questions. The topics range from the simple—how to solve a percentage problem, how to figure a tip, how to balance your checkbook—to the complex—the formula for the present value of an annuity, an installment loan formula, and believe it or not, a simple explanation of Einstein's famous formula, $E = mc^2$. You will also find here important numerical facts and definitions: everything from the definitions of gross domestic product and the federal deficit to windchill and heat index tables and the meaning of barometric pressure. Regardless of the complexity of the topic, all explanations are in plain English with a minimum of technical jargon.

The first part of the book is a review of all the math topics you need in your day-to-day life. This is *not* a review of high school mathematics. High school math teachers often try to persuade students that what they're studying will prove useful, but let's face it, students are generally on the mark when they ask rhetorically, "When are we ever going to use this?" Few adults will ever need to use geometry proofs, trigonometry, advanced algebra, pre-calculus, or calculus. In fact, although simple algebra can come in handy, you can really get by without it.

Here are topics you do need. *Basic arithmetic* (chapter 1) is useful for doing things like balancing your checkbook and dealing with big numbers in the millions and billions. *Fractions, decimals, and percents* (chapter 2) have endless applications: cooking, tipping, discounts, markups, mortgage rates, investments, etc. You use *ratios and proportions* (chapter 3) whenever you change the scale of something, like with a scale drawing or a map, or when you adjust a recipe for different numbers of people. You will want to have a basic understanding of *powers* (like $3^2 = 3 \times 3 = 9$) and *roots* (like $\sqrt{9} = 3$) to be able to work with financial formulas, among other things (chapter 4).

Another fundamental is *basic geometry* (chapter 5)—shapes are all around us, and every adult should understand the few simple formulas for perimeter, area, and volume, and the various units of measure for these quantities: inches, feet, miles, square feet, square yards, acres, cubic feet, gallons, etc. Sample problems include estimating how many square yards of carpeting you'll need to buy, and figuring the amount of fertilizer you need for your lawn. Chapter 6 will review the many units of *measurement* in the U.S. and metric systems and how to calculate *conversions* within each system and from one system to the other. You need to have a basic understanding of *probability and odds* (chapter 7) for gambling, dice games, card games, and the lottery, and to grasp the meaning of statements like "there's a 25 percent chance of rain tomorrow," or the often-quoted probability that a woman has a one-in-nine chance of contracting breast cancer sometime in her life. The media inundates us with medical studies, opinion polls, political polls, etc., and thus we need a basic understanding of *statistics* (chapter 8) to separate the wheat from the chaff. Chapter 9 will explain the ways in which *charts and graphs* we see in the media are often misleading.

If you read part I carefully, I'm confident that you will come away with the feeling that you can handle most, if not all, of the math problems you encounter in your day-to-day life. Those of you who do not need this mathematics refresher course can skip part I or read only the chapters you need.

Parts II, III, and IV contain straightforward explanations of a hundred or so frequently encountered practical math problems. Simply look up your math question in the table of contents or the index. You'll find here explanations of things like converting between U.S. dollars and foreign currency, tips for helping your children with math, explanations of casino games, calculating mortgage payments, understanding credit card rates, and how to compute a pitcher's earned run average.

Do the Math

One of my objectives is to give you the tools you need to become mathematically self-reliant, so that as you go about your day-to-day affairs, you'll consider the math when making your decisions. You should know, for example, that flying from Chicago to Miami is *much* safer than driving. You may decide to drive anyway, for any number of reasons—the scenery, you enjoy driving, etc.—but you should know the relative accident statistics. You should be aware that if you carry a large credit card debt (at, say, a 19.8 percent APR) month after month without paying down the debt, you are throwing money down the drain at a truly alarming rate. When you do the math, you'll see that it rarely makes sense to take advantage of the "convenience" of a credit card unless you know that you'll be able to pay the balance down to zero in the near future. You may decide to buy that new computer or big-screen TV anyway, but you should be aware of the financial implications. Before you decide to buy a low-deductible health insurance plan—so that you'll "never have to worry about medical bills again"—you should know that you'll probably come out ahead if you buy a high-deductible plan. Before you go to the casino, you should know that roulette and craps are games of luck, not skill, and that the odds are against you. When it comes to math, ignorance is *not* bliss.

Then Ignore the Math

You should do the math, but the math won't always give you the answer you seek. Say you're buying a house and you've narrowed your choices down to two homes. The most important factors to you are location, price, the neighborhood, and the quality of the schools. You rate each of these two homes on each of the four factors, on a scale from 1 to 10, and house A comes out ahead of house B on three of the four factors, or even on all four factors, yet for some unexplained reason you still prefer house B. What should you do? Go with the math or your gut? *Go with your gut.* Why ignore your careful analysis? I suspect that what happens in situations like this is that we're subconsciously considering more factors or assigning them different weights than we are aware of or are able to articulate. Let's say house B came out on top only on the schools issue and only by a little. If you nevertheless prefer house B, it may be because you are aware subconsciously that the schools factor is more important than the other three combined. What if you prefer house B even when house A comes out ahead on all four factors? The likely explanation is that one or more factors that you weren't aware of or had decided weren't important or "shouldn't" be important—like a beautiful porch or the number of trees on the property—really *are* important to you.

Now, does this mean that your analysis was a waste of time? Not at all. If you had not done any analysis and had made your decision only on instinct, you might end up in the wrong house. Let's say you don't have any children yet but are planning to raise a family, and thus you absentmindedly neglect to consider the schools issue. If you buy the house you like and then later learn that the schools are the worst in the country, you will wish you had done a thorough analysis before buying. The moral of the story is that in complex situations like this, you should do the math *and* listen to your gut instincts. Both are important. You can't make an informed decision unless you do the math. And you should also listen to your instincts because, in the words of mathematician and philosopher Blaise Pascal, "The heart has its reasons."

A Note on Calculator Use, Mental Computation, and Estimation

Calculators are great. I have several, I use them often, and couldn't get along without them. Everyone should know how to use them. They're fast, they never make mistakes—assuming, of course, that you punch the right buttons—and there are many math problems that are either too difficult or too time-consuming to do by hand. Throughout this book, I'll go through the calculator steps needed for solving various problems. *But,* I think it's unwise to use a calculator for every computation you do. When you use calculators for even the simplest of computations, your math muscles atrophy and you are more likely to view mathematics as a foreign, mysterious language that you will never really understand, an esoteric code that only a calculator can "understand." In contrast, when you work with numbers mentally or with pencil and paper, you strengthen your facility for math, and math will gradually come to make more and more sense to you. You will learn that you can do math with your common sense.

If you have forgotten the times table up to 9 times 9—perhaps because you have been using a calculator even for problems like 9 times 4 or 8 times 6—you owe it to yourself to relearn it. You should also be able to multiply numbers like 40 times 25 in your head. Four quarters make a dollar, right? So, of course, 4 times 25 is 100, and since 40 is 10 times as big as 4, the answer is 10 times as big as 100, or 1000. And 30 times 120 should be easy to do mentally: multiply 3 by 12 to get 36 and then add two zeros to get 3600. What about ¼ of 120?—half of 120 is 60, and half of that is 30. When you take a few seconds to think about how problems like this work rather than just pushing buttons on your calculator, your confidence in your math abilities will grow.

In the final analysis, you should do what's comfortable for you. It won't be the end of the world if you decide to use a calculator even for 2 times 3 or 5 times 4. It certainly is reassuring to know

Calculator Models

I strongly recommend that you get a calculator like Texas Instruments' TI-34 II (about $15 to $20). It has several great features and is easy to use. Unlike most calculators, it has two lines to display: one for the problem you enter and one for the answer it gives you. This allows you to check whether you've entered the entire problem correctly, and also to see the problem and the answer at the same time—and that can make a big difference. It also has buttons that will convert between fractions, decimals, and percents—like ⅕ = 0.2 = 20%—and between mixed numbers and improper fractions—like 3¼ = ¹³⁄₄. It will also add fractions, reduce fractions, and give you the remainder when you divide numbers. And it probably has every other feature you're likely to need. Whatever calculator you choose, try to find one with all or most of the above capabilities. If you'll be doing a lot of financial math (present value, future value, annuity and amortization formulas, etc.), you might also want to pick up a business calculator. Texas Instruments' BA-35 Solar is a good one (about $20 to $25).

that the calculator can't err. And if you're working on an important project where accuracy is absolutely critical, it may make sense to use the calculator, or at least to use it to check your answers. But your confidence and competence in mathematics will likely increase if, at least for the easy stuff, *you* do the math.

Whether you do a problem in your head, on paper, or with a calculator, it's a good idea to also estimate a rough answer to the problem. Estimating builds confidence in math because when you estimate, you have to rely on your own grasp of a problem rather than just following memorized rules and formulas. Estimating is also a good way to catch errors. You shouldn't just blindly accept the answer you get with pencil and paper or with a calculator. Make sure that the answer agrees with your estimate and that it doesn't fly in the face of common sense. If you don't have a rough idea of what kind of answer to expect, you might push the wrong button on your calculator, get a ridiculous answer, and not realize that it's wrong.

A Few Suggestions to Those Who Never Liked Math or Whose Math Is Rusty

Whether you have never liked math or feel that you've forgotten most of the math you learned in high school, I'm confident that if you work through part I of this book patiently and thoroughly, you'll come away with a solid grasp of all the mathematics you need for practical math problems. Even if you've always hated math, you'll find that the math presented in part I is manageable. You may find that my explanations bring math down to earth and make it easier to grasp than you experienced in school.

There are many reasons for not liking math—for feeling like a fish out of water whenever you deal with numbers. You may have had a bad experience in school that made you feel that you weren't good at math. You may have found math boring, meaningless, or irrelevant—and it's difficult to learn anything we believe is unimportant to us—or your teachers or parents may not have pushed you to succeed in math. And, for girls and women, although things are getting better all the time, there still remains in our culture a gender bias that expects more of boys than girls when it comes to math, science, and technology. The good news is that once you have a real desire to learn mathematics, none of the above will matter much. Everyone can learn math, we're hardwired for it.

When the right approach is taken, math is something we can grasp with our common sense; it need not seem strange or esoteric. Two strategies that make math easier, for example, are to *make math concrete* and to *learn why things are true*. Math concepts make more sense to us when we see the connection between what may seem like a foreign or abstract rule or formula and the concrete reality of the world around us. For example, adding, subtracting, multiplying, and dividing negative numbers confuse some people. This is understandable because negative numbers can seem abstract—we can't have -5 apples, for example. Some people might be confused about how to add -8 and -5. For example, they might mistakenly use the *multiplication* rule that *two negatives make a positive* for this *addition* problem. But this problem needn't involve learning or remembering any abstract rules. You can think of negative numbers like debt. Two negatives add up to a bigger negative in precisely the same way that two debts add up to a bigger debt. That's all there is to it. When you make connections like this between seemingly strange math concepts and the familiar things from your day-to-day life, math gets so much easier.

Learning why things are true also makes math easier to grasp. For example, do you remember the formula for the area of a triangle? No? I'm shocked! It's *Area* = ½ × *base* × *height*, or $A = \frac{1}{2}bh$. Now, *why* does this formula work? Consider the diagram below:

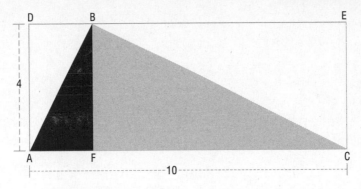

$$Area_{\text{rectangle ADEC}} = base \times height \text{ (or } length \times width\text{)}$$
$$= 10 \times 4$$
$$= 40$$

$$Area_{\text{triangle ABC}} = \frac{1}{2} \times base \times height$$

$$= \frac{1}{2} \times 10 \times 4$$

$$= 20$$

We can see that the area of the triangle is half of the area of the rectangle because triangle ABF (shaded black) is half of the rectangle on the left (rectangle ADBF), and triangle FBC (shaded gray) is half of the rectangle on the right (rectangle FBEC). Therefore, since the area of a rectangle equals *base* times *height* (which means the same thing as *length* times *width*), the area of a triangle must be half of that, or half of *base* times *height*. In short, the formula for the area of a triangle is based on the simple fact that a triangle takes up half the area of a rectangle. When you learn the logic underlying mathematical ideas like these, math becomes far less intimidating.

PART I

Getting Back to Basics

Your instincts years ago were right. Most of what you learned in high school math you *don't* need, namely, most of algebra, geometry proofs, trigonometry, and calculus. What you *do* need is the math you studied through sixth or seventh grade—basic arithmetic, fractions, decimals, percentages, ratios, proportions, simple geometry, and some facility for estimating, mental computation, and calculator use. You also need a few high school topics such as powers and roots, which are used frequently in financial math. And probability, odds, and statistics are necessary to understand games of chance, as well as the many studies and surveys we see in the media. Are you ready? Let's get started.

CHAPTER 1

The Fundamentals

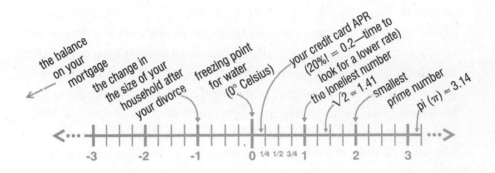

Take a good look at this number line. It's the foundation for everything in this book and, if you've never liked math, the source of your frustrations. There they are, the numbers—the building blocks of mathematics. All the numbers are there: your height, weight, and age, your annual income, your mortgage balance and credit card interest rate, the number of stars in the Milky Way galaxy, and the weight of a proton. (Actually, there are numbers that can't be found on the number line. These so-called imaginary numbers are used in electrical engineering, among other things. But since this is a book of practical math, let's not go there.) Let's review the basic types of numbers.

Whole numbers, integers, fractions, and decimals. The *whole* numbers are 0, 1, 2, 3, . . . and so on. The whole numbers and their opposites (negative numbers) are called *integers*, that is . . . -3, -2, -1, 0, 1, 2, 3, . . . *Fractions* and *decimals* are all the numbers in

3

between the integers: numbers like -⅗, -0.00126, ¹⁄₁₀₀ (or 1%), 2.8, and π (the Greek letter "pi"), which equals approximately 3.14. Fractions and decimals are obviously of great practical importance. We use them whenever we're dealing with a fraction or a percentage of something.

Negative numbers. To the left of zero are, of course, the *negative* numbers. In a sense, negative numbers seem strange and abstract—how can there be less than nothing? (This bizarre quality of the negative numbers may explain why as late as the seventeenth century, two millennia after the sophisticated mathematics of the Babylonians, Chinese, and Greeks, there was disagreement over whether negative numbers were legitimate.)[1] In another sense, however, negative numbers are quite ordinary and practical. How can we have less than nothing? When we're in debt. One of the easiest ways of understanding the arithmetic of positive and negative numbers is by using the analogy of money and debt.

Prime numbers. The *prime* numbers are numbers that can't be divided evenly by any other numbers. For example, 28 is not prime, because 2, 4, 7, and 14 all go into 28. But 17 is prime, because no numbers go into it except for 1 and 17 itself. The first several prime numbers are 2, 3, 5, 7, 11, 13, 17, 19, 23 . . . and so on. Prime numbers have always interested mathematicians. It was proven, for example, over two thousand years ago that the list of prime numbers never ends. They remain an important topic, but they have very little practical significance. With the exception of the small ones like 2, 3, 5, and 7, we rarely see prime numbers in everyday life, for several reasons. We live in a world of round numbers (100 cents in a dollar, 60 minutes in an hour, etc.), repetition (the eight-hour workday is repeated five times, resulting in a forty-hour work-week, and since 8 times 5 is 40, 40 is not prime), and things that

---

[1] Morris Kline, *Mathematics, the Loss of Certainty* (Oxford University Press, 1980), 114–15.

Negative Numbers

When you learned the rules for negative numbers in math class, they may not have made sense to you. You may have felt that you simply had to take them on faith and memorize them. But when you see the connection between positive and negative numbers and money and debt, the rules agree with what your common sense tells you. Why does -10 plus -5 equal -15? Because if you have a $10 debt and a $5 debt, altogether you're $15 in debt. Now, say you have a checking account or a debit card that allows you to carry a positive or a negative balance. Why does 10 minus 40 equal -30? Because if you have a $10 balance, then spend $40, your new balance will be -$30. Why does -50 minus 20 equal -70? Because if your balance is -$50 and then you spend $20, your new balance will be -$70. Why does 20 minus -30 equal 50? To subtract means to take away, so subtracting a negative is like taking away a debt or debit. Say your checking account balance is $20 after an erroneous $30 charge was made against your account. When you bring this error to the bank's attention, they will take away the $30 debit and your balance will go up to $50. And that's why subtracting a negative is the same as adding a positive. One last example: why does a positive times a negative equal a negative? Why, for example, does 6 times -5 equal -30? Well, multiplication is repeated addition, that is, 6 times 5 equals 5 + 5 + 5 + 5 + 5 + 5 (6 times), which adds up to 30. Therefore, 6 times -5 is like adding up six $5 debts: -$5 + -$5 + -$5 + -$5 + -$5 + -$5 (6 times), which comes to $30.

Another good analogy for positive and negative numbers is temperatures above and below zero on a thermometer. A thermometer is just like the number line standing straight up. So -5 minus 10 equals -15 because if it's 5 below zero and the temperature falls 10 degrees, it will then be 15 below zero. And -12 plus 8 equals -4 because if it's 12 below zero and the temperature goes up 8 degrees, the new temperature will be 4 below zero. Using the analogies of money and debt or temperatures can make negative numbers much easier to grasp. And, by the way, this is a great way to help your children understand negative numbers.

are arranged in equal rows (try buying a box of candy with a prime number of pieces). For everyday math, you do not need to concern yourself with prime numbers.

Rational and irrational numbers. Lastly, all numbers on the number line are either *rational* or *irrational*. Rational numbers are those that can be expressed as a fraction. Numbers like ⅒, ½, and ¾ are rational, as are 4½ (because it can be written as 9⁄2) and 5 (because it can be written as 5⁄1). Decimals that terminate, like 0.2 and 3.8, are also rational, because they can also be expressed as fractions—0.2 equals 2⁄10 or ⅕; and 3.8 equals 3 8⁄10, which equals 38⁄10. Conversely, the *irrational* numbers are those like $\sqrt{2}$ and π that can't be expressed exactly as fractions: $\sqrt{2}$ equals 1.414213 . . . ; π equals 3.141592 . . . , which is very close to 22⁄7, but no fraction is *exactly* equal to π. Irrational numbers like this are decimals that go on forever without a repeating pattern of digits. If there is a repeating pattern, as in 0.3333 . . . , which equals ⅓, then the number is rational. (To explain this any further would be definitely *irrational*.)

Like prime numbers, irrational numbers have little practical significance. In fact, it's almost impossible to use irrational numbers in the real world because we can't measure anything to the accuracy of a decimal number that goes on indefinitely, and we can't use a never-ending decimal in a calculation. Irrational numbers are thus theoretical numbers for pure mathematics. (So why am I telling you about them? I'm a math teacher—I can't help it!) In the everyday world, we don't need accuracy beyond a couple or a few decimal points. And when you round off an irrational number to a couple decimal points, it becomes a rational number. For example, if you need to know the circumference of a circle that is 5 feet across, you use the formula *Circumference* = π × *diameter*, and you can round off π (an *irrational* number) to 3.14 (a *rational* number). The circumference will be approximately 3.14 × 5, or 15.7 feet, and your answer will be good enough.

$$\pi \approx \frac{22}{7} \approx \frac{355}{113}$$

Pi (π) equals about 3.14. To 10 decimal places, it equals 3.1415926535 . . . The decimal never ends. (If you're curious, you can probably find a Web site that shows pi to 1000 or 10,000 decimal places.) The fraction $^{22}/_{7}$, which equals about 3.143, is a good approximation of pi and is certainly close enough for any problem you might want to do. I find it remarkable that as far back as the fifth century A.D., Tsu Chung-Chin discovered the *much* better approximation of $^{355}/_{113}$, which equals about 3.1415929 and is within one hundred-thousandth of 1 percent of pi! I'd like to know how he did it.

More Rational or Irrational Numbers?

Irrational numbers may be impractical, but they certainly are plentiful. Consider the numbers between zero and one. It's very easy to show that there are an infinite number of rational numbers in this interval. There's ½, ⅓, ¼, ⅕, etc. This list goes on forever. Then there's ⅔, ¾, ⅘, ⅚, etc., not to mention others like $^{3}/_{7}$, $^{58}/_{101}$, etc., etc. So the number of rational numbers is infinite. That's quite a lot, wouldn't you say? *But,* it turns out that not only is the number of irrational numbers between zero and one also infinite, it's an infinity of a higher order—yes, there are in fact different levels of infinity. And get this—there are so many more irrationals than rationals, that if you were to pick a number between zero and one at random, it's not merely very likely that you'd pick an irrational number, the probability of picking an irrational is actually 100 percent! And, thus, the probability of choosing a rational number is zero percent! Hard to believe, but true.

Well, enough about numbers you'll never use. Let's return to ordinary, everyday numbers.

Addition, Subtraction, Multiplication, and Division

I hesitated putting a discussion of addition, subtraction, multiplication, and division in this book, thinking this material was too basic. And on top of that, most people will use a calculator to, say, add a long column of numbers or multiply 37 by 62 or divide 300 by 22. But, as I mentioned in the preceding "Note on Calculator Use," if you've forgotten how to add, subtract, multiply, or divide on paper, you really owe it to yourself to relearn these basic operations. And you might want to review these topics so you can help your kids with them. Enough throat-clearing? Okay, here we go.

ADDITION

Let's add the following numbers:

Step 1) Add the numbers in the ones column:

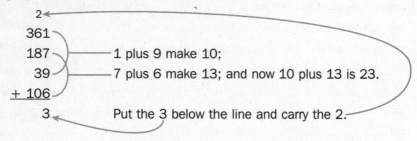

```
     2
   361
   187 ─── 1 plus 9 make 10;
    39 ─── 7 plus 6 make 13; and now 10 plus 13 is 23.
 + 106
     3      Put the 3 below the line and carry the 2.
```

(Note: looking for groups of numbers that add up to ten [like the 1 and 9 in the ones column] saves time and reduces errors.)

Step 2) Add the numbers in the tens column:

```
  12
 361          2 and 8 make 10;
 187          6 and 3 make 9;
  39          and then 10 plus 9 is 19.
+106          Put the 9 below the line and carry the 1.
 693
```

Step 3) Add the numbers in the hundreds column:

1 + 3 + 1 + 1 equal 6.
Put the 6 below the line
and we've got our answer: 693.

SUBTRACTION

Now let's subtract 357 from 6031.

```
 6031
-357
```

Step 1) In the ones column we want to take away 7 from 1, which is impossible, so we must "borrow" 1 ten from the 3 tens in the tens column. This leaves 2 tens in the tens column and turns the 1 in the ones column into 11 (because 1 plus 10 is 11). (By the way, to call this "borrowing" is about as accurate as when we ask someone to "borrow" a sheet of paper. This is *taking,* not borrowing.) Why does this "borrowing" work? Because all we're doing is rewriting the original number in a way that's different from but equivalent to the original number: 6031 equals 6000 plus 30 plus 1. After "borrowing" the ten, we now have 6000 plus 20 plus 11, which still adds up to 6031. So far, we've got the following:

$$
\begin{array}{r}
2\,11 \\
6\,0\,3\,1 \\
-\;3\,5\,7 \\
\end{array}
$$

Step 2) Now take 7 away from 11 and write the answer, 4, below the line:

$$
\begin{array}{r}
2\,11 \\
6\,0\,3\,1 \\
-\;3\,5\,7 \\
\hline
4
\end{array}
$$

Step 3) Now we'd like to take 5 away from 2 in the tens column, but, again, this is impossible, so we have to borrow from the hundreds column. This time, however, since there is a zero in the hundreds column, and since you can't take blood from a turnip, we can't borrow yet. First, we have to borrow a thousand from the 6 thousands in the thousands column. (This works because we're taking away a thousand from the thousands column and adding 10 hundreds [which equals a thousand] to the hundreds column.) See below:

$$
\begin{array}{r}
5\,10\;\;2\;\;11 \\
6\,0\,3\,1 \\
-\;3\,5\,7 \\
\hline
4
\end{array}
$$

Step 4) Now we can borrow what we need for the tens column. We borrow 1 hundred from the 10 hundreds in the hundreds column, leaving 9 hundreds in the hundreds column and turning the 2 in the tens column into a 12 (we're taking away 1 hundred from the hundreds column and adding 10 tens [which equals 1 hundred] to the tens column). We've arrived at the following:

9 12

5 1̸0 2̸ 11

6̸0̸3̸1̸

−357

4

Now we can do the final subtraction:

Step 5) 5 from 12 is 7,
3 from 9 is 6,
and we bring down the 5 in the
thousands column because there
are no thousands in 357 and thus no
thousands to take away from the 5.
So there it is: 6031 minus 357 equals 5674.

9 12

5 1̸0 2̸ 11

6̸0̸3̸1̸

−357

5674

MULTIPLICATION

Now for multiplication. Before you can do long multiplication, you've got to learn the times table. If you know the times table up to 9 times 9, skip this discussion. If you've forgotten some or all of the products up to 9 times 9 (I'm shocked!), you can either memorize the table (it's only 36 numbers) or use the tips and shortcuts discussed below. But before we get to the times table, let's review the definition of multiplication: multiplication is repeated addition. In other words, 3 times 12 means the same thing as three 12s, or 12 plus 12 plus 12. Using this definition, you could reconstruct the full table or parts of it if you forget some products. For example, let's say you forget what 6 times 7 is. You can get the answer by simply adding up six 7s: $7 + 7 + 7 + 7 + 7 + 7 = 42$.

Here's the table:

×	2	3	4	5	6	7	8	9
2	4							
3	6	9						
4	8	12	16					
5	10	15	20	25				
6	12	18	24	30	36			
7	14	21	28	35	42	49		
8	16	24	32	40	48	56	64	
9	18	27	36	45	54	63	72	81

Multiplying by 2. This is easy. Two times something is the same as doubling it or adding it to itself. For example, 2 times 7 is the same as 7 plus 7, which, of course, equals 14. If you want some help for memorizing even this simple fact (I'm shocked again!), here's a tip: think about money; $7 plus $7 is a $5 bill and two singles plus another $5 bill and two more singles, for a total of 2 fives and 4 singles, or $14. (By the way, converting numbers into money like this is a great aid to doing math in your head.) The other products involving a 2 are equally easy.

Multiplying by 5. This is also simple. One way to multiply by 5 is to simply count by fives: 5, 10, 15, 20, 25, 30, 35, 40, 45. Or you can use the fact that 5 times an even number ends in a zero, and 5 times an odd number ends in a 5. Now, consider money again: 7 times 5 is 35 because seven 5s is one more than six 5s, and six $5 bills is the same as three $10 bills, which comes to $30. Then the seventh $5 bill brings the total to $35.

Multiplying by 9. There are several simple patterns that make multiplying by 9 a snap. Consider the last row of the products in the table: 18, 27, 36, 45, 54, 63, 72, and 81. The first pattern is that the tens digit in the product is one less than the number we're multiplying by 9. For example, the answer to 9 times 6 (54) begins with a 5 (one less than 6), and the answer to 9 times 8 (72) begins with a 7 (one less than 8). The second pattern is the fact that the digits in each of the products add up to 9: the 1 and the 8 in 18 add up to 9, the 2 and the 7 in 27 add up to 9, etc. Let's do a couple products. If we want to multiply 9 by 7, we know that the answer will begin with a 6 (one less than 7) and that the answer must end with the number that when added to 6 makes 9. Since 6 plus 3 equals 9, the answer is 63. Nine times 8 must begin with a 7 (one less than 8), and since 7 plus 2 is 9, the answer is 72.

There are a couple more patterns about the 9's products:

$$18, 27, 36, 45, 54, 63, 72, 81$$

First, the tens digits increase from left to right (1, 2, 3, 4, etc.) and the ones digits decrease from left to right (8, 7, 6, 5, etc.). And second, this list of products is a palindrome! In other words, it's precisely the same read forwards or backwards, like the Napoleonic palindrome: "Able was I ere I saw Elba."

Multiplying by 4 and 8. To multiply a number by 4, you just double the number then double the result. To multiply by 8, you just double three times. For example, to multiply 6 by 4, just double 6 (that's 12), then double 12 (that's 24). To multiply 7 by 8, double 7 (14), then double 14 (28), then double 28 (56).

Well, that takes care of all but six numbers on the table. I don't have any tips for these, so you'll have to memorize them: $3 \times 3 = 9$, $3 \times 6 = 18$, $3 \times 7 = 21$, $6 \times 6 = 36$, $6 \times 7 = 42$, and $7 \times 7 = 49$.

Long Multiplication
This process is very easy once you've learned the times table. Let's multiply 6817 by 524.

$$
\begin{array}{r}
6817 \\
\times\ 524 \\
\hline
\end{array}
$$

Step 1) We multiply 6817 by the 4 in 524; 4 times 7 is 28, so we write
the 8 below the 4 and carry the 2. See below.

$$
\begin{array}{r}
2 \\
6817 \\
\times\ 524 \\
\hline
8
\end{array}
$$

Now we multiply 4 by 1, which equals 4, and add the 2 we carried, giving us 6. Write the 6 next to the 8, and this time there's
nothing to carry since our answer, 6, is only a single digit.

$$
\begin{array}{r}
2 \\
6817 \\
\times\ 524 \\
\hline
68
\end{array}
$$

Next comes 4 times 8, which is 32, so write the 2 next to the 6
and carry the 3 (above the 6 in 6817). Finally, multiply 4 by 6 and
add the 3 we carried; this comes to 27. Now, we would usually
write down the 7 in the bottom row and carry the 2, but this time,
since 6 is the leftmost digit in 6817, we write all of 27 below the
line. See below.

$$
\begin{array}{r}
3\ \ 2 \\
6817 \\
\times\ 524 \\
\hline
27268
\end{array}
$$

Step 2) Now we multiply 6817 by the 2 in 524. Since this 2 is really 20,
or 2 *tens,* we write the first number we obtain in the tens column
(below the 6 in 27268). First is 2 times 7, or 14. Write the 4
below the 6 and carry the 1. See below.

$$\begin{array}{r} \overset{\overset{1}{\cancel{2}}}{6817} \\ \times\ 524 \\ \hline 27268 \\ 4 \end{array}$$

Notice that when we carry the 1, we cross out the 2 we had carried earlier so that we keep things straight. Now continue multiplying from right to left: 2 times 1 is 2 plus the 1 we carried equals 3, so write the 3 next to the 4; 2 times 8 is 16, so write down the 6 and carry the 1; and 2 times 6 is 12 plus 1 is 13, so write the 13 in the bottom row. Here's what we've got so far.

$$\begin{array}{r} \overset{1}{3}\ \overset{1}{\cancel{2}} \\ 6817 \\ \times\ 524 \\ \hline 27268 \\ 13634 \end{array}$$

Step 3) One more row to go. Repeat the above process for the 5 in 524. Since the 5 stands for 5 *hundreds,* we write our first result in the hundreds column (below the second 3 in 13634).

$$\begin{array}{r} 4\ \ 3 \\ \overset{1}{\cancel{1}}\ \overset{1}{\cancel{1}} \\ 3\ \ \cancel{2} \\ 6817 \\ \times\ 524 \\ \hline 27268 \\ 13634 \\ 34085 \end{array}$$

Step 4) Add the three rows for the final answer.

$$
\begin{array}{r}
6817 \\
\times\ 524 \\
\hline
27268 \\
13634 \\
34085 \\
\hline
3{,}572{,}108
\end{array}
$$

DIVISION

Division is simply the reverse of multiplication: $3 \times 4 = 12$, so $12 \div 4 = 3$. Or, look at it a bit differently—3 times 4 is the same as $4 + 4 + 4$, which adds up to 12. So we see that there are three 4s in 12, or, in other words, 4 goes into 12 three times, and thus we can split 12 into three groups of 4, and that's the same thing as saying that $12 \div 3 = 4$. Twelve also equals $3 + 3 + 3 + 3$, so there are four 3s in 12, that is, 3 goes into 12 four times, and we can therefore divide 12 into four groups of 3, and that gives us $12 \div 4 = 3$. Let's look at this yet another way . . . Just kidding.

Long Division

As with long multiplication, you can't do long division—without a calculator, that is—unless you know the times table. Let's divide 1896 by 24:

$$24\overline{)1896}$$

Step 1) Look at 1896. Starting from the left, find the first number larger than 24. Since 18 is smaller than 24, we need to use the first three digits, 189. Now ask yourself how many times 24 will go into 189. Most people do this by trial and error. Make a guess, say, 8 times. And 8 times 24 is 192—too much, but just a little too much—so 7 will work: 7 times 24 is 168. Now, since we were dividing 24 into 189, write the 7 above the last digit of 189, and write the product, 168, below the 189—like this:

Casting Out Nines

There's a nice trick for checking your math, called "casting out nines," that's been known for at least a thousand years. Once you learn this trick, you can do most of it quite quickly in your head. It's much simpler than the length of the following discussion might suggest. In a nutshell, you just keep throwing out digits that add up to 9. Consider the multiplication problem in the text. Look at the digits in 6817. Since 8 plus 1 is nine, cross out the 8 and the 1. Now add what's left, 6 plus 7 is 13, and then add the 1 and the 3 in 13, for an answer of 4. You just keep going until you're down to a single digit. Do the same for 524: 5 plus 4 is 9, so get rid of the 5 and the 4. So 2 is left, and since it's a single digit, 2 is your answer. Now do the same for the answer, 3,572,108: 7 plus 2 is 9, and 1 plus 8 is 9, so get rid of those four digits. That leaves the 3, the 5, and the 0, which add up to 8. Here's what we have so far:

$$6817 \longrightarrow 4$$
$$\underline{\times\ 524} \longrightarrow \underline{\times 2}$$
$$3,572,108 \longrightarrow 8$$

Since 4 times 2 is 8, our answer checks.[2] By the way, when you're "casting out nines" like this, it doesn't matter in what order you add up the digits, nor does it matter whether you cross out digits that add up to 9. For example, with 3,572,108 you could have started anywhere, say with the 5 and the 7. And 5 plus 7 is 12, so cross out the 5 and 7 and jot down the 12, like this:

$$3,5\!\!\!/7\!\!\!/2,108$$
$$1\ 2$$

Since 1 and 2 are such small numbers, replacing the 5 and the 7 with the 1 and the 2 makes it easier to add up everything. Now add up the digits: 3 + 1 + 2 + 2 + 1 + 0 + 8 = 17. Then add the 1 and 7 in 17 and you arrive at 8, as above. *Or* you could have started by crossing out the 3, 5, and 1 because they add up to 9 and then the 7 and 2—this would leave the 0 and the 8, which, of course, add up to 8. *Or* you could have just added up all the digits in 3,572,108: 3 + 5 + 7 + 2 + 1 + 0 + 8 = 26. Then 2 plus 6 is, once again, 8. No matter how you do it, it comes out the same. The only thing that matters is that you keep going till you're down to a single digit. Casting out nines also works for addition and subtraction.

---

[2] Unfortunately, this trick isn't foolproof, but if an answer checks like above, the chances that it's wrong are extremely low.

$$\begin{array}{r} 7 \\ 24\overline{)1896} \\ 168 \end{array}$$

Step 2) Now subtract the 168 from 189, then bring down the 6:

$$\begin{array}{r} 7 \\ 24\overline{)1896} \\ 168\downarrow \\ 216 \end{array}$$

Step 3) Now divide 24 into 216. How many times will 24 go into 216? We saw above that 8 times 24 is 192. Is there room for one more 24? Yes, one more 24 added to 192 is precisely 216, so we see that 24 goes into 216 exactly 9 times. So write the 9 above the 6 and the product of 9 and 24, which is 216, below the other 216, and subtract.

$$\begin{array}{r} 79 \\ 24\overline{)1896} \\ 168 \\ 216 \\ \underline{216} \\ 0 \end{array}$$

We're done. Twenty-four goes into 1897 seventy-nine times with nothing left over. That is, 1896 divided by 24 is 79.

Now let's do a division problem where there's a remainder. Divide the following:

$$4\overline{)627}$$

Four goes into 6 one time, so we write the 1 above the 6 and the product of 1 and 4 (that's 4) below the 6 and subtract. Then bring down the 2. Next, 4 goes into 22 five times, so write the 5 above the 2 and the product of 5 and 4 (that's 20) under the 22 and subtract. Then bring down the 7, etc. The final subtraction leaves a 3, and since there are no other numbers to bring down, that ends the division problem, and the remainder is 3. Here's what it looks like:

```
    156   R3
4⟌627
    4
    22
    20
     27
     24
      3
```

As I'm sure you're aware, this remainder of 3 means that 4 goes into 627 156 times with 3 left over, which is to say that 4 times 156 equals 624, 3 shy of 627. Now, we can express this result in a few ways. We can say that 627 divided by 4 equals 156 with a remainder of 3. Or we can make a fraction by putting the remainder (3) over the divisor (4) and say that 627 divided by 4 equals 156¾. Or, since ¾ is the same as .75, we can write the answer as 156.75.

We could have obtained the decimal answer had we continued the division beyond the ones place (beyond the 7 in 627). To obtain a decimal answer, we write 627 as 627.00 (we can use as many zeros as we need). Then divide as above, except that a decimal point is placed after the 6 in 156. Thus:

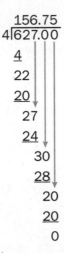

```
    156.75
4⟌627.00
    4
    22
    20
     27
     24
      30
      28
       20
       20
        0
```

Please Excuse My Dear Aunt Sally

When a single problem involves more than one operation (addition, subtraction, multiplication, etc.), the acronym PEMDAS tells us in what order to carry out the operations. Students are taught the meaningless mnemonic—*Please Excuse My Dear Aunt Sally*—to help them remember PEMDAS.

P—**Parentheses** (if there are parentheses within other parentheses, do them from inside out).

E—**Exponents** (exponents, or powers, are discussed in chapter 4).

M
D $\Big\}$ **Multiplication** and **Division** (do multiplication and division from left to right, whichever comes first).

A
S $\Big\}$ **Addition** and **Subtraction** (do addition and subtraction from left to right, whichever comes first).

Let's carry out the operations in the following expression:

$$20 - 12 \div 2 \times 3 + 4^2$$

We can skip over the "P" in PEMDAS since there are no parentheses. Next comes "E" for exponents, so replace the 4^2 with 16 (4^2 means 4 times 4, which equals 16). Multiplication and division come next. The mnemonic device is somewhat misleading here. Even though "M" comes before "D" in PEMDAS, multiplication does not take precedence over division. We do multiplication and division from left to right, regardless of the order in which they appear. So the next thing we do is $12 \div 2$, which is 6. The 6 replaces the $12 \div 2$, and then 6×3 comes next. Replacing the 6×3 with 18 brings us to the following:

$$20 - 18 + 16$$

Addition and subtraction remain. Like multiplication and division, addition and subtraction are performed from left to right in whatever order they appear. So we have $20 - 18$, which is 2; then $2 + 16$ for our final answer, 18. If you do the operations in any other order, you'll get the wrong answer. Try it.

Let's change the problem a bit:

$$(20 - 12) \div 2 \times (3 + 4)^2$$

This is identical to the original problem, except for the two sets of parentheses. We can use parentheses like this to change the order in which we perform the different operations. This time we do what's inside the parentheses first, so replace the $20 - 12$ with 8, and the $3 + 4$ with 7. Now we have

$$8 \div 2 \times 7^2$$

Exponents come next, so replace the 7^2 with 49, then do the multiplication and division from left to right: $8 \div 2$ is 4, then 4×49 is 196. If Regis Philbin asks, 196 is your final answer.

By the way, calculators automatically do operations in the proper order. So if you enter either of the above two problems in a calculator just as they appear in the text, parentheses included, the calculator will give you the correct answer. Try it.

Big Numbers

We're bombarded with big numbers every day in the media. It would be difficult to pick up a newspaper or turn on the news and not see or hear something about the stock market or some corporate takeover or government program involving millions or billions or trillions of dollars. If you've forgotten the meaning of thousands, millions, billions, and trillions and the relationships among these numbers, well, pardon me for saying this, but *get a grip!* and learn this simple topic. It really is a very easy thing to learn. And if you want to be mathematically literate, you must understand these numbers and be able to do some simple computations with them.

Here we go.

One thousand:	1000
One million:	1,000,000
One billion:	1,000,000,000
One trillion:	1,000,000,000,000

I've got a simple mnemonic device to help keep these straight. You know what a thousand is; and to remember the order of the numbers million, billion, and trillion, just think of the prefixes "mono" (1) for million, "bi" (2) for billion, and "tri" (3) for trillion. You know—"mono" as in monopoly (1 company) or monocle (1 lens), "bi" as in bicycle (2 wheels), and "tri" as in tricycle (3 wheels).

You've probably noticed the simple pattern in the numbers above: there are three more zeroes in each subsequent number. Another way of saying the same thing is that

a *million* is a thousand *thousands,*
a *billion* is a thousand *millions,* and
a *trillion* is a thousand *billions.*

Make sure you have a solid grasp of this fundamental pattern. Let's try an example. If there were 125 million[3] taxpayers in the United States and each was taxed one thousand dollars, how much would the Treasury take in? Well, since a thousand times a million is one billion, a thousand times 125 million equals 125 billion. When you multiply a number by a thousand, you add three zeros to the num-

---

[3] In this and other examples, I'm using close but not accurate numbers so that the computations are easier to follow.

ber, and adding three zeros turns thousands into millions, millions into billions, and billions into trillions.

MORE MULTIPLICATION PROBLEMS

You should have no difficulty mastering multiplication problems with big numbers. One simple shortcut you probably already know is that you can temporarily ignore the name of the number you're working with while you do the computation. For example, let's say the federal government wants to immunize the 4 million two-year-olds in the United States against a certain disease at a cost of $8 per child. What would this cost? Instead of using the number 4 million, or 4,000,000, you can temporarily ignore the word "million" or ignore the six zeros and just use the number 4. Since 8 times 4 is 32, the answer is $32 million.

Here's one more problem. Say there were 130 million taxpayers in the U.S., and the average amount paid annually in income tax was $8,000. What would the total be? That is to say, what's 130 million times 8 thousand? Let's do this two different ways.

METHOD 1.

Since 8 thousand equals 8 times a thousand, we can do this problem by first multiplying by 8 and then multiplying the answer we get by a thousand.

Step 1) Temporarily ignoring the "million" in 130 million, we multiply 130 by 8, which is 1040 (no pun intended), giving us a preliminary answer of 1040 million.

Step 2) We must multiply this number by a thousand, but that's simple if you remember from above that when multiplying by a thousand, millions become billions. So now we have a thousand times 1040 million, which equals 1040 billion.

Step 3) Since 1000 of the 1040 billions makes a trillion, our final answer is $1 trillion 40 billion.

METHOD 2.

The second method involves the very useful shortcut of counting zeros.

Step 1) Count then temporarily discard the zeros in our problem: 130,000,000 times 8000. There are a total of 10 zeros (7 zeros in 130,000,000 and 3 zeros in 8000). When we discard them, we're left with 13 times 8.

Step 2) Multiply: 13 times 8 is 104.

Step 3) Now add the 10 zeros to 104:

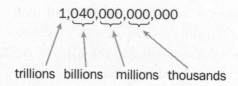

$$1,040,000,000,000$$

trillions billions millions thousands

Again, we arrive at $1 trillion 40 billion.

DIVISION PROBLEMS

The gross domestic product of the United States in 1999 was roughly $9 trillion. If there are 150 million U.S. workers, what is the average amount produced per year per worker? The answer is given by 9 trillion divided by 150 million. You'll probably want to use a calculator for this one, but even if you're going to use a calculator, it's good to be aware of the following shortcut.

When dividing 9,000,000,000,000 by 150,000,000 we can cancel the same number of zeros from each number. Canceling seven zeros from each leaves us with 900,000 divided by 15. Do this on your calculator or on paper and you'll get $60,000 per worker. Some people prefer to cancel only the zeros that come in groups of three. When we do it this way, we cancel six zeros (the equivalent of 1 million) from each number: 9 trillion then becomes 9 million (because a million millions equals a trillion), and 150 million becomes just 150. Now we divide 9,000,000 by 150 and, again, arrive at the answer of $60,000 per worker.

The world's gross product in 1999 was about 39 trillion U.S. dollars. With 3 billion workers, what does that come to per worker? We solve this by dividing 39 trillion by 3 billion. This time let's cancel nine zeros (the equivalent of 1 billion) from each number. Thus

$$\frac{39,000,\cancel{000},\cancel{000},\cancel{000}}{3,\cancel{000},\cancel{000},\cancel{000}}$$

becomes

$$\frac{39,000}{3}$$

which equals $13,000 per worker. Alternatively, we could have just noticed that 3 goes into 39 thirteen times, and since there are a thousand billions in a trillion, the answer is 13 times a thousand, or $13,000.

PERCENT PROBLEMS

If a report were to claim that 10% of the world's population of 6 billion lives on less than 50 cents per day, how many people is that? Before answering this question, let's do an easier variation of the problem: what's 10% of 600 billion? Well, 10% of something is the same as ⅒ of it. And we can calculate ⅒ of something by dividing it by 10. So what's 600 billion divided by 10? Like we did above, we can temporarily ignore the word "billion" and simply divide 600 by 10, which is 60 (when you divide by 10, all you do is take off one zero; to divide by 100, take off two zeros; to divide by 1000, take off three zeros, etc.). So our answer is 60 billion. Now let's take 10% of that. All we have to do, again, is take off a zero: 6 billion. Now we've arrived at our original problem: what is 10% of 6 billion? We'd like to simply take off a zero, but there are no zeros in the number 6. So, recalling that a billion is a thousand millions, think of 6 billion as 6000 millions. Now just take off a zero, and we have our final answer, 600 million. We could also have written out the original number, 6,000,000,000, and simply taken off one of the 9 zeros, leaving 8 zeros—600,000,000—and giving us, again, 600 million.

Now that you see how to compute 10% ($\frac{1}{10}$) of big numbers, you should have no trouble computing 1% ($\frac{1}{100}$) of these numbers. Just take off two zeros instead of one, or, what amounts to the same thing, move the decimal point two places to the left. Let's start with 850 trillion—take 1% of that, then 1% of the answer, then 1% of that answer, etc. What's 1% of 850 trillion? There aren't two zeros in 850, so just move the decimal point two places to the left—8.50,—giving us an answer of 8.5 trillion: 8 trillion is 8000 billion, so 8.5 trillion is 8500 billion. To figure 1% of that, take off two zeros: that's 85 billion. Then 85 billion is 85,000 million, and 1% of that is 850 million, etc.

With a little practice, you should have no difficulty understanding the relationship among millions, billions, and trillions, and you should be able to do computations like those above. It's easier than it appears at first. You'll even be able to do many such computations in your head, at least approximately. Once you can do that, you'll have a handle on the daily news stories involving big numbers. You'll know, for example, not to worry about a federal program that costs taxpayers $10 million—if you've got an average tax bill, that's less than a dime of your money. But, on the other hand, when Congress is debating whether to increase defense spending by $130 billion over five years, you'll know—assuming, again, that you have an average tax bill—that that means $1000 out of your pocket.

CHAPTER 2

Fractions, Decimals, and Percents

You can't possibly do everyday math without understanding fractions, decimals, and percents. They're everywhere. They come up in situations involving tipping, taxes, inflation, finance, mortgages, credit cards, sales, cooking, sports, gambling, measurement—you name it. Why are they so common and thus so important? Well, we need them whenever we want to describe or determine part of something, like half a pound of butter or 15 percent of a dinner tab, and everywhere you turn, there are things that don't come in whole numbers.

Fractions, decimals, and percents are very closely related. The fraction ¼ is the same as the decimal 0.25, which is the same as 25 percent. You probably studied these topics several times, beginning in elementary school. And if you don't like math, it's quite likely that one of the culprits is this three-in-one topic. I'm not sure that anyone knows why, but a great number of students never fully grasp fractions, decimals, and percents when they study them in elementary school, and then from that point on, these topics continue to be a nagging frustration because they come up constantly in the study of all levels of mathematics.

Fractions

Do you like Italian food? Great! The best way to understand fractions is to use the visual aid of a pizza cut into slices. This may seem too elementary, but it's important to understand fractions in this visual way. The denominator (the bottom number in a fraction) tells you how many slices the pizza is cut into; the numerator (the top number) tells you how many pieces you get.

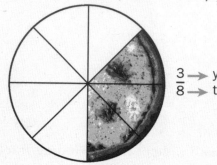

$\dfrac{3}{8}$ → you get 3 slices
→ the pizza is cut into 8 slices

That's it. Plain and simple, $\frac{7}{10}$ means you have the equivalent of 7 pieces of a 10-slice pizza; $\frac{3}{20}$ means you have the equivalent of 3 pieces of a 20-slice pizza. If the numerator is larger than the denominator, you have more than one whole pizza. Like $\frac{21}{8}$, for example, where you have 21 slices from pizzas cut into 8 pieces each. Since two 8-slice pizzas would be 16 slices, and 21 is 5 more than that, you have two whole pizzas plus $\frac{5}{8}$ of another, or $2\frac{5}{8}$.

$\frac{21}{8}$ or $2\frac{5}{8}$

You can also use this pizza visual aid to get a good feel for fraction-to-percent conversions. You know what ¼, ½, and ¾ of a pizza look like, right? These fractions equal, as you know, 25%, 50%, and 75%.

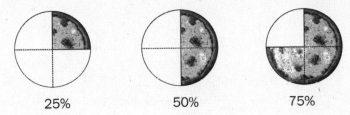

Add to these the benchmarks involving tenths of a pizza. For example, 10% of a pizza (⅒ or 1 slice from a 10-slice pizza) looks like this:

10%

And 60% (⁶⁄₁₀ or 6 slices from a 10-slice pizza) looks like this:

60%

Here's another visual aid that you might find handy for estimating fraction-to-percent conversions. Let's use ⅚ as an example. Take a piece of regular lined paper. On one of the lines mark a starting point, and then put down six more evenly-spaced marks from left to right. We want *six* intervals because our number is five-*sixths*. The marks should be roughly a quarter inch apart, but that's not really important. What is important is that they're evenly spaced. And you'd be surprised how easy it is to mark down equal intervals if you take some care to be reasonably accurate. Just check to make sure that your intervals don't gradually shorten or lengthen from left to right. Your paper should look like this:

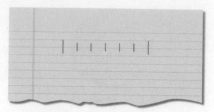

Now, on a line just below this line, put two marks immediately below the first and last marks—like this:

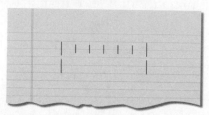

Next, cut this bottom interval in half, then cut the two halves in half, then cut the four quarters in half—this will produce *eighths* on the bottom line. Again, if you mark this bottom line carefully—really trying to cut each interval exactly in half—you'll find that, with a little practice, it's very easy to produce extremely accurate eighths. You might want to cover the top line with your hand while you're working on the bottom line so the marks on the top line don't play tricks on your eyes and affect your accuracy. Here's what we've got so far:

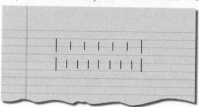

(By the way, this type of diagram and the pizza diagrams would be great things to work on with your children when they're studying fractions. Every student should understand fractions visually as well as numerically.)

Finally, write down 25%, 50%, and 75% at the quarter marks on the lower line; and then mark the remaining eighths with 12.5%, 37.5%, 62.5%, and 87.5%. Here's the final diagram:

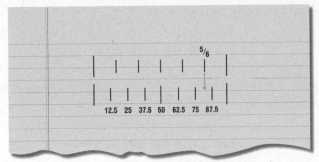

Now you can use the lower percent scale to estimate the sixths on the upper line. The ⅚ mark on the upper line is in between the 75% and 87.5% marks—perhaps a bit closer to the 87.5% mark—so a good estimate would be about 82% (the exact percentage is 83⅓%).

I promise you that drawing and marking this little diagram is *much* easier and faster than explaining how to do it. Try it. See how you like it. And try it with your kids. Quick: ⅔₃ is about what percent?

ADDING, SUBTRACTING, MULTIPLYING, AND DIVIDING FRACTIONS

Let's begin with multiplication and division because they're so easy. To multiply two fractions, simply multiply straight across the top and straight across the bottom.

$$\frac{2}{3} \times \frac{4}{5} = \frac{8}{15}$$

So 2 times 4 is 8, and 3 times 5 is 15. That's all there is to it. Here's one more:

$$\frac{6}{5} \times \frac{3}{8}$$

This time we can reduce before we multiply because there's a number (2) that goes into one of the numerators (the 6) and also goes into one of the denominators (the 8). So we divide the 6 and the 8 by 2 (6 ÷ 2 = 3 and 8 ÷ 2 = 4):

$$\frac{\overset{3}{\cancel{6}}}{5} \times \frac{3}{\underset{4}{\cancel{8}}}$$

Now multiply straight across:

$$\frac{3}{5} \times \frac{3}{4} = \frac{9}{20}^{1}$$

Dividing fractions is also very easy. There's just one extra step. Let's divide ¼ by ⅔:

$$\frac{1}{4} \div \frac{2}{3}$$ **Step 1)** Flip the second fraction and change from division to multiplication.

$$= \frac{1}{4} \times \frac{3}{2}$$ **Step 2)** Multiply straight across.

$$= \frac{3}{8}$$

Addition and subtraction of fractions is a bit more involved because we first have to find the least common denominator (LCD). Let's add ¾ and ⅙. To find the least common denominator, take the larger of the two denominators (the 6) and run through its multiples (6, 12, 18, etc.) until you find one that the other denominator goes into evenly. Since 4 goes into 12, 12 is the LCD. If you're adding more than two fractions, the process is the same except that you have to find a multiple of the largest denominator that all of the other denominators go into evenly.

$$\frac{3}{4} + \frac{1}{6}$$ **Step 1)** Convert each fraction into twelfths. Since 4 goes into 12 three times, multiply the top and bottom of ¾ by 3; and since 6 goes

---

[1] Note that you can also do the reducing after you multiply. First, multiply: ⅗ × ¾ = ¹⁸⁄₄₀. Now, since 2 goes into the numerator and the denominator, divide the top and bottom by 2. This gives us, again, ⁹⁄₂₀.

into 12 two times, multiply the top
and bottom of ⅙ by 2.

$$= \frac{3}{4} \times \frac{3}{3} + \frac{1}{6} \times \frac{2}{2}$$

$$= \frac{9}{12} + \frac{2}{12}$$

Step 2) Add the numerators; the denominator
stays the same.

$$= \frac{11}{12}$$

If you don't want to bother finding the LCD, any common denominator will do. An easy one to use is the product of the denominators. Let's add ¾ and ⅙ again using this alternate method. The product of 4 and 6 is 24, so we'll use 24 as the common denominator.

$$\frac{3}{4} + \frac{1}{6}$$

$$- \frac{3}{4} \times \frac{6}{6} + \frac{1}{6} \times \frac{4}{4}$$

Step 1) Convert each fraction into 24ths.

$$= \frac{18}{24} + \frac{4}{24}$$

Step 2) Add the numerators.

$$= \frac{22}{24}$$

$$= \frac{11}{12}$$

Step 3) Reduce: divide top and bottom by 2.
(Note: if you use the LCD, you'll
often, but not always, avoid having to
reduce the answer.)

Some people like to use the following shortcut:

$$\frac{3}{4} + \frac{1}{6}$$

$$= \frac{3 \times 6 + 4 \times 1}{4 \times 6}$$

$$= \frac{18 + 4}{24}$$

$$= \frac{22}{24}$$

$$= \frac{11}{12}$$

Let's take one last look at the above problem, ¾ + ⅙. I want to use the pizza diagrams again to show you why we need a common denominator and what's really going on when we add fractions. Why can't we just add ¾ and ⅙ without using a common denominator? Consider the following diagrams:

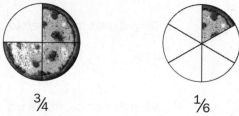

¾   ⅙

What do we have if we add up these slices of pizza? We have a total of four slices, but they're not all the same size. If you try to describe this by saying, "Well, I've got four slices—three bigger ones and one small one," that doesn't describe the total accurately. To determine a precise total, we need to cut the slices into smaller slices so all the slices are the same size. Observe what happens when we cut each of the slices on the left into three smaller pieces and cut the one slice on the right in half.

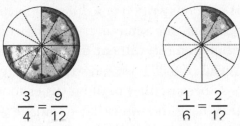

$$\frac{3}{4} = \frac{9}{12} \qquad\qquad \frac{1}{6} = \frac{2}{12}$$

Now all the slices are the same size—*twelfths*. We have 9 slices of a 12-slice pizza on the left and 2 slices of a 12-slice pizza on the right. Altogether we have 11 slices of a 12-slice pizza, or, in other words, eleven-twelfths ($^{11}/_{12}$). You could take the two slices on the right and move them over onto two of the three empty spaces on the left pizza—like this:

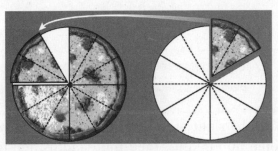

$$\frac{9}{12} + \frac{2}{12} = \frac{11}{12}$$

Subtracting fractions works the same as adding them except that in the final step you subtract the numerators rather than adding them. Thus:

$$\frac{7}{8} - \frac{2}{8} = \frac{5}{8}$$

Decimals

Decimals are just fractions written in a different form—and, as we'll see in the next section, the same is true of percents. The world could get along fine (almost) without decimals. Instead of 2.5, we can write 2½; instead of 0.003, we can write ³⁄₁₀₀₀, etc. But decimals do serve a purpose because they're often easier to work with than fractions. And they have the somewhat mundane advantage over fractions in cases like ³¹¹⁄₁₀₀₀ where it's faster and more convenient to write 0.311.

Let's briefly review the fundamentals of numbers written in decimal form and then go over addition, subtraction, multiplication, and division of decimals. Consider the number 12.5163.

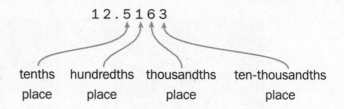

Immediately to the right of the decimal point is the tenths place. After that come hundredths, then thousandths, ten-thousandths, hundred-thousandths, etc. As we move to the right, each place represents a fraction that's ten times smaller than the one before. In other words, after tenths come hundredths, which are ten times smaller than tenths; after hundredths come thousandths, which are ten times smaller than hundredths, etc.

In the number 12.5163, there are five tenths (⁵⁄₁₀), one hundredth (¹⁄₁₀₀), six thousandths (⁶⁄₁₀₀₀), and three ten-thousandths (³⁄₁₀,₀₀₀). So, altogether, the number 12.5163 equals

$$12 + \frac{5}{10} + \frac{1}{100} + \frac{6}{1000} + \frac{3}{10,000}$$

But the easier way to write the number (and to think about it) is

$$12 \; + \; \frac{5163}{10,000}$$

Lastly, you can use this same denominator, 10,000, and put the original number, with the decimal point removed, in the numerator, like this:

$$\frac{125,163}{10,000}$$

This last version of the number is called an *improper fraction*. That's a fraction where the numerator is greater than the denominator. Let's look at a couple more examples.

$$1.33 = 1\tfrac{33}{100}, \text{ or } \tfrac{133}{100}$$

$$0.057 = \tfrac{57}{1000}$$

$$12.5 = 12\tfrac{5}{10}, \text{ or } \tfrac{125}{10} \text{ or } 12\tfrac{1}{2} \text{ or } \tfrac{25}{2}$$

ADDITION, SUBTRACTION, MULTIPLICATION, AND DIVISION OF DECIMALS

Addition. To add a column of decimals, you merely need to line up the decimal points one above the other, add in the regular way, then put a decimal point in the answer immediately below all the others. For example, to add 1.08 + 20.565 + 1.3, line up the decimal points like this:

$$
\begin{array}{r}
1.08 \\
20.565 \\
+ \quad 1.3 \\
\hline
\end{array}
$$

Now, add in the regular way, column by column, carrying where necessary; and when you're done, put a decimal point in the answer in alignment with the other decimal points.

$$
\begin{array}{r}
1 \\
1.08 \\
20.565 \\
+\quad 1.3 \\
\hline
22.945
\end{array}
$$

Subtraction. Subtracting decimals works exactly the same except that instead of adding—hold on to your hat—you subtract.

Multiplication. Just multiply in the regular way, and then place the decimal point in the answer so that the number of digits to the right of the decimal point in the answer is the same as the total number of digits to the right of the decimal points in the two numbers you multiplied. Let's multiply 8.15 by 5.3.

$$
\begin{array}{r}
8.15 \\
\times\quad 5.3 \\
\hline
2445 \\
4075 \\
\hline
43.195
\end{array}
$$

We multiply in the regular way, just as we would multiply 815 by 53. Then we count the total number of digits to the right of the decimal points in 8.15 and 5.3 (two digits in 8.15 plus one digit in 5.3 for a total of three). So our answer should have three digits to the right of the decimal point, and thus the answer is 43.195.

Division. As with multiplication, division with decimals works just like regular long division except for locating the decimal point. Let's divide 6.264 by 1.45.

$$1.45 \overline{)6.264}$$

Step 1) Move the decimal point in the outside number all the way to the right, counting the number of places you move.

Step 2) Move the decimal point in the inside number the same number of places to the right, filling in zeros if necessary, and then put another decimal point directly above it on the line where the answer will go. So far, we've got this:

$$1.45. \overline{)6.26.4}$$

Step 3) Divide as usual.

$$
\begin{array}{r}
4.32 \\
145 \overline{)626.4} \\
\underline{580} \\
464 \\
\underline{435} \\
290 \\
\underline{290} \\
0
\end{array}
$$

Let's do one more: 5 divided by 0.04.

$$0.04 \overline{)5}$$

Move the decimal point in the 0.04 two places to the right, then move the decimal point in the 5 two places to the right and fill in two zeros (there's sort of an imaginary decimal point just to the right of the whole number 5 [like this: 5.]). Then put the decimal point for the answer above the line. Here's what we have so far:

$$0.04. \overline{)5.00.}$$

Now, just divide 500 by 4. The answer is 125.

Percents

Like decimals, percents are also just fractions written in a different form. I said the world could almost get along without decimals; well, we could definitely get along without percents because the word "percent" is simply a synonym for the word "hundredth." Twenty percent of 80, for example, means exactly the same thing as twenty-hundredths of 80, or $^{20}\!/_{100}$ of 80. Wherever you see the word "percent" you can substitute the word "hundredth" without changing the meaning one bit. I'm guessing that the reason the term "percent" and the idea of a percent exist is that people like using the round number 100—there are 100 cents to the dollar, 100 centimeters in a meter, 100 years in a century, etc. So, since people found it convenient to divide things into hundredths, the idea of this special amount, this special fraction ($\frac{1}{100}$) came about—and thus we have the term "percent." But just remember, there really isn't anything special about it. It's just a simple fraction—a hundredth.

Let's go over a few percent problems. The most common type of problem is something like

what is 15% of 80?

You can do this two ways. First, you could change 15% to the fraction $^{15}\!/_{100}$ and then multiply by 80 (the word "of" in "15% of 80" can be read as "times").

$$\frac{15}{100} \times 80$$

$$= \frac{15}{100} \times \frac{80}{1} \qquad (80 = {}^{80}\!/_1)$$

$$= \frac{1200}{100} \qquad \text{(multiply straight across the numerator and straight across the denominator)}$$

$$= \frac{12}{1} \qquad \text{(just cancel the two zeros on the top and bottom of } {}^{1200}\!/_{100})$$

$$= 12$$

Most people prefer the following method: change the percent to a decimal and then multiply (15 percent or 15 hundredths is written in decimal form as .15 or 0.15). So, the solution is simply:

$$0.15 \times 80 = 12$$

Do this by hand:	Or just use your calculator:
80	press 15 [%] 80 [enter or =]
× 0.15	or
400	0.15 [×] 80 [enter or =]
80	
12.00	

This second method illustrates the following rule of thumb for converting percents to decimals and decimals to percents. To convert a percent to a decimal, move the decimal two places to the left (for example, 5.2% equals 0.052). To convert a decimal to a percent, move the decimal two places to the right (for example, 0.326 equals 32.6%).

The type of percent problem we just did—what is 15% of 80?— is one of the three ways a basic percent question can be asked, and it's by far the most common (it's where we know the percent [15%]

and the "whole" [80] and want to compute the "part" [which we learned is 12]). Let's look at the other two ways, using the same example from above. The second type of question is "12 is what percent of 80?" (Here we know the part [12] and the whole [80] and want to compute the percent.) And the third and least common type of question is "15% of what is 12?" (Here we know the percent [15%] and the part [12] and want to compute the whole.)

The method for the second question type—"12 is what percent of 80?"—is easy to remember when you consider that another way of asking the same thing is "12 is what *fraction* to 80?" To solve, you just write the fraction, ¹²⁄₈₀, and then divide:

$$\frac{12}{80} = 0.15 = 15\%$$

Here's an easy-to-remember method for doing the third type of question. *And if you like the idea of learning just one rule and not having to keep the three question types straight, you can use this method for all three types.* When you get a type-three question like "90 is 60% of what?" you can solve it with the following equation:

$$\frac{is}{of} = \frac{percent}{100}$$

The *of* stands for the number or unknown in the question immediately after the word "of." The *is* stands for the number or unknown next to—or very close to—the word "is." And the *percent* stands of course for the percent. If you prefer, you can use the equivalent equation,

$$\frac{part}{whole} = \frac{percent}{100}$$

You may remember this equation from school. It makes a lot of sense since the word "whole" corresponds to 100% of something, and the word "part" corresponds to the fraction or percent of something. But one drawback of these terms is that in some problems, the *part* is larger than the *whole*.

Let's do a couple examples using the $\frac{is}{of}$ equation. Again, 90 is 60% of what? (Or this could be phrased as "60% of what is 90?")

Step 1) Plug 90 into *is*, 60 into *percent*, and the unknown, *x*, into *of* since that's the thing we don't know.

$$\frac{is}{of} = \frac{percent}{100}$$

$$\frac{90}{x} = \frac{60}{100}$$

Step 2) Cross-multiply (this is called "cross" multiplication because we draw the following cross or *X* around the numbers and then multiply each pair of numbers):

$$\frac{90}{x} = \frac{60}{100}$$

$$x \cdot 60 = 90 \cdot 100$$

$$x \cdot 60 = 9000$$

(We used the times dot here because the times "×" would get confused with the unknown *x*.)

Step 3) Divide:

$$x = \frac{9000}{60}$$

$$= 150$$

Thus, 90 is 60% of 150.

Let's try it again with a type-two question: 120 is what percent of 160? (Or this could be phrased as "what percent of 160 is 120?")

Step 1) Plug 120 into *is*, 160 into *of,* and *x* into *percent:*

$$\frac{is}{of} = \frac{percent}{100}$$

$$\frac{120}{160} = \frac{x}{100}$$

Step 2) Cross-multiply:

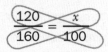

$$160 \cdot x = 120 \cdot 100$$

$$160 \cdot x = 12{,}000$$

Step 3) Divide:

$$x = \frac{12{,}000}{160}$$

$$= 75$$

Thus, 120 is 75% of 160.

PERCENT INCREASE AND PERCENT DECREASE

Now let's turn to one of the most practical categories of percent problems—percent increase and percent decrease. Examples include discounts and markups, the inflation rate or the Dow Jones average or the crime rate going up or down a certain percent, and getting a 5% raise at your job. We saw above that 15% *of* 80 is 12. So what's 15% *more than* 80? Well, that's just 80 increased by 12, which is 92. (If a retailer bought an item for $80 and marked it up 15%, the price would be $92.) And what's 15% *less than* 80? That's just 80 decreased by 12, which is 68. (If an $80 item is on sale for 15% off, the sale price would be $68.)

The above approach is an easy way to think about and to solve problems where you want to increase or decrease a number by a given percent. You just compute the percent of the number, then add or subtract. But it's a good idea to understand the following alternate method as well (it's used frequently in financial math). Let's do the same questions again. What's 15% more than 80? (Or what's 80 increased by 15%?)

Step 1) Change 15% to a decimal: that's 0.15.
Step 2) *Add* this to one: 1 plus 0.15 is 1.15 (this is the decimal form of 115%).
Step 3) Multiply: 80 × 1.15 = 92.

And what's 15% less than 80? (Or what's 80 decreased by 15%?)

Step 1) Change 15% to a decimal: that's 0.15.
Step 2) *Subtract* this from one: 1 minus 0.15 is 0.85 (this is the same as 85%).
Step 3) Multiply: 80 × 0.85 = 68.

This second method illustrates the important distinction between the expressions "percent *of*" and "percent *more than*" (or "percent *less than*"). Once again, 15% of 80 is 12, and thus 15% more than 80 is 92. Now, you know that 100% of anything is itself, right? So 80 is 100% of 80. And since 92 is 15% more than that, 92 is 115% *of* 80. That's why we added 1 and 0.15 above. Have you got it? We can express the same relationship in two different ways. We can say that 92 is 15% *more than* 80 or that 92 is 115% *of* 80. And, by the same token, we can say that 68 is 15% *less than* 80 or, since 15% less than 100% is 85%, that 68 is 85% *of* 80. It's important that you pay careful attention to this distinction when reading a percent question and when expressing your answer.

One advantage of the second method is that after doing steps 1 and 2 (which are usually effortless), you get the answer with a single computation (step 3). If a retailer, for instance, wants to mark down several items in her store by 15%, she can do each item with a single computation—multiplying each price by 0.85. With the first method, on the other hand, she'd have to do two steps for each item: multiplying the price by 0.15 and then subtracting this amount from the price.

Close but No Cigar

"My portfolio fell 15% last year, but then it rose 15% this year. So at least I recouped my losses."

Oddly enough, going down and then up the same percent, or vice versa, is not a wash. As we saw in the text, you compute a 15% drop by multiplying by 0.85. A 15% gain is computed by multiplying by 1.15. Say you invest $1000 in the stock market. If the value of your portfolio falls 15%, your investment would drop to $1000 × 0.85, or $850. If it then goes up 15%, you'd have $850 × 1.15, or only $977.50. This amounts to an average loss of about 1.1% per year for the two years. Sorry.

When you want to compute either the percent increase or the percent decrease between two numbers, use this formula:

$$percent\ change = \frac{difference}{initial\ value}$$

If a retailer buys an item for $120 and marks it up to $150, what's the percent increase?

Step 1) Compute the difference: 150 minus 120 is 30.

Step 2) Plug into the formula:

$$percent\ change = \frac{difference}{initial\ value}$$

$$= \frac{30}{120}$$

$$= \frac{1}{4}$$

$$= 0.25,\ or\ 25\%$$

If the stock price of Widgets Are Us falls from \$76 to \$70, what's the percent decrease?

Step 1) Compute the difference: 76 minus 70 is 6.

Step 2) Plug into the formula:

$$percent\ change = \frac{difference}{initial\ value}$$

$$= \frac{6}{76}$$

$$\approx 0.079,\ or\ about\ 7.9\%$$

Converting between Fractions, Decimals, and Percents

Most of the following conversion rules are covered above, but I thought it would be helpful to have them all in one place.

Percent to decimal. Just move the decimal point two places to the *left*. Thus 135% becomes 1.35. There's no need to use a calculator for this simple process, but if you have a calculator with the features of Texas Instruments' TI-34 II, it will do the conversion for you:

press: 135

Decimal to percent. Move the decimal point two places to the *right*. Thus, 0.058 becomes 5.8%. Like with converting from a percent to a decimal, there's no need to use a calculator for this, but on a calculator like the TI-34 II, you can simply

press: 0.058

Fraction to decimal. Just divide. For example, to convert ⅜ to a decimal, divide 3 by 8; that's 0.375. With a calculator like the TI-34 II,

press: 3  8

Or, if your calculator doesn't have this convert-to-a-decimal button,

press: 3  8

Decimal to fraction. Let's convert 0.275 to a fraction. The digit 5 in 0.275 is in the thousandths place. Thus, 0.275 equals 275 thousandths or, in other words, $^{275}/_{1000}$. Now, just reduce: $^{275}/_{1000} = ^{11}/_{40}$. With the TI-34 II, press: 0.275 →F enter or =

If your calculator doesn't have a convert-to-a-fraction button, you'll have to reduce the fraction $^{275}\!/_{1000}$ by hand. To do this, find a number that goes into both 275 and 1000. You can see that they're both multiples of 5, so divide the numerator and denominator by 5. That gives you $^{55}\!/_{200}$. Since both of these numbers are also multiples of 5, divide again by 5. That results in $^{11}\!/_{40}$. Since no number goes into both 11 and 40 (except for 1), this is as far as you can go.

Percent to fraction. If the percent doesn't have a decimal point in it, like 80%, just put the percent over 100 and then reduce: $^{80}\!/_{100}$ reduces to $^8\!/_{10}$ which reduces to $^4\!/_5$. If the percent does have a decimal point in it, like 62.5%, convert the percent to a decimal by moving the decimal point two places to the *left*, that's 0.625, and then use the decimal-to-fraction rule from above. This will give you an answer of $^5\!/_8$. If your calculator doesn't have a convert-to-a-fraction button, you'll have to do this by hand, but with a calculator like the TI-34 II,

press: 62.5 % →F enter or =

Fraction to percent. Use the fraction-to-decimal rule from above to get a decimal, then move the decimal point two places to the *right*. For example, to convert $^3\!/_8$ to a percent, divide 3 by 8; that's 0.375. Now move the decimal point; that gives you 37.5%. With the TI-34 II,

press: 3 / 8 →% enter or =

Or, if your calculator doesn't have this convert-to-a-percent button,

press: 3 ÷ 8 enter or =

then move the decimal point two places to the right.

CHAPTER 3

Ratios and Proportions

Ratios and proportions are closely related to the topics in the last chapter: fractions, decimals, and percents. A *ratio* is basically the same thing as a fraction; it's just written in a different form. When we say, for example, that the ratio of boys to girls in a classroom is 3 to 4, or 3:4, this means nothing more or less than saying that there are ¾ as many boys as girls. A *proportion* is simply an equation where two ratios—that is, two fractions—are set equal to each other, as in

$$\frac{6}{8} = \frac{12}{16}$$

In this equation, the fraction on the left could represent a class with 6 boys and 8 girls, and the fraction on the right a class with 12 boys and 16 girls. Since the fractions are equal, we would say that the number of boys and girls in the two classes is proportional. Did you notice that both of these fractions reduce to ¾? Because they do, the ratio of boys to girls in both classes is 3 to 4.

Ratios

Let's continue with the above example. If the ratio of boys to girls in a classroom is 3 to 4, this means, of course, that there are 3 boys for every 4 girls in the class. It does *not* mean that there are exactly 3 boys and 4 girls in the class (though this is one possibility). In fact, if all we're told is that the ratio is 3 to 4, there is no way to determine the size of the class. What we do know is that regardless of the size of the class, we could arrange the students into groups or teams of 7 students each, with 3 boys and 4 girls in each group. The class might have three groups, in which case there would be 3 times 7 or 21 students—3 times 3 or 9 boys, and 3 times 4 or 12 girls. Or the class could have five groups, in which case there would be 35 students (5 × 7): 15 boys (5 × 3) and 20 girls (5 × 4), etc.

The above example is perhaps the most common type of ratio in that it expresses the ratio of a part of something to another part (boys are *part* of the class and girls are *part* of the class); the sum of two parts equals the *whole*. The following summarizes these ideas:

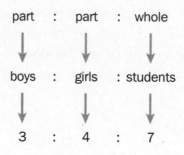

When we consider all three numbers, 3:4:7—as opposed to just the two numbers we gave originally, 3:4—we get a more complete picture of what a 3-to-4 ratio of boys to girls means. It means that for every 7 students there are 3 boys and 4 girls, and thus that ⅜ of the class are boys and ⅘ of the class are girls. These two *parts*, ⅜ and ⅘, add up to 1, or 100%, or the *whole* class.

The following example will illustrate why it's important to consider all three numbers in this type of ratio problem. Say a soccer team has the following ratio of wins to losses.

wins   :   losses

1   :   4

A common mistake here is to conclude that the team has won ¼ of its games. This error is easy to make because ¼ seems like a sensible answer—in the first example, this type of mistake would be much less likely because when the ratio of boys to girls is 3:4, there are more girls than boys, and it's therefore obvious that the class is not ¾ boys. Such a mistake is avoided when we consider all three numbers in the ratio.

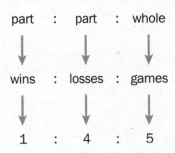

Now we see that the team has 1 win and 4 losses for every 5 games, and thus it has won ⅕ (not ¼) of its games; it has lost ⅘ of its games.

Two ratios are equivalent when their corresponding fractions are equal. For example, a ratio of 6:8 is the same as a ratio of 3:4 because 6⁄8 equals ¾. And just as 6⁄8 can be reduced to ¾ (because both the 6 and the 8 in 6⁄8 can be divided by 2), the ratio 6:8 can be reduced to 3:4. Just as with fractions, it's customary to reduce ratios as far as possible.

It Doesn't Take an Einstein

$$E = mc^2$$

It took someone of Einstein's genius to come up with $E = mc^2$, but it doesn't take an Einstein to understand it. In fact, its meaning is as straightforward as the following simple equation relating your car's mileage rate, say 32 miles per gallon, to the number of miles you can travel:

$$D = 32 \times g$$

To use this equation, you simply plug the number of gallons of gasoline into g and multiply by 32. This gives you the distance, D, the gas will take you. Einstein's equation is no harder. Note a few parallels. First, the form of the equations is exactly the same. Now, it's true that the three letters in $E = mc^2$ make it look a bit more complicated, but, actually, the letter c just stands for a number, the speed of light—about three hundred million meters per second. The equation says to square c, so if we do that and then tweak the equation a bit to convert it into familiar units, we arrive at:

$$E \approx 11,324,000,000 \times m$$

Now you can see how similar the two equations are. In both cases, you simply plug a number into the variable on the right side of the equation and then multiply to get the answer. For Einstein's equation, the input is the number of pounds of matter you have, and the answer is the number of kilowatt-hours of energy created when the matter is turned into energy—this occurs in stars, nuclear reactors, and nuclear bombs. For both equations, you input an amount of "fuel"—gasoline for the first, matter for the second—and the answers given by both equations tell you how much that amount of fuel can accomplish.

Proportions

When two ratios are equal, we have a proportion. Let's return to the above example of a classroom where the ratio of boys to girls is 3 to 4. Two possible classes with this ratio would be 9 boys with 12 girls and 15 boys with 20 girls. The ratio of boys to girls in each class is the same, in other words, because

$$\frac{\text{boys}}{\text{girls}} = \frac{\text{boys}}{\text{girls}}$$

$$\frac{9}{12} = \frac{15}{20} \quad \text{(both of these fractions reduce to ¾)}$$

the two classes are proportional with regard to the number of boys and girls.

Proportions come up frequently because they're used whenever we want to expand or reduce something (like a recipe), while keeping the amounts of the different components (like flour and sugar) in the same relation to each other. (Make sure your kids understand this fundamental concept and the following discussion.)

Say a recipe makes 5 dozen cookies and calls for 2 cups of chocolate chips. How many cups of chocolate chips do you need if you're making 8 dozen? We want the ratio of cups of chocolate chips to dozens of cookies in the bigger batch to be the same as in the recipe. In other words,

$$\underset{\text{recipe}}{\frac{\text{cups}}{\text{dozen}}} = \underset{\text{bigger batch}}{\frac{\text{cups}}{\text{dozen}}}$$

By the way, when we use words like this ("cups" and "dozen") to describe the different quantities in a proportion, all proportions will look like the above with the identical words on the left and right sides of the equation.

Now let's solve our problem.

Step 1) Plug in the numbers from the recipe and the bigger batch:

$$\frac{2}{5} = \frac{cups}{8}$$

Step 2) Cross-multiply:

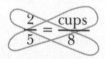

$$5 \times cups = 2 \times 8$$

$$5 \times cups = 16$$

Step 3) Divide:

$$cups = \frac{16}{5}$$

$$cups = 3\tfrac{1}{5} \text{ or } 3.2 \quad \text{(3¼ cups is close enough)}$$

So, you need about 3¼ cups of chocolate chips to make 8 dozen cookies.

The above solution technique, using cross-multiplication, is the traditional approach to problems like this. It's easy, widely used, and useful to know. But like a lot of mathematics, it doesn't register with our common sense. It's not immediately clear why cross-multiplication works—and I'll spare you the algebraic explanation. When we do it, we're just following a foreign-looking process because we were told that it works. When possible, it's always preferable to do math in a way that *does* register with our common sense. I think the following is a better way of understanding and doing proportional problems.

In the above example, we wanted to expand a recipe for 5 dozen cookies so that it would make 8 dozen. How much bigger is 8 than 5? To compute this, just divide 8 by 5. Use your calculator for this to obtain 1.6. So 8 dozen is 1.6 times as much as 5 dozen. And this number, 1.6, is the *expansion* multiplier that we'll use to increase the amounts of the ingredients of the recipe. Thus, the 2 cups of chocolate chips become 2 times 1.6, or 3.2 cups. And if the recipe called for 2¼ cups of flour, we would need 2¼ times 1.6, or 3.6 cups (call it about 3½ cups).

The same method works when we want to reduce a recipe. If we had wanted to make only 3 dozen cookies, we would compute a *reduction* multiplier. Divide 3 by 5—whether you're expanding or reducing, you compute the multiplier by dividing your new amount by the original amount. Three divided by 5 is 0.6. So we use 0.6 to multiply the amounts of each ingredient. The 2 cups of chocolate chips in the recipe would become 2 times 0.6, or 1.2 cups (about 1¼ cups) for our batch of 3 dozen. The 2¼ cups of flour would become 2¼ times 0.6, or 1.35 cups (about 1⅓ cups). As you can see, one advantage of this method over the cross-multiplying method is that after figuring the multiplier, you just use it over and over for the entire list of ingredients. This is especially easy if you use a calculator.

Why don't we do the last computation from above (2¼ times 0.6) with a calculator. If your calculator lets you enter fractions, enter 2¼ × 0.6. With Texas Instruments' TI-34 II, for example, you would do the following:

press: 2 $\boxed{unit}$ 1 $\boxed{/}$ 4 $\boxed{\times}$ 0.6

This will appear on the display as

$$2 \; \llcorner \; \frac{1}{4} \; \times \; 0.6$$

Then press  and the answer will appear—1.35. If your calculator doesn't allow you to enter mixed numbers like 2¼, do the fol-
lowing:

press: 2 ＋ 1 ÷ 4 [enter or =]

This converts 2¼ into the decimal 2.25. Then just press ✕ 0.6 [enter or =]
for the final answer.

CHAPTER 4

Powers and Roots

After addition, subtraction, multiplication, and division, the next most basic thing we can do with numbers is to compute a power or a root. A power tells you how many times to multiply a number by itself. Taking a root is the reverse process. In terms of day-to-day math, powers—and, to a much lesser extent, roots—come up most often in financial math problems such as computing compound interest.

Raising a number to a power (also called an "exponent") is a simple idea. 4^2 ("4 squared") means 4×4, or 16. In something like 5^3 ("5 cubed," "5 to the third power," or just "5 to the third"), the 3 tells you to multiply 5 by itself 3 times: $5 \times 5 \times 5$—which equals 125. And 2^6 equals $2 \times 2 \times 2 \times 2 \times 2 \times 2$, or 64. Just as multiplication is nothing more than repeated addition (4×3 means the same thing as $4 + 4 + 4$), "exponentiation" is nothing more than repeated multiplication (4^3 means the same thing as $4 \times 4 \times 4$). That's all there is to it. Make sure you remember that the 3 in 5^3, for instance, tells you to multiply 5 by itself 3 times and that 5^3 does *not* equal 5 times 3.

Taking a root of a number is the reverse of exponentiation. Since $4^2 = 16$, the square root of 16 (written as $\sqrt{16}$) equals 4. The square root of a number means the second root, but by convention we do not write a 2 in the root symbol like $\sqrt[2]{16}$ as we do for third roots, fourth roots, etc. Since 5^3 equals 125, the third root of 125 (written as $\sqrt[3]{125}$) equals 5. Thus, the following two equations express the same mathematical relationship:

$$4^2 = 16$$

$$4 = \sqrt{16}$$

As do

$$5^3 = 125$$

$$5 = \sqrt[3]{125}$$

With roots, make sure you don't make the mistake of thinking that something like $\sqrt[3]{125}$ means 125 divided by 3.

These computations are a snap with a calculator. To square a number, just enter the number, press the $\boxed{x^2}$ button, then press $\boxed{\frac{enter}{or =}}$. For the square root of a number, use the $\boxed{\sqrt{}}$ button instead. Higher powers and roots are also easy. Let's do 5^3 and $\sqrt[3]{125}$ with a calculator. The buttons you push vary a bit depending on the calculator model, but the process is the same. To calculate 5^3,

1) press 5

2) press $\boxed{\wedge}$ or $\boxed{y^x}$ or $\boxed{x^y}$

3) press 3

4) press $\boxed{\frac{enter}{or =}}$

And to compute $\sqrt[3]{125}$,

1)   press   3

2)   press $\boxed{\sqrt[x]{}}$, or $\boxed{\sqrt[x]{y}}$, or $\boxed{\sqrt[y]{x}}$, or $\boxed{x^{\frac{1}{y}}}$, or $\boxed{y^{\frac{1}{x}}}$

3)   press 125 (If your calculator has a $\boxed{\sqrt[3]{}}$ button, you can just press 125 $\boxed{\sqrt[3]{}}$ or $\boxed{\sqrt[3]{}}$ 125, then $\boxed{\begin{smallmatrix}enter\\or=\end{smallmatrix}}$; also, depending on the calculator model you use, you may have to enter the 125 before the 3.)

4)   press $\boxed{\begin{smallmatrix}enter\\or=\end{smallmatrix}}$

Scientific Notation

Mathematicians, scientists, and engineers use scientific notation for numbers far bigger or smaller than you'll ever have occasion to use. The distance to the Andromeda galaxy, the nearest galaxy similar to our own, the Milky Way, is roughly 2 million light-years. Since one light-year (the distance light travels in a year) is about 6 trillion miles, the distance to Andromeda is 2 million times that, or about 12,000,000,000,000,000,000 miles. This number is too cumbersome, so you can use scientific notation to write it as 1.2×10^{19}. The 19th power of 10 tells you that the original number has 19 digits to the *right* of where the decimal point is in the number 1.2—like this: 12,000,000,000,000,000,000.

19 digits

The weight of a proton is about .000000000000000000000000166 grams. Instead of this eyesore, you can write it with scientific notation as 1.66×10^{-24}. The *negative* 24th power of 10 tells you that the original number has 24 digits to the *left* of where the decimal point is in the number 1.66—like this: .000000000000000000000000166. Very large and very small numbers are

24 digits

easier to write, read, and comprehend when they're written in scientific notation.

Exponents are used when calculating the end result after something repeatedly grows or shrinks by the same percent, say once a day, once a month, or once a year. For example, if a $1000 investment grows 8% each year, what is it worth after five years? As we saw in the last chapter, to compute an 8% increase, we convert 8% to a decimal (0.08), add it to 1 (that's 1.08), then multiply. So here's what happens to the $1000 growing at 8% per year:

after one year: $1000 × 1.08   = $1080
after two years: $1080 × 1.08   = $1166.40
after three years: $1166.40 × 1.08 ≈ $1259.71
after four years: $1259.71 × 1.08 ≈ $1360.49
after five years: $1360.49 × 1.08 ≈ $1469.33

We can write this series of multiplications in one line:

$$\$1000 \times 1.08 \times 1.08 \times 1.08 \times 1.08 \times 1.08$$

And this is the same as

$$\$1000 \times 1.08^5$$

Which equals, again, $1469.33.

To close this chapter, let's do one more financial calculation. If you're hoping for an average annual return of 10% in the stock market, and you want to end up with $100,000 twenty years from now, what would you have to invest today? This is similar to the above problem where we computed

$$\$1000 \times 1.08^5 = \$1469.33$$

By this time, since we don't know what we must start with, we'll put the word "investment" where the $1000 is. Our annual multiplier this time is 1.10 because 10% converted to a decimal is 0.10, then that added to one is 1.10. And we use the 20th power for 20 years. That gives us:

$$investment \times 1.10^{20} = \$100,000$$

Now solve:

Step 1) Calculate 1.10^{20}: that's about 6.727.

Step 2) Divide \$100,000 by 6.727. You'd need to invest about \$14,865; why not make it \$15,000?

A Googol and a Googolplex

Powers can express huge numbers with great economy. A googol, 10^{100}, is a one followed by 100 zeros. This is *way* more than the number of protons, neutrons, and electrons in the universe. But a googol is a veritable pipsqueak next to the awesome googolplex. A googolplex is 10 raised to the googol power, or $10^{10^{100}}$; that's a one followed by a googol zeros. How big is a googolplex? Suffice it to say that if each zero in a googolplex were no bigger than a grain of sand, there wouldn't be enough room in the entire universe just to write it down.

Believe it or not, mathematicians have used numbers *much* bigger than a googolplex. For instance, they have long known a formula for estimating the number of prime numbers up to a given number. This formula always gave an answer a bit too high. Well, in 1933, Samuel Skewes proved that eventually this formula had to produce an underestimate of the number of primes. And he showed that this had to occur at some point before the number $10^{10^{10^{34}}}$. How big is that? I'm out of superlatives.

CHAPTER 5

Basic Geometry

There isn't much geometry that you need for day-to-day life. Understanding area problems is the main thing, and that's easy—for instance, determining the area of your backyard for grass seed or your floors for carpeting. Next, there are a few formulas for perimeter and volume that may come in handy. And I'll go over things like converting from square feet to square yards and from cubic feet to gallons. Lastly, I'll briefly cover two other useful ideas: the Pythagorean theorem and the slope of a line.

Let's begin with perimeter, area, and volume. Keep in mind that:

- **Perimeter** is *one*-dimensional like *string*. The perimeter of a room—or any other shape—is simply the length around the outside edge of the shape. You could think of perimeter as a measure of how much string you'd need to lay along the outside of the shape.
- **Area** is *two*-dimensional like *paper*. The area of a floor—or any other shape—is the amount of flat space it covers. You

could think of area as a measure of how much paper you'd need to cover the shape in question.

- **Volume** is *three*-dimensional like *water*. The volume of a backyard pool—or any other shape—tells you how much space is *inside* it. You could think of volume as a measure of how much water the object would hold.

When you consider the formulas below, notice the following pattern. Since volume is *three*-dimensional, you multiply *three* dimensions together, for instance, *length* × *width* × *height*, or *radius* × *radius* × *radius*. Area is *two*-dimensional, so you multiply *two* dimensions, for example, *length* × *width*, *base* × *height*, or *radius* × *radius*. And since perimeter is *one*-dimensional, you don't multiply dimensions by each other—instead, you add them, like *length* + *width* + *length* + *width*.

Perimeter Formulas

Perimeter is simple. You just add up the lengths along the outside edge of the shape in question. This will be easy as long as the sides of the shape are straight. So there's really no point to memorizing the rectangle formula below. But because it could be tricky to measure around the outside of a circle, the circle formula might come in handy.

Perimeter of rectangle = 2 × length + 2 × width

Notice that this is the same as just adding up the four sides: *length + width + length + width*. Also notice that, as mentioned above, you are not multiplying a dimension by a dimension here, as you will below with the area and volume formulas.

Circumference of circle = π × diameter

The Greek letter pi, π, equals about 3.14. An easy way to remember the above formula is to picture a circle inside of a square: Obviously, the distance around the square is more than the distance around the circle. And you can see that the distance around the square is four times as long as its width. The distance around the circle is a little less than that, namely, about three times its width.

Area Formulas

Area questions are by far the most frequently encountered geometry problems.

Area of rectangle = length × width

This is the only formula you'll need for most area problems. Either the shape in question will be a rectangle, or, if not, you'll be able to divide it into rectangular sections. This is called—can you guess?—the *rectangular sections method*. Consider, for example, the L-shaped room below:

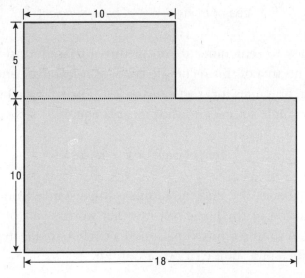

To compute the area of this room, just divide it as shown above into a 10'-by-18' rectangle and a 5'-by-10' rectangle. The large rectangle has an area of 10 times 18, or 180 square feet; the small one, 5 times 10, or 50 square feet. Add these up for the total area: 180 plus 50 is 230 square feet. Alternatively, you could have subtracted the missing 5'-by-8' corner (40 square feet) from the whole (imaginary) rectangle (15' by 18', or 270 square feet): 270 minus 40 gives you, again, 230 square feet.

You would also use the rectangular sections method in a problem like estimating the amount of wallpaper you'd need for a room. Walls, doors, and windows are generally rectangular, so you'd use the rectangle formula to compute their areas. And this time, you'd obviously *subtract* the areas of the doors and windows from the areas of the walls.

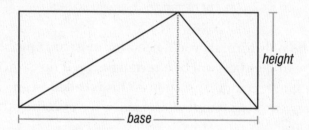

Area of triangle = ½ × *base* × *height*

This is easy to remember if you picture a triangle inside of a rectangle. The area of this rectangle is *base* × *height* (*base* and *height* are just different names for *length* and *width*). The triangle takes up half of the rectangle's area, and thus its area equals ½ × *base* × *height*.

Area of circle = π × *radius*²

Pi equals about 3.14, and the radius is the distance from the center to the outside of the circle, or, in other words, half of the circle's diameter. A simple approximation of a circle's area is that it's about ¾ of the area of a square drawn around it.

A Circle's about ¾ of a Square

Simple elegance is everywhere in mathematics. Consider the following connections between circles, squares, spheres, and cubes. Here's a circle inscribed in a square.

And can you picture the same idea with a sphere inside of a cube—like a basketball that fits perfectly in a box? Well, the circumference of the circle is about ¾ of the perimeter of the square; and the area of the circle is also about ¾ of the area of the square. For the sphere, use the number ½ instead of ¾. The surface area of the sphere is about ½ of the surface area of the box, and the volume of the sphere is also about ½ of the volume of the box. And in all four of these approximations, the error is exactly the same. In each case, the exact circle or sphere answer is 4.7% larger than the approximation; this error amount comes from the ratio of π to 3, which equals about 1.047. By the way, the same rule also applies to ellipses inside of rectangles (the rule works for area but not for perimeter) and three-dimensional ellipses inside of boxes (the rule works for volume but not for surface area).

Surface area. Another type of area problem involves the *surface area* of a three-dimensional shape, like a box. You don't need a formula for this because all you have to do is add up the areas of the six rectangular "faces" on the outside of the box. A box has the same size rectangles on its top and bottom, two equal rectangles on the front and back, and two more identical rectangles on the right and left. Just add up these six areas.

Area conversions. Since there are 3 feet in a yard, there are 3 times 3, or 9 square feet in a square yard (see diagram below). So to convert from square yards to square feet, you multiply by 9. To convert from square feet to square yards, you divide by 9.

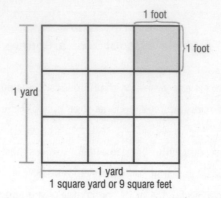

1 square yard or 9 square feet

For example, the area of a 12-foot-by-16-foot room is 12 times 16, or 192 square feet. To convert this to square yards, divide by 9: 192 divided by 9 gives you 21⅓ square yards.

Since there are 12 inches in a foot, there are 12 times 12 or 144 square inches in a square foot (see diagram below). Thus, to convert from square feet to square inches, you multiply by 144. To convert from square inches to square feet, divide by 144.

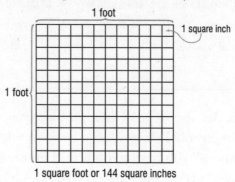

1 square foot or 144 square inches

Volume Formulas

You need volume formulas to figure things like the amount of water needed to fill an aquarium or a backyard pool or the amount of soil you need for a garden. Here are the formulas.

Volume of box = length × width × height

Pizza Geometry

Let's say your local pizza place sells 10-inch, 12-inch, 14-inch, and 16-inch pizzas. You and three of your friends are hungry; you don't think one 16-inch pizza will be enough, but two 14-inchers are too much. What should you get—a 16-inch and a 10-inch, or a 14-inch and a 12-inch, or three 10-inchers, or what? And which option is the best value?

The amount of food in a pizza depends on a pizza's *area*, not its *diameter*, so you want to be able to compare the areas of different-size pizzas. The area of a circle equals π (pi) times the radius squared—in other words, about $3.14 \times r^2$—but you can disregard the 3.14 because that multiplier affects the different-size pizzas in the same way—it's a wash. So to compare various pizza sizes, you merely need to divide the diameters in half then square the results:

10-inch pizza:	$10 \div 2 = 5$;	$5^2 = 25$
12-inch pizza:	$12 \div 2 = 6$;	$6^2 = 36$
14-inch pizza:	$14 \div 2 = 7$;	$7^2 = 49$
16-inch pizza:	$16 \div 2 = 8$;	$8^2 = 64$

This shows us that the four pizza sizes, 10-inch, 12-inch, 14-inch, and 16-inch, compare in size in the same way as do the numbers 25, 36, 49, and 64. The table reveals some comparisons that may surprise you. Two 10-inch pizzas (2 times 25 is 50) is almost exactly the same amount of food as one 14-inch pizza (49); thus, it never makes sense to pay a lot more for two 10-inch pizzas instead of getting one 14-inch pizza. And if you've got a hungry family, a 16-inch plus a 14-inch (64 plus 49 is 113) is more pizza than three 12-inchers (3 times 36 is 108), so don't pay more—which you probably will—for three 12-inchers.

Let's return to your party of four. Now you should be able to answer the question I posed: how do the three options compare—a 16-inch plus a 10-inch, a 14-inch plus a 12-inch, and three 10-inchers? For the 16-inch plus 10-inch option, add 64 to 25; that's 89. For the 14-inch plus 12-inch option, add 49 to 36; that's 85. For three 10-inchers, multiply 25 by 3; that's 75. You'll have to check the prices at your pizza place to be sure, but of the above three options, you'll probably get the most for your money with the 16-incher plus the 10-incher, or perhaps with the second option.

You use this, for instance, to determine the volume of an aquarium. Say the aquarium is 20" by 10" by 10"; that's $20 \times 10 \times 10$, or 2000 cubic inches (see below for converting cubic inches to gallons).

After a box shape, the next most common shape is something with the same shape on its bottom and top (actually, a box also fits this description). For example, if the bottom and top are equal circles, you've got a cylinder, and if the bottom and top are equal triangles or equal hexagons, etc., you've got a prism. Cylinders and prisms have the same formula:

Volume of cylinder or prism = area of base × height

A circular pool is cylindrical. Say it's 3 feet deep and 12 feet across. How much water do you need to fill it?

Step 1) Figure the area of its base, which is a circle:

$$
\begin{aligned}
\textit{Area of circle} &= \pi \times \textit{radius}^2 \\
&\approx 3.14 \times 6^2 \\
&\approx 3.14 \times 36 \\
&\approx 113 \text{ square feet}
\end{aligned}
$$

Step 2) Multiply this by the height (which means the same thing here as depth):

113 times 3 is 339 cubic feet; let's call it 340 cubic feet.

Volume conversions. Since there are 3 feet in a yard, there are $3 \times 3 \times 3$ or 27 cubic feet in a cubic yard. And since there are 12 inches to the foot, there are $12 \times 12 \times 12$ or 1728 cubic inches to the cubic foot. To convert from the big thing to the small thing—cubic yards to cubic feet or cubic feet to cubic inches—*multiply* by 27 or 1728. To convert from the small thing to the big thing, *divide* by 27 or 1728. The following conversion is also useful:

1 cubic foot ≈ 7.5 gallons

And here are some conversions involving the weight of water. You may have occasion for determining the weight of the water in a large aquarium or in a waterbed, or the weight of water you're carrying on a long hike.

1 pint of water weighs about 1 pound
1 gallon of water weighs about 8⅓ pounds
1 cubic foot of water weighs about 62 pounds

Pythagorean Theorem

You probably won't have too much occasion to use the Pythagorean theorem, but let's go through it briefly—at a minimum, you can help your kids with it (they certainly *will* need it). The lengths of the three sides of any right triangle are related by the following equation.

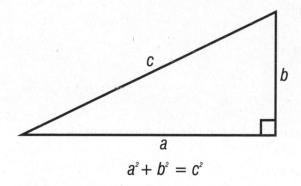

$$a^2 + b^2 = c^2$$

Let's do a problem. Say you cut diagonally across a park on your walk to work. If the park is 2 blocks by 3 blocks, how long is your shortcut, and how many blocks does the shortcut save you?

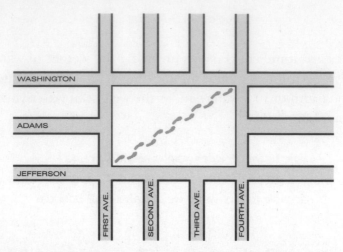

Step 1) Plug 2 and 3 into *a* and *b* in the formula (*a* and *b* are interchangeable; it doesn't matter which number you plug into which unknown):

$$a^2 + b^2 = c^2$$

$$2^2 + 3^2 = c^2$$

Step 2) Simplify:

$$4 + 9 = c^2$$

$$13 = c^2$$

Step 3) Use your calculator to take the square root of 13:

$$\sqrt{13} = c$$

$$3.6 \approx c$$

So the shortcut is about three and a half blocks long and you save about a block and a half compared with walking around the park.

Slope

The slope of a line is simply a measure of its steepness. Consider the following diagram:

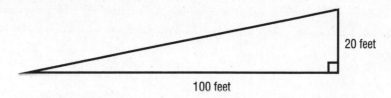

If you walked up this hill, you'd go up 20 feet vertically, and traverse 100 feet horizontally. The slope of this hill is the ratio of this vertical distance (called the *rise*) to the horizontal distance (called the *run*). Here's the formula:

$$Slope = \frac{rise}{run}$$

For this hill, we have,

$$Slope = \frac{20'}{100'}$$

$$= \frac{1}{5} \text{ or } 0.2$$

Slope is used to measure, among other things, the steepness of roads, railways, rooflines, and stairways.

CHAPTER 6

Measurement and Conversion

In this brief chapter, we'll first go over a few rules for how to use units of measure when doing computations. Then we'll discuss the U.S. and metric systems of measurement and how to do conversions within each system and from one system to the other. And last, we'll discuss how to use your body to measure things.

Units of Measure

When using units in computations, make sure you first convert each number to the proper unit. All lengths must be converted into the same unit, all weights must be expressed in the same unit, etc. For example, if you want to figure the area of an eight-inch-by-six-foot piece of material, you must first convert the eight inches into feet (if you want the answer in square feet) or convert the six feet into inches (if you want the answer in square inches). One inch is ¹⁄₁₂ of a foot, so eight inches is ⁸⁄₁₂ of a foot, and ⁸⁄₁₂ reduces to ⅔. So the area is ⅔ foot times 6 feet, which equals 4 square feet. In a problem like this, make sure you don't make the mistake of converting 8 inches into 0.8 feet. Remember:

*8 inches is **not** 0.8 feet*

And, by the same token,

*1 hour and 12 minutes (or 1:12) is **not** 1.12 hours*

You can't use 1:12 in a computation. Either convert it into 72 minutes or convert it into hours: 1 hour and 12 minutes is 1¹²⁄₆₀ hours, which reduces to 1⅕ hours or 1.2 hours.

Let's try a problem. How much gas do you need to drive 31.8 miles if your car gets 28.5 miles per gallon? If you're not sure how to do this problem, I've got two tips for you. First, use your common sense: just think for a moment what 28.5 miles per gallon means. As you know, it means that you can drive 28.5 miles for each gallon of gas. From this fact, it's clear that you'll need a little more than one gallon to go 31.8 miles. And this tells you that you can't get the answer by multiplying 28.5 by 31.8 or by dividing 28.5 by 31.8 (because when you divide a smaller number by a bigger number, you get an answer *less* than one). Thus, the solution must be given by dividing the bigger number by the smaller number: 31.8 divided by 28.5 is about 1.1, and an answer of 1.1 gallons agrees with what your common sense tells you.

The second tip is to try to make up a similar problem with numbers that make the solution obvious to you. Using round numbers usually helps. For example, if the problem had been, "How much gas do you need to drive 100 miles if you can get 25 miles per gallon," you probably would have seen the solution right away—4 gallons. And why is the answer 4 gallons? Because, of course, 25 goes into 100 four times, or, in other words, 100 divided by 25 is 4. Now, after doing this simplified version of the problem, just go back and do the original problem the same way. In the original problem, we have 31.8 miles instead of 100 miles and 28.5 miles per gallon instead of 25 miles per gallon. So since we got the answer to the simplified problem by doing 100 divided by 25, the solution to the original problem is 31.8 divided by 28.5, which, again, equals about 1.1 gallons.

U.S. System of Measurement

LENGTH

12 inches	=	1 foot
3 feet	=	1 yard
36 inches	=	1 yard
5280 feet	=	1 mile
1760 yards	=	1 mile
1.15 miles	≈	1 nautical mile
5,878,000,000,000 miles	≈	1 light-year

AREA

144 square inches	=	1 square foot (there are 12 inches in a foot, so there are 12 times 12, or 144 square inches in a square foot)
9 square feet	=	1 square yard (there are 3 feet in a yard, so there are 3 times 3, or 9 square feet in a square yard)
43,560 square feet	=	1 acre
640 acres	=	1 square mile
27,878,400 square feet	=	1 square mile
10 acres	=	an ⅛-mile-by-⅛-mile square

VOLUME

3 teaspoons	=	1 tablespoon
2 tablespoons	=	1 ounce
8 ounces	=	1 cup
2 cups	=	1 pint
2 pints	=	1 quart
4 quarts	=	1 gallon
16 ounces	=	1 pint
32 ounces	=	1 quart
128 ounces	=	1 gallon
4 cups	=	1 quart
16 cups	=	1 gallon
1.8 cubic inches	≈	1 ounce
1.1 tablespoons	≈	1 cubic inch
7.5 gallons	≈	1 cubic foot
1728 cubic inches	=	1 cubic foot (there are 12 inches in a foot, so there are 12 times 12 times 12, or 1728 cubic inches in a cubic foot)
27 cubic feet	=	1 cubic yard (there are 3 feet in a yard, so there are 3 times 3 times 3, or 27 cubic feet in a cubic yard)

WEIGHT

16 ounces	=	1 pound
2000 pounds	=	1 ton

SPEED

1.47 feet/second	≈	1 mile/hour
1.15 miles/hour	≈	1 knot (1 knot equals 1 nautical mile/hour)

Here's how to convert from one U.S. unit to another. Just use the above tables and your common sense. In the above tables, each unit in the left-hand column is a smaller unit than the corresponding unit in the right-hand column. Now, it's obvious that if you have, say, 3 gallons of something, you have *more* than 3 cups of it because cups are *smaller* than gallons, and if you have 60 inches of something, you have *less* than 60 feet of it because feet are *bigger* than inches. So here's the rule:

To go from a big unit to a small one, multiply.
To go from a small unit to a big one, divide.

Converting 5000 yards into miles, for instance, is going from a small thing (yards) to a big thing (miles), so we divide. Thus, 5000 divided by 1760 is about 2.84 miles. That's all there is to it.

In the interest of saving space, I didn't list every possible conversion in the above tables, so you'll have to do an extra step if you want to convert from, say, teaspoons to cups or vice versa. Since there are 3 teaspoons in a tablespoon, 2 tablespoons in an ounce, and 8 ounces in a cup, there are 3 times 2 times 8, or 48 teaspoons in a cup. Now you can use the number 48 to convert between teaspoons and cups.

One last item. Here's an old hiker's maxim:

A pint's a pound the world 'round.

In other words, a pint of water weighs about a pound. Thus, a cup of water weighs about half a pound, a quart of water weighs about two pounds, a half a gallon weighs about four pounds, and a gallon weighs about eight pounds. Knowing these simple facts makes it easy to estimate the weight of anything that has a density close to water[1]—

---

[1] In other words, anything that has a *specific gravity* of 1. My apologies if that reminds you of your high school chemistry class.

and many things do. Most liquids weigh about the same as water, as do most fruits and vegetables (unless they have a lot of air in them, like lettuce). Animals and people also are about as dense as water. Here are a few examples. If you see a watermelon that looks about as big as three one-gallon milk containers, then it weighs about three times eight or twenty-four pounds. Or you might see a dog that looks about as big as four gallons. So it weighs about four times eight or thirty-two pounds. And since a liter is very close to a quart, a liter of Coke weighs about two pounds. Lastly, here's a somewhat depressing thought to close this section. If you gain just eight pounds, the extra weight you're carrying around is as heavy and as big as a gallon of milk!

The Metric System

The metric system, which is used in just about every country of the world except the United States, is much easier to learn and to use than the U.S. system because everything is based on multiples of 10. For example, there are 100 centimeters in a meter, 1000 meters in a kilometer, and 1000 grams in a kilogram. There are none of the "unround" numbers you find in the U.S. system: 36 inches in a yard, 5280 feet in a mile, 128 ounces in a gallon, etc. Hopefully, the U.S. will one day get with the program, but don't hold your breath.

All units in the metric system use the same prefixes. On the following list, the commonly used prefixes are in bold. These are the ones you should definitely know.

milli:	**one-thousandth**
centi:	**one-hundredth**
deci:	one-tenth
deka:	ten
hecta:	one hundred
kilo:	**one thousand**

In addition to these, the following prefixes are used in computer contexts, among other things:

mega: one million (1,000,000)
giga: one billion (1,000,000,000)
tera: one trillion (1,000,000,000,000)

LENGTH

1000 millimeters	=	1 meter
10 millimeters	=	1 centimeter
100 centimeters	=	1 meter
1000 meters	=	1 kilometer
9,461,000,000,000 kilometers	≈	1 light-year

AREA

100 square millimeters	=	1 square centimeter
10,000 square centimeters	=	1 square meter
10,000 square meters	=	1 hectare
100 hectares	=	1 square kilometer
1,000,000 square meters	=	1 square kilometer

VOLUME

1 milliliter	=	1 cubic centimeter
1000 milliliters	=	1 liter
1000 liters	=	1 cubic meter

WEIGHT

1000 grams	=	1 kilogram
1000 kilograms	=	1 metric ton

SPEED

3.6 kilometers/hours	=	1 meter/second

To convert from one metric unit to another you use the same method discussed in the section on U.S. units.

U.S./Metric Conversions

Let's begin this section with a mnemonic device for remembering a few U.S./metric conversions:

$$1.1 \text{ yards} \approx 1 \text{ meter}$$
$$1.1 \text{ quarts} \approx 1 \text{ liter}$$
$$2.2 \text{ pounds} \approx 1 \text{ kilogram}$$

These are approximate conversions, but they're close enough for practical purposes. To help you remember this, notice the following. "Meter" rhymes with "liter"; "yards" almost rhymes with "quarts" (I realize that may sound a bit silly, but with mnemonic devices, silly works); add up 1.1 and 1.1 and you get 2.2; the units *meter, liter,* and *kilogram* are three of the most fundamental of all metric units; and lastly, to remember that the numbers 1.1, 1.1, and 2.2 belong on the left side of the above mnemonic, recall that a meter is a little longer than a yard—you may know that a meter stick is about 3½ inches longer than a yardstick or that the 100-meter dash is a little longer race than the 100-yard dash or that a 25-meter swimming pool is a bit longer than a 25-yard pool.

If you can remember just these three conversions and the common metric prefixes listed above, you can derive any of the other U.S./metric conversions you might need, in the event that you don't have the complete U.S./metric table handy. For example, let's say you want to know how many centimeters make an inch:

Step 1) Since there are 36 inches in a yard and about 1.1 yards in a meter, there are 36 times 1.1 or about 39.6 inches in a meter.

Step 2) There are 100 centimeters in a meter, so now we know that:

$$39.6 \text{ inches} \approx 100 \text{ centimeters}$$

Step 3) You want to know what 1 inch equals, so divide both sides of this equation by 39.6:

$$\frac{\cancel{39.6} \; \textit{Inches}}{\cancel{39.6}} \approx \frac{100 \; \textit{centimeters}}{39.6}$$

$$1 \; \textit{inch} \quad \approx \quad 2.5 \; \textit{centimeters}$$

The complete U.S./metric table is in the appendix.

The Mars Climate Orbiter

If you think converting between U.S. units and metric units is no big deal—I mean, does it really matter whether you call a gallon of milk a gallon or 3.8 liters?—check this out. The Mars Climate Orbiter, launched on December 11, 1998, was lost when it crashed into Mars about a year later due to failure to properly convert English units into metric units! Price tag: $125 million!

Using Your Body to Measure Things

If you find yourself wanting to measure something when you're away from your home and you don't happen to have a tape measure in your back pocket, you can use your body to measure things (and see the appendix for a list of common objects that can be used for measuring). I recommend that you take a 3-by-5 index card—fold it in thirds and it'll fit nicely in your wallet—or an old business card, and copy onto it some of the numbers discussed below that you think you'll be likely to use. You could also mark up the edges of the card so you can use it like a ruler. You could mark one edge in inches and the other in centimeters, like this:

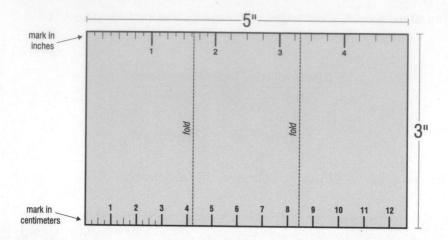

While you're at it, why not add to this card a few other facts like the Fahrenheit/centigrade conversion formulas from chapter 22 and the tipping shortcuts from chapter 19.

On the back of the card, you could put information about using your body to measure things. Spread your hand out as wide as possible and measure the distance from the tip of your thumb to the tip of your little finger. Record this measurement on your card. Next, measure your fingers—looking for a couple measurements that come out to an exact number of inches. For example, you may find that the first or second segment of your little finger is exactly an inch, or that the first and second segments (together) of your index finger measure exactly two inches, or that your entire index finger is exactly four inches, or that the total width of your four fingers is three inches, etc. Perhaps the distance from the tip of your middle finger to your elbow is a nice round number. Now spread your arms out and measure the distance from the tip of your fingers to the tip of your fingers.

Next, measure your foot. The most accurate way to do this is to walk heel-to-toe, heel-to-toe, etc., for six or eight steps, measure this distance, then divide by the number of steps. Let's say this is 9½ inches. You may find it handy to record both this length and also its equivalent in feet—that's about 0.79 feet (0.8 feet is close enough). Now you can use this measurement to walk off the distance across a room, for instance. After walking across the room, you just multiply your foot measurement by the number of steps. But there are a couple other ways you can do it. If, say, four of your steps is exactly three feet or five steps is exactly four feet, you might want to record and use that fact. Or, instead of walking heel-to-toe, heel-to-toe, you can leave a gap of 2½ inches (for the 9½-inch foot) between each of your steps so that each step equals one foot. With practice, you can get quite precise in eyeballing this gap amount.

You can, of course, also pace off a distance with regular steps. One way to do it is to make each of your steps one yard long. After you do it a few times, you'll get the feel and look of these yard-long strides. The other method is to walk normally for six or eight strides, measure that distance, then divide by the number of steps to determine the length of one of your normal strides. Because the length of your strides can vary quite a bit—especially the first step before you get going—try to walk as naturally as possible at your normal pace, and try to make your first step the same as the rest. And, if you really want an accurate length, take fifteen or twenty steps instead of six or eight, or do the six or eight steps a few times and average the results. Record your natural stride length on the card. Well, there you have it. Carry the card in your wallet, and you'll never be at a loss about measuring things.

CHAPTER 7

Probability and Odds

(Brace yourself.)

Probability, odds, and chance pop up everywhere. You hear things like there's a 25 percent chance of rain tomorrow, that you have a one-in-ten-thousand chance of contracting such-and-such an illness, or a one-in-ten-million chance of winning the lottery—or, if you believe Chicago baseball fans, the comparably low odds of the Cubs winning the World Series. Probability questions also arise at the races, at the casino, and in card and dice games like bridge, poker, and backgammon. Mathematical literacy requires knowledge of at least the fundamentals of this ubiquitous topic.

Part I: Basic Principles

Six Probability Rules

1) A probability is always a percent from 0% to 100% or a number from 0 to 1. The probability that something will happen is always in the range of 0% to 100%, or, if you convert these percentages to ordinary numbers, the range is from 0 to 1. A probability of 0% means that something can't possibly happen; a probability of 100% means that the thing in question will definitely happen. As you know, a 50% probability means that something is equally likely to occur or not occur, and a 25% probability means that something will happen, on average, one time out of four.

2) Probabilities always add up to 100%; or, if you use numbers rather than percents, they add up to 1. Since something must either happen or not happen, the probability of it happening plus the probability of it not happening must add up to 100% or 1. For example, if there's a 25% chance of rain tomorrow, it follows that there's a 75% chance that it won't rain. A related idea is that if we list the probabilities of all the mutually exclusive things that might happen in a given situation, their probabilities must add up to 100%. If we toss two coins for instance, there are three possible outcomes: two heads, two tails, and one head with one tail. Thus, the probabilities of these three results must add up to 100%, which they do: the probability of two heads is 25%, two tails is also 25%, and one head with one tail is 50%. We'll return to this problem below.

3) The basic probability formula. The beginning point for determining a probability is the simple formula,

$$probability = \frac{number\ of\ \text{``successes''}\ or\ \text{``winners''}}{total\ number\ of\ possibilities}$$

For example, what's the probability of rolling a 5 with a single die? Since there is just one 5 on the die, and thus just one way to "succeed" or "win"—in other words, just one way to get what we want—and since there are a total of six numbers that can come up on the die, the formula gives us,

$$probability = \frac{1}{6}\ \text{(or about 17\%)}$$

Here's another one. What's the probability of drawing a face card from a deck of cards? There are 12 face cards in the deck: four jacks (one in each of the four suits: clubs, diamonds, hearts, and spades), four queens, and four kings. And there are a total of 52 cards. So we have,

$$probability = \frac{12}{52} = \frac{3}{13} \text{ (about 23\%)}$$

Et tu, Brute?

Take a breath. Believe it or not, mathematicians have calculated that there's over a 99 percent probability that you just inhaled at least one molecule of air from Caesar's dying breath when he turned to Brutus and asked, "Et tu, Brute?" (If you like, you can substitute your favorite historical figure from the same era or earlier.) Hard to believe? Look at it this way. Say you put one drop of red food coloring in a gallon of water and stir. In a matter of moments, the entire gallon will be a bit pink, and if you draw a teaspoon of water from the gallon, it will contain some of the coloring. Now, granted, the earth's entire atmosphere is a great deal more than a gallon, but the air from Caesar's breath has had about two thousand years to thoroughly mix throughout the atmosphere, and there are so many billions of air molecules in one of your breaths—actually, it's billions of billions—that it's close to certain that at least one of the molecules you inhaled passed through Caesar!

4) The multiplication rule. I'm going to try to keep this as simple as possible, but there are a few unavoidable complications with this rule. The basic idea, though, is quite straightforward: when you want to compute *the probability that two or more things will happen*, you *multiply* their probabilities. It's easy to apply this rule to sequential events. For example, what's the probability that the next four shower gifts you'll buy will be for baby girls? For each birth, the probability of having a girl is 50% or ½—actually it's about 48.5%, but let's keep this simple and call it an even 50%. So the probability of four girls in a row is given by the multiplication rule:

$$\frac{1}{2} \times \frac{1}{2} \times \frac{1}{2} \times \frac{1}{2} = \frac{1}{16} \text{ (about a 6\% chance)}$$

By the way, the probability of tossing four coins in a row and having them all come up heads is computed the same way.

Here's another example. What's the probability of dealing three hearts in a row from a deck of cards? Well, the probability of dealing the first heart is $\frac{13}{52}$ because there are 13 hearts and a total of 52 cards; this reduces to ¼. We could have also reasoned that the probability is ¼ because we need to deal a heart, which is one out of four suits. After the first heart is dealt, the probability changes for the next heart because now there are only 12 hearts left out of a total of 51 cards—this gives us $\frac{12}{51}$. After two hearts are dealt, there are 11 hearts left out of 50 cards so the probability is $\frac{11}{50}$. Thus, using the multiplication rule, the probability of dealing three hearts in a row is:

$$\frac{13}{52} \times \frac{12}{51} \times \frac{11}{50} = \frac{11}{850} \text{ (or about 0.013 or 1.3\%)}^{[1]}$$

So far so good. But it gets a bit complicated with problems like the following. What's the probability of tossing three coins simultaneously and getting one heads and two tails? You can use the multiplication rule with problems like this involving *simultaneous* events as well as with problems like the above involving *sequential* events, but you've got to be careful. You can't just say, "Well, I want one heads (that probability is ½) and two tails (each has a probability of ½), and thus the answer is ½ times ½ times ½, which equals ⅛." This is wrong because there are three different ways to get one heads and two tails—any one of the three coins could be the one heads

---

[1] If, after dealing each card, we had replaced it in the deck, the probability of dealing the second and third hearts would be the same as the probability of dealing the first one—¼. And thus the probability of dealing three hearts in a row would be ¼ times ¼ times ¼, which equals $\frac{1}{64}$ or about 1.6%.

you get. With problems like this, it can be instructive to consider how the same problem would work sequentially. If you flip one coin three times and you want to get one heads and two tails, you could get HTT or THT or TTH. The probability of each one of these three possibilities can be figured like the other sequential problems we did above. The probability of tossing HTT is ½ times ½ times ½, which equals ⅛. The probabilities of the other two possibilities work the same way, so they're each also ⅛. And since we want any one of the three things to happen, we add up the individual results: ⅛ plus ⅛ plus ⅛, which comes to ⅜ (this is the addition rule—see below). This result, ⅜, is the probability of tossing three coins simultaneously and getting one heads and two tails.[2] Had the question instead been, "what's the probability of tossing three coins simultaneously and getting three heads," there would not have been this complication because there's only one way to get three heads: HHH. In this case, the answer is the same whether it's three heads sequentially or three heads simultaneously: ½ times ½ times ½, or ⅛. To make a long story short, when you want to use the multiplication rule for simultaneous events, you've got to ask whether there's more than one way to get what you want. If there is, you add up the individual probabilities.

5) The addition rule. When you want to compute *the probability that any one of several things happens*, you *add* their probabilities. To use the addition rule, the events in question must be *mutually exclusive*. For instance, the Yankees, the Red Sox, and the Tigers are all in the American League. So, obviously, only one of them can win the pen-

---

[2] We could have solved this problem a different way using the basic probability formula (rule 3 above),

$$probability = \frac{number\ of\ ``successes"\ or\ ``winners"}{total\ number\ of\ possibilities}.$$

The number of successes—in other words, the number of ways of getting one heads and two tails—is three: HTT, THT, and TTH. And the total number of possibilities when tossing three coins is eight: HHH, HHT, HTH, HTT, THH, THT, TTH, and TTT. So the formula gives us the answer—⅜. The formal, mathematical way of computing this answer is $_3C_1/2^3$ . . . whoah . . . sorry . . . I'm supposed to be keeping this simple, right?

nant in any given year, in other words, the Yankees winning, the Red Sox winning, and the Tigers winning—these are mutually exclusive events. So to compute the probability of any of them winning, you just add up each of the probabilities. If you estimate that the Yankees have a 20% chance of winning the pennant next season, that the Tigers have a 15% chance, and that the Red Sox have a 5% chance, then the probability of any of them winning would be 20% plus 15% plus 5%, which comes to 40%.

When you play craps, rolling a 2, 3, or 12 on your first roll is called *craps*—you lose. What's the probability of "crapping out" like this? Rolling a 2 or a 3 or a 12 are mutually exclusive events—since you can't roll more than one of them at the same time—so we just add up their probabilities. There's just one way to roll a 2 (1, 1), out of a total of 36 possible rolls, so the probability of rolling a 2 from the basic probability formula (rule number 3 above) is $\frac{1}{36}$. There's also one way of rolling a 12 (6, 6), so its probability is also $\frac{1}{36}$. And there are two ways of rolling a 3, (1, 2 and 2, 1), so that probability is $\frac{2}{36}$. Thus, the probability of crapping out on your first roll is

$$\frac{1}{36} + \frac{1}{36} + \frac{2}{36} = \frac{4}{36}, \text{ which reduces to } \frac{1}{9} \text{ (about 11\%)}$$

Alternatively, we could have just counted up the total number of losing rolls—the one way of rolling a 2 plus the one way of rolling a 12 plus the two ways of rolling a 3—for a total of 4 losing rolls out of 36 possible rolls. This gives us, again, a probability of $\frac{4}{36}$.

Here's a problem that illustrates an important principle. If we toss three coins, what's the probability that we get either one or two heads? This would be a somewhat complicated problem if it weren't for the following nice shortcut. *Figuring out the probability of not getting the desired result is often easier than computing the probability of what we want.* Then, since the probability of something happening plus the probability of it not happening must add up to 100% (rule number 2 above), you can subtract the probability that something *won't* happen from 100% to give you the probability that it *will* happen. There are four mutually exclusive things that can happen when we toss three coins: we can get zero, one, two, or three heads. Let's figure the probability that we *don't* get what we want—one or two heads—namely, that we get either three heads or three tails. The probability of tossing three heads is simply ½ times ½ times ½, which equals ⅛, or 12.5%. The probability of tossing three tails works the same way, so that's also 12.5%. Now we use the addition rule to compute the probability of tossing either three heads or three tails: 12.5% plus 12.5% equals 25%. Since this is the probability of *not* getting the desired result, the probability that we *do* get the desired result—either one or two heads—is 100% minus 25%, which equals 75%.

6) When you can't use the addition rule. When you have two or more events that are *not mutually exclusive* and you want to compute *the probability that at least one of them happens,* you can't just add up their individual probabilities. For example, let's say your church runs a raffle once a year. Since it's for a good cause, you always buy *lots* of tickets—10% of all the tickets sold. That gives you a 10% or 1-in-10 chance of winning the raffle each year. If you plan on playing for five years, you might think that you have a 50% chance of winning at least once because adding up 10% five times is 50%. But you *can't* use the addition rule here because winning the raffle in different years are not mutually exclusive events; in other words, you could win more than once. It's easy to see why you can't use the addition rule in problems like this if you consider what would happen if you entered the raffle 15 times. If you use the addition rule to add up 10% fifteen times, you'd get an answer of 150%, which is impossible because no probability can be more than 100% (rule number 1 above). And not only can't the answer be 150%, it can't even be 100%, because as everyone knows, if you have a 10% chance of winning and you play 15 times, that may make it quite likely that you'll win at least once, but it certainly doesn't give you a guaranteed, 100% chance of winning.

For problems like this, you use the method introduced above, namely, you compute the probability of *not* getting the desired result and then subtract that number from 100%. To use this method, the events in question must be *independent*—as are the events in the above problems because winning or not winning the raffle in any given year has no effect on whether you win the raffle another year. So what is the probability of winning at least once if you enter the raffle five times? To answer this, we'll figure the probability of *not* winning at least once—in other words, not winning at all. We'll then subtract that probability from 100%. First, compute the probability of *not* winning a raffle. Since the probability of winning is 10%, the probability of not winning is 90% or 0.9. Next, use the multiplication rule to figure the probability of *not* winning five times in a row.

$$0.9 \times 0.9 \times 0.9 \times 0.9 \times 0.9 = 0.59 \text{ (or about 59\%)}$$

And now just subtract this from 100%. That gives us the answer—about 41%. And what if you played 15 times? Use the multiplication rule to compute the probability of not winning 15 times in a row. To multiply 0.9 by itself 15 times, use the 15th power:

$$0.9^{15} \approx 0.21 \text{ (or about 21\%)}$$

Subtracting this from 100% gives us the answer: there's about a 79% chance of winning at least once if you play 15 times.

One more example. Let's say you estimate that the Yankees have a 40% chance of winning the American League pennant next season and that the Braves have a 30% chance of winning the National League pennant. (No disrespect to either team, but these percents are wildly optimistic—as they would be if applied to any team in any given year.) Assuming these probabilities are correct, what would be the probability of at least one of the two teams winning the pennant? Since these events are not mutually exclusive, we can't add their probabilities for an answer of 70%. Instead, since these events are independent, we can use the above method. The Yankees have a 40% chance of winning, so they have a 60% or 0.6 chance of not winning, and the Braves have a 30% chance of winning and thus a 70% or 0.7 chance of not winning. Now we use the multiplication rule to compute the probability of both of them *not* winning their respective pennants:

$$0.6 \times 0.7 = 0.42 \text{ (or 42\%)}$$

Just subtract this from 100% for the final answer: there is a 58% chance that the Yankees, the Braves, or both will win their pennants.

A final comment. Use the method described above if you want the exact answer, but for a quick approximation, just add up the individual probabilities and then make the following correction:

If the answer you get is less than 10%, make no correction.
If the answer you get is from 10% to 19%, subtract 1%.
If your answer is in the twenties, subtract 2%.
If your answer is in the thirties, subtract 3%.

Don't use this shortcut if your answer is 40% or above, because the error grows rapidly from that point on. Let's do an example. Say you entered the raffle described above three times with a 10% chance of winning each time. To approximate your chances of winning at least once, just add up the individual probabilities: 10% plus 10% plus 10% is 30%. Now, because your answer is in the thirties, subtract 3% for a final answer of 27%. Compare this with the answer given by the exact method. Since the probability of winning the raffle is 10%, the probability of *not* winning is 90% or 0.9. So we multiply 0.9 by itself three times—0.9 times 0.9 times 0.9 equals 0.729 or 72.9%—and then subtract this from 100%. This gives us an exact answer of 27.1%. Our approximation was only a tenth of one percent off. The shortcut method could give you an error of as much as 4%, but the error will usually be much smaller, and, in any event, the answer will be good enough.

Four Counting Principles

The following four principles show you how to determine the total number of ways something can occur—the total number of possibilities. Figuring the number of possibilities is interesting in its own right, and is often necessary when doing probability problems.

1) The fundamental counting principle. Let's illustrate this simple idea with an example. If the menu at your favorite restaurant lists 3 salads, 8 entrees, and 4 desserts, how many times could you eat there without repeating the same meal (assuming that you always order all three courses)? The fundamental counting principle gives the answer. Just multiply: 3 times 8 times 4 equals 96. With 96 different meals, you wouldn't have to repeat a meal until your 97th visit. This principle works whenever you have to choose among options, then choose again, then choose again, etc.

If you run into a friend and learn that both of you had just eaten at the restaurant referred to above, what is the probability that both of you had the same meal? Well, whatever meal you had, there is just one way for your friend's selection to match yours—out of a total of 96 possible meals. So the basic probability formula gives us the answer: ⅟₉₆, or about a 1% chance. (For sticklers, this answer assumes that both you and your friend order all three courses and the unrealistic assumption that each of you is equally likely to pick any of the 3 salads, any of the 8 entrees, and any of the 4 desserts.)

2) The factorial button ![!]. If you have, say, 6 things, how many different ways can you order them or line them up? Well, you have 6 choices for what to put first, then, after that's selected, 5 choices for what to

Let's Make a Deal

The field of probability produces many puzzles with remarkable, counterintuitive answers. A famous one is based on the old TV game show *Let's Make a Deal*. The show's host, Monty Hall, would select two contestants from the audience. They'd come down from their seats to join Monty, and then each would choose one of three doors; they couldn't both choose the same door. Behind one of the doors was something like a shiny new car; behind the other two were things like a bale of hay or a donkey. Obviously, both contestants couldn't win; one or both of them had to lose. Before Monty revealed the winning prize, he'd open a losing door that a contestant had picked to show him or her what he or she had "won." This losing contestant would then sit down, leaving the other contestant standing with his or her door and one other still unopened.

Here's the puzzle. At this point in the game, with one contestant left and two unopened doors, one of which hides the winning prize, what is the probability that the contestant will win? Believe it or not, the answer is *not* 50%. Yes, there is one prize, and yes, there are two doors, but the probability is *not* one in two (or ½ or 50%). The chances that this remaining contestant will win are ⅔, or 2 in 3, or about 67%. In *odds* terminology, the odds that this contestant will win are 2-to-1.

This answer seems so strange to some people that they refuse to believe it. They insist that the answer is 50%. But I promise you, the answer is about 67%. The rigorous mathematical explanation is beyond the scope of this book, but here's an explanation that some find persuasive. Let's say the game is played 300 times in a year. How many prizes would you expect the game show to give out? Well, each time the game is played, two people pick from three doors. So there's a 2-in-3 chance that someone will win. And so, over a span of 300 games, we'd expect there to be a winner about two-thirds of the time, or about 200 times out of the 300. Now, every time the game is played, there is a loser who is asked to sit down, and every time there is one contestant still standing with two unopened doors. If the probability of this contestant winning was only 50%, that would mean that time after time the probability of someone winning would be 50%. And if that were true, we'd expect only about 150 winners in 300 games. But we know that there must be about 200 winners. And the only way for that to happen is if the remaining contestant has a 2-in-3 chance of winning each time the game is played.

If you're still not convinced, you're not alone. You can find more complete explanations of this puzzle in several books and articles and on the World Wide Web.

put second, then 4 choices for what to put third, etc. The total number of different orders is given by the fundamental counting principle:

$$6 \times 5 \times 4 \times 3 \times 2 \times 1 = 720$$

You can compute this in one step with the *factorial* button ⊞ on your calculator:

press: 6 ⊞ ⊞

The answer again is 720.

In some problems, we can use the factorial button to compute the number that we need for the denominator in the basic probability formula. For example, if you put a CD with 10 tracks in a CD player and select "random play," what is the probability that the tracks will be played in the same order as they appear on the CD case? Since the total number of ways to list the 10 tracks is given by 10 factorial (10!), and since there is only one way to list the 10 tracks in the desired order, we have

$$\text{probability} = \frac{\text{number of "successes" or "winners"}}{\text{total number of possibilities}}$$

$$= \frac{1}{10!}$$

$$= \frac{1}{3{,}628{,}800}$$

That's only one chance out of about three and a half million. Don't bet on it!

3) Combinations. Both this and the following principle, permutations, involve situations where you want to figure out the total number of ways you can choose some or all of the items from a list.

When you're choosing some items and also putting them in some order or ranking or giving them some designation, that's a *permutation* problem. If the order of the things you choose doesn't matter, it's a *combination* problem. Let's go through an example.

If you have to select three people out of five to serve on a committee, how many different groups of three could you choose? This is a *combination* problem because the question doesn't involve any type of ordering or ranking of the three people you choose. In other words, selecting, say, Ann, Bob, and Connie to be on the committee means the same thing as selecting Bob, Connie, and Ann. If your calculator has a combinations button, $_nC_r$, as many do, you can do this problem in one step, and you can then skip the explanation below of how to do the problem the long way—unless you're just dying to learn another formula. We want to compute $_5C_3$ (the C is for "combinations," but you can read this as "5 *choose* 3," which is a good way to remember how to use the combinations button because out of 5 things you're choosing 3). On your calculator,

press: 5  3

This gives you an answer of 10. Let's say you have to choose three from the following five people: Ann, Bob, Connie, Dave, and Elaine. Here are the 10 groups of three you could choose:

1)	Ann	Bob	Connie
2)	Ann	Bob	Dave
3)	Ann	Bob	Elaine
4)	Ann	Connie	Dave
5)	Ann	Connie	Elaine
6)	Ann	Dave	Elaine
7)	Bob	Connie	Dave
8)	Bob	Connie	Elaine
9)	Bob	Dave	Elaine
10)	Connie	Dave	Elaine

Now let's do the problem the long way. Here's the combinations formula for 5 choose 3:

$$_5C_3 = \frac{5!}{(5-3)! \times 3!}$$

$$= \frac{5!}{2! \times 3!}$$

You can finish this computation with your calculator or by hand. Both ways are quite easy. With your calculator,

press: 5 ⊡ ➗ (2 ⊡ ✕ 3 ⊡) enter or =

And it's a snap to do this with pencil and paper because so many numbers cancel:

$$_5C_3 = \frac{5!}{2! \times 3!}$$

$$= \frac{5 \times 4 \times 3 \times 2 \times 1}{2 \times 1 \times 3 \times 2 \times 1}$$

$$= \frac{5 \times 4 \times \cancel{3} \times \cancel{2} \times \cancel{1}}{2 \times 1 \times \cancel{3} \times \cancel{2} \times \cancel{1}}$$

$$= \frac{20}{2}$$

$$= 10$$

4) Permutations. As stated above, when you're selecting items from a group *and* putting them in an order or giving them some designation, you have a permutation problem. Let's do a variation of the above committee problem. Like above, you have to choose three people out of five to serve on the committee. But this time, you also have to give each of the three a committee office: president, secretary, or treasurer. How may different ways could you fill these positions? This is a permutation problem because order *does* matter. In other words, unlike above, selecting Ann, Bob, and Connie (for president, secretary, and treasurer, respectively) is *not* the same as selecting Bob, Connie, and Ann.

If your calculator has a permutations button, , just

press: 5 $_nP_r$ 3 enter or =

This gives you an answer of 60. Let's consider where these 60 possibilities come from. Refer to the above list of the 10 possible groups of three—the solution to the combination problem. Let's consider the first possibility: Ann, Bob, and Connie. How many different ways can you assign these people to the three positions— president, secretary, and treasurer? That answer is given by the factorial rule. It's just 3!, which equals 3 times 2 times 1, which is 6. Here are the six possibilities:

	President	Secretary	Treasurer
1)	Ann	Bob	Connie
2)	Ann	Connie	Bob
3)	Bob	Ann	Connie
4)	Bob	Connie	Ann
5)	Connie	Ann	Bob
6)	Connie	Bob	Ann

Each of the other nine groups of three from the combinations problem can also be assigned to the three offices in six different ways. Thus, the total number of permutations is 10 times 6, which gives us, again, an answer of 60.

If your calculator doesn't have a permutations button, you'll need to use the formula. Here's the permutations formula for $_5P_3$:

$$_5P_3 = \frac{5!}{(5-3)!}$$

As with the combinations formula, this computation can be finished easily with your calculator or with pencil and paper.

Part II: Probability and Gambling

If you want to see probability in action, go to a casino. Every spin of the roulette wheel, every toss of the dice in craps, every card dealt in blackjack, and every pull of the slot machine arm involves probability and odds. Unfortunately, no matter how well you understand probability, you can't overcome the house advantage every casino enjoys. You might come out ahead, of course, if you get lucky, but regardless of your skill or your knowledge of probability, the odds are against you. Understanding probability can, however, help you to lose less than you would if you gamble without knowing the math. And a grasp of probability can help you win at card and dice games like poker, bridge, and backgammon where you only have to beat your opponent and there's no casino taking a cut of the action.

PROBABILITY VERSUS ODDS

There is a simple connection between the probability that you'll win something and the *odds* that you'll win. Recall from above the basic probability formula:

$$probability = \frac{number\ of\ ``successes"\ or\ ``winners"}{total\ number\ of\ possibilities}$$

Thus, your probability of winning is given by the ratio of *winners* to *total*. Your *odds* of winning, on the other hand, is given by the ratio of *winners* to *losers*. For example, the probability of rolling a 3 with

The Birthday Problem

How large a group of people would you need so that there would be better than a 50-50 chance of two of them having the same birthday? One common response to this probability problem is 183 people, because there are 365 days in a year and half of that is 182.5. What's your guess?

The remarkable answer is 23 people! With a group of 23, the probability of at least one match is 50.7%. With 30 people, the chance of at least one match is 70.6%. With 40 people, 89.1%. For 50 people, it's 97.0%. For 100 people, bet the farm on a match—the chances are 99.99997%. And with 183 people? The chances of at least one match are 99.9999999999999999999995% (yes, that is correct to 23 decimal places). If you could gather together a new group of 183 randomly selected people once every second, you would expect to wait on average, oh, only about 66 quadrillion years before finding a group without a match. That's in the neighborhood of 5 million times as long as the age of the universe. To complete this experiment, you'd have to relocate to another star system because our sun would have burned out *long* before then.

Let's come back down to earth. If you're somewhat incredulous about these results, you can do a simple test. As stated above, the probability of finding a match with 40 people is about 90%. Just ask your son or daughter to check on the birthdays of all the kids in two different classrooms—that should be at least 40 students. Or check the birthdays of the first 40 people in your address book. About 9 out of 10 readers who try this test will find at least one match in the group.

The complete mathematical explanation of these results is a bit complicated, so I'll just give you the following commonsense way of understanding why matches occur so much more frequently than you'd expect. Let's assume that the first 18 people in a group don't have a common birthday. Now add one more to the group. What are the chances that this 19th person will have the same birthday as one of the other 18? The chances are 18 out of 365, or about 1 in 20. If there's no match, add a 20th person, then a 21st, etc. As the group gets bigger and bigger, the chances of the next added person matching a birthday will increase, but let's keep it simple and assume the chances remain 1 in 20 for each new person. And 1 in 20 or $\frac{1}{20}$ over and over adds up very fast. With just 10 more people, it adds up to about 10 in 20, or 50% (actually, if you do the math, it's only about 40% [rule number 6, page 95]). So you see that adding just 10 people to a group of 18 gives you far many more chances of matching a birthday than you'd expect.

a single die is ⅙ because there is one way to roll a 3 out of a total of six numbers that can come up. The odds of rolling a 3 are 1-to-5 because there is one "winning" number and five "losing" numbers. While both probabilities and odds are technically ratios, probabilities are written as a fraction or a percent whereas odds are written like 1-to-5 or 1:5. Odds are often expressed as the odds *against* winning. Thus, the odds of rolling a 3 might be expressed as "5-to-1 against" or simply "5-to-1." Gamblers would refer to rolling a 3 as a "5-to-1 shot."

It's very easy to convert from a probability to odds or vice versa. If the probability of winning is 30%, what are the odds of winning?

Step 1) If the probability is given as a fraction, go to step 2; if the probability is given as a percent, convert it to a fraction and reduce: $30\% = {}^{30}\!/_{100} = {}^{3}\!/_{10}$.

Step 2) Subtract the numerator from the denominator: 10 minus 3 is 7.

Step 3) The odds are thus 3-to-7 or 3:7, or 7-to-3 *against* winning.

Now let's do the reverse—converting odds to a probability. In craps, you can win on your first roll by rolling a 7 or an 11. There are 8 ways of doing this: six 7s—(6, 1), (5, 2), (4, 3), (3, 4), (2, 5), and (1, 6)—and two 11s—(6, 5) and (5, 6). Since there are 36 possible outcomes when two dice are tossed, that leaves 28 rolls that don't win on the first roll. This gives us the odds: 28-to-8 *against.* Because 4 goes into both 28 and 8 evenly, this ratio can be reduced in the same way that you would reduce a fraction. Thus, 28-to-8 reduces to 7-to-2 *against.* Here's how to convert this to a probability:

Step 1) Add: 7 plus 2 equals 9, so 9 is the denominator.

Step 2) Take the 2 from the odds of 7-to-2 *against;* so 2 is the numerator. Thus, the probability of rolling 7 or 11 is ²⁄₉.

By the way, since the probability of something happening and the probability of it not happening must add up to 1 (rule 2 above), the probability of *not* rolling 7 or 11 is 1 minus ⅔, which equals ⅞. Now, did you notice the simple pattern among all the numbers in this problem?

Probability of rolling 7 or 11: $^2/_9$

Probability of *not* rolling 7 or 11: $^7/_9$

Odds of rolling 7 or 11:   2-to-7

$$\frac{2}{9} \ + \ \frac{7}{9} \ = \ \frac{9}{9} \ = \ 1$$

If you bet on the Super Bowl with a friend and give him or her 3-to-2 odds, that means that you put up \$3 to your friend's \$2. Assuming this is a fair bet, it follows that your odds of winning are 3-to-2 and your friend's odds of winning are 2-to-3. And, since 3 plus 2 is 5, your probability of winning would be ⅗ or 60%; your friend's would be ⅖ or 40%. Lastly, it also follows that if you made such a bet with your friend five times, you'd expect to win three times (that's 60% of the time), and lose two times (40% of the time). You'd win \$2 for each of the three wins—that's a total of \$6; and you'd lose \$3 for each of the two losses—losing \$6. Because this nets to zero, we call this a fair bet.

Unfortunately for you and me, casino games are *not* fair bets. For instance, in American roulette[3]—which has a 0 and a 00 in addition to the numbers from 1 to 36—the probability of any particular number coming up is 1/38 because there is one winning number out of 38 total numbers. Thus, the *true* odds of your number coming up are 37-to-1 (against). But the *house* odds or *payoff* odds

---

[3] European roulette has a 0 but no 00 and is thus a better deal for casino patrons.

are only 35-to-1. If it were a fair bet, you'd put up your $1 to the casino's $37. But the casino only puts up $35. And this is why, in the long run, they win and we lose.

One final point about odds before we move on. As mentioned above, the casino pays 35-to-1 for a winning single-number bet in roulette. If you bet $1 and win, the casino pays you $35 *plus* the $1 you placed on the table. (If you bet $10, you get $350 plus your bet, etc.). You win $35, not $36, because it wouldn't make sense to count the $1 you bet as part of your winnings, but as you reach out your hands over the roulette table with a big grin on your face, you will be hauling in $36 worth of chips; for this reason, payoff odds of 35-to-1 are sometimes referred to as 36-*for*-1—you bet $1 and collect $36 if you win. Be aware of this difference in terminology: 1-to-1 is the same as 2-for-1; and 14-to-1 is the same as 15-for-1, etc. Make sure you don't make the mistake of thinking that 3-for-1 means 3-to-1; a 3-for-1 bet pays only $2 for each dollar you bet—that's a payoff of 2-to-1.

EXPECTED RETURN

If you spend any time at casinos, the most important thing for you to understand about probability is the idea of *expected return*. And there are two important things for you to understand about expected return. First, *all* casino games have expected returns less than 100%, which means that, in the long run, *you should expect to lose money;* it doesn't matter how well you understand the many games you can play and the various bets you can place; the law of averages is against you. And second, you will tend to lose less if you make bets with high expected returns.

Here's how expected return works. If you repeatedly make a bet with an expected return of 80%, you should expect to win only 80% of what you bet, and, thus, 20% of the money you bet or 20 cents per dollar bet. In this case, we would say that the "house advantage" is 20%. An expected return of 95% means that, in the long run, you'll probably lose about 5% of the money you bet or 5 cents of each dollar bet, etc. Notice that I said, "in the long run." On any given night at the casino, you could, of course, win big. You could also lose your shirt—doing much worse than what the expected return predicts. What the expected return tells you is what would likely happen if you played night after night after night—and the longer you play, the more accurate the expected return's prediction will be. Again, anything can happen on a particular night; the expected return tells you what will happen on an average night. An expected return can be expressed as a percent (say 94.7%), or its numerical equivalent (that's 0.947).

The expected returns of all casino games are less than 100%, but they vary quite a bit. All roulette bets, with one minor exception, have expected returns of about 94.7%. Keno is really bad, with an expected return of about 75% to 80%. Slot machines vary from about 75% to about 99%. In craps, some bets have the relatively good expected return of 98.6%; others have a much worse return of 83%. Contrary to what some people believe, none of the above games involves any skill—they are all games of pure chance. Blackjack, in contrast, involves quite a bit of skill. And if you learn the best strategies, you can reduce the house advantage to as little as half of a percent—an expected return of 99.5%—quite "high." (However, the average player's expected return is probably more like 98%.) In fact, if you count cards,[4] you can actually achieve an expected return over 100%—about 101%. But—surprise, surprise— the casinos don't like this, and if they catch you counting cards, which they will, they'll politely (the first time) ask you to leave.

The difference between an expected return and 100% can be viewed as the price of placing a bet. For example, if you place 24 one-dollar bets at keno some evening, each with an expected return

---

[4] Counting cards means keeping track mentally of the number of 10s and face cards dealt. At some point, if the portion of 10s and face cards still in the dealer's deck becomes higher or lower than normal, you can take advantage of this by both changing your strategy for when you decide to take more cards and changing the amount you bet.

of 80%, you should expect to lose about 20% of the $24 you bet—that's $4.80. The result would be the same if the casino increased your odds of winning to the point where keno was a *fair* game—which is to say its expected return would be 100%—but then charged you $0.20 to place a dollar bet. Looking at it this way, a $1 roulette bet costs you about a nickel, a $10 roulette bet costs about 50 cents, $10 craps bets cost anywhere from about 15 cents to $1.70, etc.

Before going to a casino, you might want to do the following experiment, which will give you a good handle on how expected returns work. As discussed in the above section on odds, the odds of rolling a 2 with a single die are 5-to-1 (against). In a fair bet between you and a friend, if you're trying to roll the 2, you'd put up your $1 to your friend's $5. In the long run, you'd win once for every five times you lost, and your winnings and losses would tend to cancel each other out. But if there were a casino game, the casino would pay maybe $4, instead of $5, when you rolled a 2. In the long run, for every six times you placed your $1 bet, you'd win $4 once and lose your $1 five times. This nets to a one dollar loss for every six dollars you bet. That's an expected return of about 83%. Now here's the experiment—it will take you all of five or ten minutes. Take a single die and roll it over and over, keeping a tally of the results. On the first roll, if a 2 comes up, jot down $4; otherwise record −$1. Then keep a running total—adding $4 for each 2 you roll and subtracting $1 for any other number. It's impossible to predict exactly what will happen. Every time you try this, the result will be different. But you'll certainly see your running total going up and down. You may be in the red for a while, then the black, then the red, then the black, etc. But after five or ten minutes, what will likely happen is that you'll be down $10 or $20, and, if you keep at it, you'll find your fortunes, in the words of Bruce Springsteen's song, "going down, down, down—going down, down, down." You'll stay in the red and may never see black territory again. You'll witness firsthand the inexorable pull of the law of averages. Expect the same when you go to the casino.

I'm not trying to discourage you from going to the casino; a little gambling can be great fun. So by all means go, and try your hand at all the games. But before you go, make sure you understand the principle of expected return. During the course of an evening, you could place a hundred bets or two hundred or more. If at least most of the time you make bets with the best expected returns, you'll probably leave with more money in your pocket—that's "more" as in more than if you ignore this, not "more" as in more than you came with.

GAMBLING FALLACIES

Fallacy #1. Numbers are "*hot*" or numbers are "*due*." There are two widely held misconceptions about games of chance. One is that if certain numbers keep coming up on the dice, or the roulette wheel, or at keno, etc., that these numbers are "hot" and are bound to keep coming up. A related notion is that if it's been a long time since certain numbers have come up, then these numbers are "due"—in other words, they're overdue and are a good bet to come up soon. If you believe in either of these "principles," you've certainly got a lot of company. Unfortunately—and I hate to be the bearer of bad news—probability simply doesn't work that way.

> *Nothing is ever hot.*
> *Nothing is ever due.*

Betting on "hot" numbers is called, in gambler's parlance, "chasing the old man." And betting on numbers that are "due" is "letting the old man chase you." Neither system works one bit. Period. As mathematicians say, "dice have no memory." Every roll of the dice or spin of the roulette wheel is completely independent of what happened before. Some night at the casino, you might see someone at the craps table roll 7 four times in a row. But that would have *no effect whatever* on the probability of his rolling a 7 on his next roll. The probability of his rolling a 7 on his fifth roll is ⅙—precisely the same as the probability of anyone rolling a 7 on any toss of the dice.

Fallacy #2. If you've had some bad luck, you're bound to have some good luck so that everything evens out. Related to the misconception that numbers are overdue is the belief that if you've had a long run of bad luck, you're due to soon have a run of good luck. This is also untrue. All you can ever expect from the gods of chance is *average* luck—beginning *now*. Most people will have some runs of unusually good luck and some runs of unusually bad luck. But, regardless of how things have gone for you in the past, the laws of probability say that all you can look forward to is average luck. Say you play bridge once a week. You might get more than your fair share of lousy hands for a month or two or even more. Unfortunately, this would not "entitle" you to start getting lots of good hands. It is true that after a long run of bad luck, "your luck is bound to change," but that's only because it's bound to change from bad to *average*, not because it's likely to change from bad to good.

The misconceptions that numbers are due and that good luck should follow bad luck are based on a misunderstanding of the law of averages. The law of averages does not say that things tend to even out in the long run. But this "long run" always begins at the present moment. The law of averages never looks back in time. It does *not* say that future events will balance out what has already occurred. It says only that beginning *now*, things will probably average out in the long run.

Fallacy #3. You can win at the casino with the right betting system. You might get lucky some night at the casino and come away a big winner. If you keep going back, however, you'll probably end up in the red. True, there is a small number of lucky souls who will end up in the black after a lifetime of gambling, but that's only because, given the millions who gamble, some are bound to beat the odds. All of this is simply the laws of chance at work. The only way you can exercise any control over the laws of chance is to make bets with the best expected return. You'll still probably lose, but this will increase your odds of winning and, in any event, will tend to minimize your losses. But there is no way to overcome the casino's advantage. There is no surefire way to win.

People have tried to beat the casino with several betting systems: D'Alembert, Martingale (doubling your bet after each loss), Labouchere, and others. They all sound good, but are all based on faulty logic. Rather than go over the details of these and other systems people have concocted, let me cut to the chase and state emphatically—

No betting system works.

I recently saw an interview with Peter O'Toole in which he described going to a Beirut casino with Omar Sharif during the filming of *Lawrence of Arabia.* He said that they lost several months' worth of wages—even going so far as to sell their passports to raise more cash—because Sharif "had a system." If a friend of yours wants to take you to a casino because she has a "sure-fire" system, tell her that you'll be happy to tag along and that since she's so sure about her system, you'll help her win even more by playing with her money. Bring only enough of your own money so that you can buy her a drink at the end of the evening to help her drown her sorrows.

CHAPTER 8

Statistics

(Brace yourself again.)

The media inundates us with studies, surveys, polls, top ten lists, the risks of this and the risks of that. We hear things like the Dow is up, the NASDAQ is down, women have a one-in-nine chance of contracting breast cancer sometime in their lives, the "average" American watches 26 hours of TV per week, has two children, and each year earns $55,000, drives 11,000 miles, and drinks 300 beers. We hear dire warnings about the economy, pollution, nuclear energy, global warming, terrorism, AIDS, little kids killing with guns, the cutting down of the rain forests, and the possibility that cell phones cause brain tumors. I seem to remember a study a while back about some connection between caffeinated coffee and some illness. Did you switch to decaf? Well, I guess it's time to switch back, because on the heels of this study was some report about the adverse effects of decaffeinated coffee.[1] And recently I read that there's something in semisweet chocolate that's actually good for

---

[1] I hope it goes without saying that I'm being somewhat facetious here. I don't remember either coffee study well, and it's possible, of course, that they're both bad for you; it's also possible that—taken in moderation—neither will do you much harm.

you. It's enough to make your head spin. The purpose of this chapter is to give you the tools you need to sort through such statistics, to separate the wheat from the chaff.

Part I: Basic Principles and Definitions

Average, mean, median, mode. You learned long ago how to compute an average: add up all the items and divide by the number of items. For example, to compute the average of the nine numbers 6, 8, 8, 11, 12, 20, 20, 20, and 21, you add them up and divide by nine:

$$\frac{6 + 8 + 8 + 11 + 12 + 20 + 20 + 20 + 21}{9} = 14$$

average or *mean*

This is the most common type of average. Technically, it's called the *mean,* and usually if you see the word "average" it means this type of average. But there are two other types of average, the *median* and the *mode.* The median of the above numbers is 12 because it's the middle number when the numbers are listed from least to greatest. If there are an even number of numbers in the list, there will be two numbers in the middle; in that case, the median is the mean of the two middle numbers.

6, 8, 8, 11, 12, 20, 20, 20, 21

median

The mode of this group of numbers is 20 because it occurs more frequently (three times) than any of the other numbers in the list.

6, 8, 8, 11, 12, 20, 20, 20, 21

mode

For a list of numbers, there is always a single mean and a single median. However, it's possible for there to be no mode, or, if there's a tie for the most frequent number, there can be more than one mode.

The whole idea behind an average, say the average U.S. household income or the average height of U.S. women, is to give an idea of what's typical or representative of the group—roughly speaking, an average gives some sort of middle value. But there is no single way to compute such a representative number that works in all cases. Each of the above three types of averages has advantages and disadvantages depending on the group of numbers you're trying to describe. For instance, say you hosted a dinner party for seven couples, including your close personal friends Bill and Mandy Gates. Let's say the annual household incomes were $40,000, $50,000, $75,000, $80,000, $110,000, $150,000, $180,000, and $5,000,000,000 (guess who). If a nosy neighbor later asked you what the average income of your guests was, and you told her the ordinary average (the *mean*) of about $715 million, she'd get a strange idea of what your guests were like. For this group of numbers, the *median* of $80,000 gives a much better idea of a typical guest.

As a general rule, the type of average you're used to, the *mean*, works pretty well in many cases—for example, a student's grade point average, your average monthly phone bill, and the average height of a five-year-old boy—but the mean is probably overused. The *median* gives a better typical number if there are some numbers in the group way above or way below the middle that skew the mean—like in the Bill Gates example. The median also works better in the frequent cases where, because all the numbers must be positive, it's impossible to have really low numbers to balance out the really high ones. I'd better explain that. The median U.S. household[2] income in 1999 was about $41,000.[3] Anyone earning a

---

[2] Statistical Abstract of the United States: 2001, 6. "A 'household' comprises all persons who occupy a 'housing unit,' that is, a house, an apartment or other group of rooms, or a single room that constitutes 'separate living quarters.'" A single person living alone also constitutes a "household."
[3] Ibid., table 664.

million or more per year is at least $959,000 above that median number. But it's impossible to earn that same amount less than the median income because that would be less than zero. So this is a case where the very small percentage of households earning more than a million per year distorts the average upward. That's why you often hear reference to the *median* U.S. household income—it gives a better indication of a typical household than the mean. The *mean* U.S. household income in 1999 was about $55,000[4]—but that's a far cry from what's "average" if you take that to mean a typical income or one that's near the middle. In fact, a household income of $55,000 in 1999 was in the top 37% of all household incomes, almost in the top third of incomes.

In some cases, the *mode* gives a very good typical value. In general, the larger the group of numbers, the more telling the mode will be. It is very instructive to learn, for example, that, among U.S. families with children, the mode is one—because that tells us that a one-child family is more common than any other.

Consider the following histogram of the number of sex partners of 25- to 44-year-old women as a final illustration of mean, median, and mode.

First, note that the "6–9" column and the "10 or more" column do *not* show an upward trend. They're tall columns simply because many different numbers are grouped together in each column. If each column represented one number, the graph would probably look something like the second histogram, where each column gets shorter and shorter as you go to the right. By the way, the slight increase in the percentage for four partners to the percentage for five partners shown in the first chart is probably some sort of survey error. It's unlikely that the number of women who have had five partners is greater than the numbers who have had four.

---

[4] Ibid., table 664.

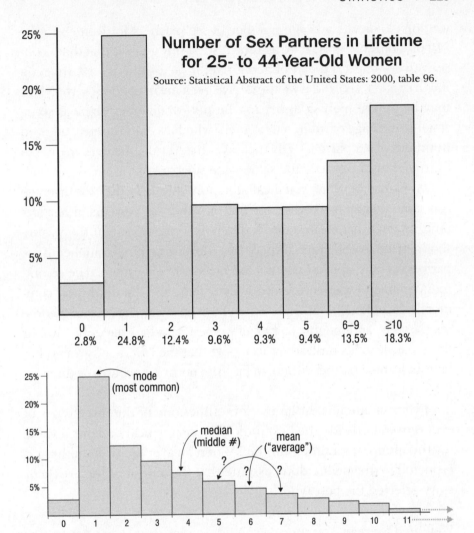

Number of Sex Partners in Lifetime for 25- to 44-Year-Old Women
Source: Statistical Abstract of the United States: 2000, table 96.

0	1	2	3	4	5	6–9	≥10
2.8%	24.8%	12.4%	9.6%	9.3%	9.4%	13.5%	18.3%

mode (most common)

median (middle #)

mean ("average")

The graph immediately above is a good one to keep in mind whenever you hear "average" numbers reported in the media. It shows one of the many situations where the true picture given by the actual data is quite different from the idea you might get from the reported "average." According to the above data, the *median* number of sex partners for 25- to 44-year-old women is four. (The 50th percentile is located just barely into the "4" column, which goes from the 49th to the 59th percentile.) The *mean* can't be computed exactly from this data because we don't know the average number of sex partners for women in the "10 or more" category. If we assume it's 13—my guess is that that's conservative—we get a mean of about five; if we assume it's 19, we get a mean of about six; and if we use 24, we get a mean of about seven. This may be on the high side, but maybe not—remember, there is some small percentage of women (and men) who have had dozens and even hundreds of sex partners. (By the way, whatever the mean is, the mean for men must be exactly the same—see sidebar.)

Now imagine that you hear a report that says that the average American woman has had six (or five or seven) sex partners in her lifetime. Doesn't that create quite a different impression than the picture shown in the second graph? Notice that the most common number of sex partners is one—for just about a full quarter of all women. The second most common experience is two sex partners, and the third most common is three. Roughly 40% of women have had zero, one, or two lifetime sex partners, and roughly half of all women have had zero, one, two, or three partners. It's misleading to report that the "average" woman has had six lifetime partners when, in fact, the norm is one, two, or three.

Every situation is different. Sometimes one of the three types of averages will provide the best indication of a typical or central value for the group, sometimes another. When an average of something is reported in the media, don't assume that the author of the article or story selected the best type.

Weighted average. You use a weighted average when you want to give certain numbers in a group more weight than others. For example, let's say a student's semester math grade is made up of the following components: the homework average makes up 5% of the final grade, the quiz average 15%, the test average 60%, and the semester exam 20%. These percentages—5%, 15%, 60%, and 20%—will be used to weight the student's scores. Notice that these weights add up to 100%. Here are the student's scores in the four categories: homework average 95%, quiz average 93%, test average 85%, and semester exam 88%. To compute his semester grade, you simply add up the weighted scores as follows:

$$\textit{weighted average} = 0.05 \times 95\% + 0.15 \times 93\% + 0.60 \times 85\% + 0.20 \times 88\%$$
$$= 87.3\%$$

By the way, this gives the same result as computing the *mean* or regular average of five 95s, fifteen 93s, sixty 85s, and twenty 88s. When you look at it this way, you can see that the weighted average of a group of numbers is basically the same thing as the mean, except that you're not figuring the mean of just one of each of the numbers—instead, you're computing the mean of numbers, some or all of which are repeated within the group. If you did compute the mean of one each of the numbers 95, 93, 85, and 88, you'd get the wrong answer of 90.25%. This wrong answer is higher than the correct answer of 87.3% because in this second computation, the 95, for example, counts as much as the 85, but in the computation of the weighted average, the 95 is weighted less than the 85.

Percentile, quartile, quintile, decile. Say a list of scores is ranked from lowest to highest; a *percentile* is one of the marks that divides the scores into 100 groups of 1% each. The first percentile is the dividing point between the lowest 1% of scores and all the rest. Test scores are usually reported as *above* a certain percentile. If your child scores above the 70th percentile on a standardized test, for example, that means she's between the 70th and the 71st percentile marks—in other words, she scored better than 70% of the test takers and worse than 29%. The 50th percentile is the same as the median of a group of numbers. The *quartiles* divide a list into four groups of 25% each. *Quintiles* divide a list into five groups of 20% each, and *deciles* divide a list into ten groups of 10% each. For example, the fourth quintile for U.S. family[5] income in 1999 was \$88,082.[6] (The fourth quintile is the same as the eighth decile and the 80th percentile.) This tells us that 80% of U.S. families in 1999 had an income lower than \$88,082 and that 20% of the families had an income higher than that.

---

[5] Statistical Abstract of the United States: 2001, 6. "The term family refers to a group of two or more persons related by birth, marriage, or adoption and residing together in a household."
[6] Ibid., table 670.

The Battle of the Sexes

I have a feeling that many readers will find it hard to believe that

*The average woman has the same number of
different sex partners as the average man.*

Let's do the math. Imagine a world where there are only 10 men and 10 women. We'll label the men A through J and the women A through J, and we'll draw a line connecting a couple every time a new liaison occurs. A year after the beginning of this hypothetical world, we arrive at the following:

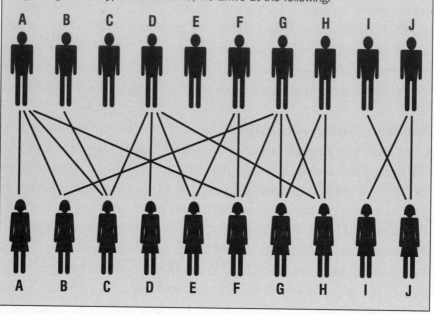

As you can see, man A has had four sex partners: women A, B, C, and F; man B has been monogamous (so far); but his partner, woman C, has not been; man C is a virgin (so far), etc., etc. Now we get to the critical point. There are 20 total lines in the diagram, and, since each line goes to one man and one woman, there are 20 lines pointing to men and 20 lines pointing to women. Now bear with me. As a group, the men have had a total of 20 sex partners, and, as a group, the women have also had 20. So, since there are 10 men and 10 women, the average number of sex partners for both the men and the women is equal to 20 divided by 10, or 2.

As time goes on, there'll be more and more romances, and it should go without saying that whenever a man has sex with a new woman, there's a woman (his partner, of course) who's having sex with a new man. Every time we draw a new line, the total number of lines pointing to men increases by one and the total number of lines pointing to women also increases by one. Thus, at any point in time, the group totals must be equal, and since for the men and the women, the average equals the total divided by 10, the averages for men and women will always be the same.

As you can imagine, this argument works exactly the same in our world of six billion people. (Well, okay, it's not exact because there aren't precisely the same number of men and women in the world—but it's close enough.) Well, was I right? Does this result surprise you?

Normal distribution or bell curve, and standard deviation.

Consider the following graph of the heights of 18- to 24-year-old U.S. women.[7]

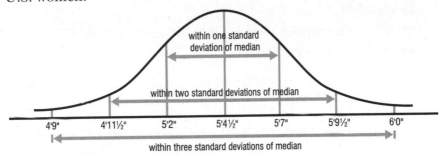

within one standard deviation of median

within two standard deviations of median

4'9" 4'11½" 5'2" 5'4½" 5'7" 5'9½" 6'0"

within three standard deviations of median

---

[7]The data in the graph is from Daniel S. Yates, David S. Moore, and George P. McCabe, *The Practice of Statistics* (W. H. Freeman and Company, 1999), pp. 75–77.

Many sets of data fall into this shape—the so-called *normal* distribution or bell curve. When a set of numbers is normally distributed, the mean, median, and mode are all equal and are right in the middle of the bell shape. IQ scores, weights of newborn girls (or boys), batting averages, and annual rainfall in Chicago are all normally distributed or very close to it. For such data, it's helpful to know the *standard deviation*, which tells you how tightly bunched all the numbers are around the middle value. For the preceding graph, the average height is 5'4½" and the standard deviation is 2½". This means that if you start at 5'4½" and go down 2½" and up 2½"—obtaining a range of 5'2" to 5'7"—68% or about two-thirds of the women will have heights in this range. For all normal distributions, the following rules hold:

> **68%** of the values are within *one* **standard deviation** of the middle value,
> **95%** of the values are within *two* **standard deviations** of the middle value, and
> **99.7%** of the values are within *three* **standard deviations** of the middle value.

Applying these rules to the above graph gives us the following:

> **68%** of the women have heights between 5'2" and 5'7" (within 2½" of 5'4½"),
> **95%** have heights from 4'11½" to 5'9½" (within 2 × 2½" or 5" of 5'4½"), and
> **99.7%** of the women have heights between 4'9" and 6'0" (within 3 × 2½" or 7½" of 5'4½").

For IQ scores, the mean is 100 and the standard deviation is 15. So this tells us that:

> **68%** of the population have IQs between 85 and 115 (within 15 of 100),
> **95%** of the population have IQs between 70 and 130 (within 2 × 15 or 30 of 100), and
> **99.7%** of the population have IQs between 55 and 145 (within 3 × 15 or 45 of 100).

POLLS

Just before I began writing this chapter, George W. Bush *finally* won the presidential election 36 days after the election on November 7, 2000. So not only did we have to listen to the daily dose of standard pre-election polls, we were treated to post-election poll results that told us, after each new lawsuit or other development, what percentage of people thought Gore should stick it out, what percentage thought he should throw in the towel, what percentage thought we should do away with the electoral college, etc., etc. What can we conclude on the basis of such polls? How accurate are they? Can we trust the results?

Much of the mathematics of polling is complex and beyond the scope of this book, but you should understand at least the following basics. Say the results of a poll a week before the election were 50% for Bush and 44% for Gore with a margin of error of 2%. What does this tell us? To understand these results, we first need to know precisely what question or questions people were asked. Let's say the pollsters asked 2000 likely voters, "If you voted today, who would you vote for?" The results—Bush: 50%, Gore: 44%, and undecided: 6%—tell us the following:

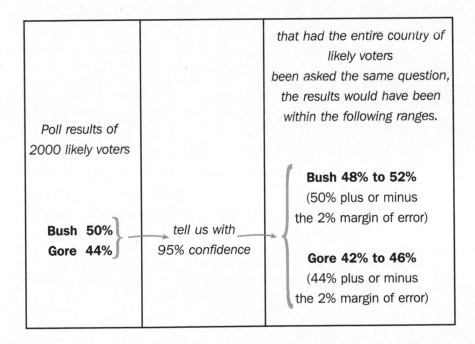

that had the entire country of likely voters been asked the same question, the results would have been within the following ranges.

Poll results of 2000 likely voters

Bush 50%
Gore 44%

tell us with 95% confidence

Bush 48% to 52%
(50% plus or minus the 2% margin of error)

Gore 42% to 46%
(44% plus or minus the 2% margin of error)

Many people find it surprising that pollsters can make valid predictions about all likely voters in the country—around 100 million people—on the basis of the opinions of a mere 2000 people. But, in fact, such conclusions are valid—though a full explanation is beyond the scope of this book. Here's the simple formula.[8] To be 95% confident about the opinions of the whole country, a poll of 2000 people will produce the following margin of error:

$$\textit{margin of error} \approx \frac{1}{\sqrt{2000}}$$

$$\approx \frac{1}{44.7}$$

$$\approx 0.0224 \text{ (or about 2\%)}$$

You just put the number of people in the poll under the square-root sign. A poll of 10,000 people will cut the margin of error in half:

$$\textit{margin of error} \approx \frac{1}{\sqrt{10,000}}$$

$$\approx \frac{1}{100}$$

$$\approx 0.01 \text{ (or 1\%)}$$

This margin of error calculation is straightforward and precise. To this extent, polling is an exact science—though perhaps "exact" is an odd word to use here since we're talking about an exact calculation of a margin of *error*. What makes polling an inexact science,

---

[8] This is a shortcut, approximate formula, and thus the *approximately-equal-to* symbol, "≈." The true formula is a bit more complicated. Was it presumptuous of me to think you wouldn't mind?

however, are all the other types of errors that can occur. Bear in mind the following limitations of this poll and others like it. By the way, I'm discussing political polls here, but a similar analysis applies to any opinion poll or survey.

- First, with regard to the precise computation of the margin of error, don't forget that a margin of error of 2% tells us that the responses of the whole country would probably have been within 2% of the poll results—but only 95% of the time. It's not guaranteed. Granted, 95% is pretty high, but it's a far cry from certainty. Five percent of the time—that's 1 time out of 20—the error will be larger than 2%, and things that happen "only" 5% of the time happen all the time.

- The 2000 people polled will never be a *perfectly* random sample, and, therefore, they will not be a perfectly fair, unbiased cross-section of the whole country. It's impossible to come up with a truly random sample of 2000 likely voters. Here are just two of the many difficulties. Some voters don't have a phone, and since most polls are conducted over the phone, the poll results won't reflect the voting behavior of people without a phone. Also, the voting patterns of people correlate somewhat with the type of jobs they hold and thus with their work schedules; their work schedules affect what time of day they're home to answer phone calls. So the poll can be affected by the time of day people are called. There is no end to this type of polling imperfection, and, unlike the precise calculation of the margin of error, the extent of this type of error can't be determined exactly.

- Even if we assume that the 2000 people polled are a perfectly random sample from the entire country of likely voters, there's another class of errors that can skew the poll results, namely, that people do not always respond to polls honestly and accurately. There are several causes. Some people are embarrassed to say "undecided" because they think they should have made up their minds only so-and-so many days before an election. To avoid this embarrassment, they make up an answer. The same thing goes for people who are too embarrassed to admit that they've decided not to vote for anyone. Other people may try to respond to questions in the way they think will make the pollster happy—just to be "nice." These are just some of the reasons why someone's responses to a poll may not exactly mirror the choices he or she makes in the privacy of a voting booth. And the resulting polling errors, like the other category of errors discussed above, cannot usually be measured precisely.

• On top of all these problems, some polls are conducted by organizations that have a vested interest in the result. Sometimes this is obvious, as in the case where a candidate's own campaign conducts a poll. Sometimes the polling organization might have a neutral-sounding name but in fact be very political. And in other cases, the organization might be basically apolitical—like one of the major networks—but nevertheless have an institutional culture that favors certain political views. These political preferences can affect the way the poll is conducted. Regardless of who conducts a poll, there are many subtle ways in which biases can creep into the polling process and reduce its accuracy. Personal biases of those who write the poll questions, for example, can make for leading questions, and biases of the pollsters can come through in the tone of voice they use when conducting the poll, which can affect how people respond.

The bottom line is that polls usually aren't as precise as they seem. When we hear a poll result of 52% to 44% with a 2% margin of error, that sounds very exact and mathematical, but, as explained above, that's not the whole picture. Perhaps the following caveat would give a truer picture of a poll's accuracy: "The poll results are 52% to 44% with a 2% margin of error at the 95% confidence level, but it's only under ideal conditions that we can be 95% confident that the true numbers are within 2% of the poll results. The true error span is probably larger than ± 2% due to limitations that are inherent in this and every poll, but, unfortunately, this additional error amount can't be calculated precisely." I suspect, however, that the public would tire of hearing this.

Now, I don't mean to suggest that polls are usually misleading or wrong. If done correctly by disinterested experts, they can be quite accurate and tell us much valuable information. And pollsters and statisticians are always looking for ways to minimize and compensate for the above-described errors. As a result, polls are becoming more and more reliable. But just remember that even when the very best pollsters are involved, polls are less than perfect.

Part II: Statistics in the News and Common Statistical Errors

Headline: MURDERS UP FOURTH YEAR IN A ROW
Headline: DOW FALLS RECORD NUMBER OF POINTS
Headline: TOXIC CHEMICAL UP 278% IN LOCAL DRINKING WATER!
Headline: LINK DISCOVERED BETWEEN TEA AND ARTHRITIS

Can you guess what these hypothetical headlines have in common apart from the fact that they sound alarming? Give up? Okay, here it is: while they may be reporting something significant, they may be next to meaningless or even totally meaningless, and without knowing the numbers behind the headlines, there's no way to tell.

The point I want to make in this section and the next chapter on charts and graphs is that just because you see some study or report on TV or in the newspaper, don't assume it's meaningful. Many of the statistical reports we see in the media are misleading, just plain wrong, or accurate but pointless. Sometimes this is intentional, when, for instance, the author of the report or finding has an agenda of some sort and is trying to put a certain spin on the numbers. Other errors are probably unwittingly committed by reporters or journalists who either don't understand the math or who have deadlines to meet and are under pressure to produce a dramatic headline or story. Some statistical information has been presented in the same inferior or erroneous way for so many years that the practice continues through sheer force of habit. You've got to be an educated consumer of statistical reports; be skeptical of studies you see in the media. Always ask yourself, "How might this report or finding be wrong or misleading?" and "Are these results meaningful?" What follows is a discussion of just some of the many ways statistical information is erroneously interpreted or reported. Be on the lookout for them!

Don't ignore inflation. If you found a great bargain, but then learned that your friend bought the very same item for less—25 years ago—would you be upset? Of course not! Comparing today's prices with those of 10, 25, or 50 years ago, without taking inflation into account, is obviously comparing apples to oranges. It just doesn't make any sense. If you want to compare prices from different years, you've got to level the playing field by converting all prices into *today's* dollars. But despite this obvious fact, the media continues to ignore inflation and report things like, "*Titanic:* top-grossing movie of all time." Since this "fact" ignores inflation, it's total nonsense. When inflation is factored in, *Gone with the Wind* is number one and *Titanic* is number five.[9] That ranking is the only meaningful one.

---

[9] This isn't as simple as I at first thought. It's complicated by the fact that *Gone with the Wind* has been earning money much longer than *Titanic.* But if my criticism of the media is unfair in this instance my point is still valid: that they do at times ignore inflation and, thus, make absurd claims.

How should one characterize mistakes like this? Well, words like "silly," "stupid," and "idiotic" come to mind. There really is no way to be kind about it. Such statements are no less ridiculous than your friend telling you she's taller than you because you're only 68 inches tall (5'8") while she's 165 *centimeters* tall (about 5'5"). Perhaps this seems more ridiculous because it's a comparison between inches and centimeters, whereas the *Titanic* statement at least compares dollars to dollars. But last year's dollars are *not* this year's dollars, and in fact the *Titanic* statement really is every bit as absurd as your friend's claim. For the life of me, I can't figure out why such statements persist. They're an insult to the intelligence of every reader and viewer. When will the media finally wake up? Don't hold your breath.

Average may not be typical. As discussed earlier in this chapter, the *median* or the *mode* of a set of numbers is often a better indication of what's typical than the *mean* or ordinary average.[10] This happens frequently in cases where there is an absolute minimum number like zero that makes it impossible for very low numbers to balance the very high numbers. For example, the "average" (mean) American probably has had somewhere between five and ten different sex partners in his or her life, but whatever the actual number is, you can be sure that the average is more than what's typical. This is because there are people like Wilt Chamberlain—if you believe him—who have had *way* more (20,000!!) than the average number of sex partners, and it's impossible for anyone to be on the low side to balance out the Wilt Chamberlains out there because it's impossible to have fewer than zero sex partners. So if you see some report about this average number of sex partners, and if your number is below this, before you start to feel unusually prudish or holy—depending on your point of view—remember that the *typical* American's number is certain to be below the average American's number.

---

[10] All three are types of averages, but the *mean* is the most common, and when the word average is used alone it means the *mean*.

When you hear that the average American drinks such-and-such number of beers per year, the average American this, the average American that, etc., etc., remember that in many of these cases, it's impossible for low numbers to balance the high numbers, so these average numbers are higher than what's typical. In such cases, the so-called average American is not really average at all in the sense of being typical or normal.

Don't confuse correlation with causation. Consider the above facetious headline about the link between tea and arthritis. We see reports of similar findings all the time. But just because there is an association or correlation between two things, it does *not* necessarily mean that one causes the other. This is obvious when you consider something like the following absurd statement: "Study finds correlation between number of churches in a city and number of murders." Actually, the statement itself isn't absurd—there is such a correlation!—it's the implication that the two things have anything to do with each other that's absurd. I'm sure you can guess what explains the correlation. It's that cities with higher populations tend to have more churches and more crime. It's the greater number of people that causes both the higher number of churches and the greater number of murders. There is no causal connection between crime and churches. Since suggesting that there is would be absurd, no one would pay any heed to such a conclusion. But when we hear things like the tea/arthritis correlation, it's very easy to assume that tea *does* cause arthritis because that sounds plausible.

When you hear about such a correlation, remember that while there may be a causal connection, which researchers may later discover, it's also possible that there's no causal connection whatsoever. Why might there be a correlation between tea drinking and arthritis absent a causal connection? Here's one of many possible explanations. Perhaps it's the case that the vast majority of people enjoy drinking some hot beverage. And perhaps as a general rule, the more tea a person drinks, the less coffee he or she drinks—think of all the people who drink mainly tea or mainly coffee. I'm not saying these things are true, but they're plausible, aren't they? Now, what if it turns out that there's something in coffee that helps prevent arthritis? If that were the case, then the higher incidence of arthritis among tea drinkers would be caused by a lack of coffee and would have absolutely nothing to do with drinking tea.

It's much easier to discover a correlation between two things than to prove that one causes the other. This may explain why we see so many studies about correlation. And discovering a correlation is often the first step in the process of proving a causal link. Just remember not to jump to the conclusion that causality has been established every time you read about correlation.

Things come in bunches and, therefore, bunches are not necessarily meaningful. In the normal course of events, it's to be expected that occasionally things will happen many times in a row or frequently in a short period of time—and thus we have the well-known aphorism. First, make sure you understand what "things come in bunches" means and what it does not mean. What it means is that over the long run—merely because of the normal, random fluctuations of things—it's likely that once in a while some things will occur several times in a row (like a coin landing on heads 6 or 8 times in a row) or that something will occur more often than average (like heads coming up 15 times out of 20). If you think about this, it's really just common sense. Consider flipping a coin. The odds of heads or tails is 50-50. So, over the long run, the law of averages says that we should expect about half of our tosses to be heads. But it doesn't follow that we should expect tosses to alternate perfectly—heads, tails, heads, tails, heads, tails, etc. Wouldn't it seem strange for this perfect pattern to persist? Of course. There is no predictable pattern with coin tosses or dice or any other random event. And because there's no predictable pattern, it follows that once in a while we'll see several heads or several tails or several 7s (when tossing two dice) in close succession. It would be peculiar if this *didn't* happen.

Now let's discuss what "things come in bunches" doesn't mean. It does not mean that there is some principle of nature or mathematics—a bunching force like the gravitational force—that tends to make things bunch up. This misconception is basically the same as the one described in the previous chapter on probability that certain numbers—on dice, for instance—are sometimes "hot." If someone rolls a 7 with two dice four times in a row, that does *not* make another 7 on his next toss any more likely than at any other time. It would be wrong to conclude that the four consecutive 7s are evidence that the "bunching force" is at work and that, therefore, more 7s are likely to follow. The fact that things come in bunches never allows you to predict anything specific about what will happen next. It only allows you to predict that *in the long run* you should expect to see some runs or clustering of certain events (you should expect to see fewer big bunches than small ones, and the farther out you look, the more bunches you should expect to see and the bigger the biggest bunch is likely to be). But when the bunches will occur or how big any particular one will be is totally unpredictable, and, furthermore, you can never know when you're in the middle of one.

Now for an example. If you flip a coin 250 times, the normal thing you should expect to see would be about eight runs of five or more consecutive heads or consecutive tails. Maybe you'd see only four such runs or as many as twelve, but to see fewer than four or more than twelve would be peculiar. The runs are caused by pure randomness. There is nothing meaningful about them. Now consider the fluctuations in the stock market. On any given day, the market can go up or down, like heads or tails—it's *very* unlikely to stay *exactly* the same. Now, I'm not saying that the fluctuations of the stock market are purely random—though there are experts who say that whether the market goes up or down on any given day is pretty much a coin toss—but just remember the above-described number of expected runs for coin tosses whenever you read that the market has gone up (or down) five days in a row. The stock market is open roughly 250 days in the year. So if the daily ups and downs of the market are like coin tosses, we'd expect to see the market rise (or fall) five or more days in a row about eight times during the year. Thus, if the market drops for five consecutive days, especially if the drops are all relatively small, don't jump to the conclusion that this is evidence that the market must be on the way down. Five straight drops in the market might be meaningful, but it could also be pure randomness at work.

Whenever anything happens several times in a row or more than an average number of times over some interval, this could be evidence of a meaningful trend, but remember that it might also just be due to the meaningless, random phenomenon that "things come in bunches."

Things tend to fluctuate and, therefore, fluctuations are not necessarily meaningful. This is the flip side of "things come in bunches." In the ordinary course of events, due to normal randomness, things fluctuate. Thus, while a change in something might be significant, it might also be a meaningless, random fluctuation. Let's say there are an average of 100 auto thefts per year in a certain city. We'll assume that the city's population and demographics are unchanging. Now, wouldn't it be peculiar if year after year there were *exactly* 100 auto thefts? Of course. Instead, we'd expect to see the numbers change from year to year, say, 94, 110, 105, 118, 90, 92, 101, 85, etc. Here's a simple rule that tells you how large you can expect such ordinary fluctuations to be. Take the square root of the average number of occurrences:

$$\sqrt{100} = 10$$

This tells us that in about 68%[11] of the years, the number of auto thefts will be within 10 of 100—in other words, from 90 to 110.

---

[11] Sixty-eight percent is the percent for one standard deviation, and, in this example, 10 is the standard deviation. These concepts are discussed earlier in this chapter (pp. 123–124).

Now double the number 10: that's 20. This tells us that in about 95%[12] of the years, the number of car thefts will be within 20 of 100—from 80 to 120. If you do the math, what follows is that it would be peculiar if we *didn't* see numbers in the 80s and in the 110s a full quarter of the time; and that only numbers more than 20 away from 100 should seem somewhat unusual.

The bottom line? If the number of auto thefts in this city jumped from 95 to 115 from one year to the next, this would not necessarily mean anything at all. While it's possible that this jump is the beginning of an upward trend, it's also possible that the increase is an ordinary, random, meaningless fluctuation. The jump from 95 to 115 should not, by itself, be alarming. Even four consecutive years with the numbers 95, 103, 105, and 108 would not be enough to show that there is a real upward trend.

Sportscaster babble. One of my pet peeves is the type of statement made by sports announcers, like, "Never in the history of baseball has a team come back to win the World Series after being down 3–0," or "In the Super Bowl, the team that has had the lead at halftime has won 30 out of 36 times," or "No basketball team that won its first 10 games of the regular season has gone on to win the NBA championship." (The first statement is true; I made the other two up.) The problem with such statements is that they are often much less meaningful than they sound; sometimes they are virtually meaningless. They are made, however, as if they will help you predict the outcome of a game or series. In fact, the proper response to these statements is often "So what?" or "Who cares?"

Take the statement about coming back from a 3–0 deficit in the World Series. Now of course it's difficult to come back after being down 3–0. The trailing team has to win four straight games. How hard is that? Well, if we assume that the teams are evenly matched—this oversimplification is usually not too far off—it's

---

[12] Ninety-five percent is the percent for two standard deviations; see footnote 11 above.

exactly as hard as flipping a coin and getting four heads in a row. That probability is 1 chance in 16.[13] So sure it's hard. But it may be no harder than winning four straight games at any point during the regular season against an equal opponent.[14] When the sportscaster makes the above statement, however, he suggests that there's some extra difficulty, some special World Series jinx that makes it virtually impossible to come back from a 3–0 deficit. One thing that makes the above statement misleading is the phrase "never in the history of baseball"—or perhaps it might be "never in the history of the World Series." What the sportscaster fails to mention is that there have only been 20 World Series in which a team has fallen behind 3–0. So none of those 20 teams has come back from 3–0 to win. To say that it's never happened "in the history of the World Series"—that's since 1903—makes it sound like none of the roughly 100 teams involved has been able to come back from being down 3–0. Now, is it odd that none of the 20 teams has come back to win? Not at all. If the probability is roughly 1 in 16, we'd expect it to happen about one time out of the 20. But for it to happen zero times or two times would not be a bit unusual.[15] Thus, the fact that it's never happened is quite an *ordinary* result. The sportscaster, by failing to do the math, erroneously suggests that it's *extraordinary*. A further indication of how sportscasters often ignore statistics and even common sense is the fact that it wouldn't be surprising to hear the above statement about the World Series (or a similar statement about a seven-game NBA playoff series) even after the team trailing 3–0 had then gone on to win one or two or even three games.

---

[13] To compute the probability of tossing four heads in a row we do this—$\frac{1}{2} \times \frac{1}{2} \times \frac{1}{2} \times \frac{1}{2} = \frac{1}{16}$.

[14] Perhaps it's a bit harder because losing the first three games may be evidence that it's not an even match. If we assume that the team trailing 3–0 has only a 45% chance of winning each subsequent game, instead of 50%, the probability of coming back to win would be $0.45 \times 0.45 \times 0.45 \times 0.45 \approx 0.041$—about 1 chance in 24.

[15] In case you're curious, the probability of one comeback out of 20 is about 36.7%, the probability of it never happening is about 27.5%, and the probability of two comebacks is about 23.2%.

But, after winning some games, the odds of a comeback obviously increase. And if the trailing team ties it up 3–3, both teams have a roughly equal shot at winning the seventh game.[16] To suggest, even after it's tied up 3–3, that it's still virtually impossible to win the series after having been down 3–0 would be just plain ridiculous.[17]

I don't mean to suggest that all such statistics cited by sportscasters are statistically flawed. Let's say that one team is trailing another by 20 points with five minutes to go in an NBA game. If we were to learn at this point that out of the last 200 times that a team has had such a commanding lead, only 10 teams have come back to win, that would be a telling fact (I made this stat up). It would give us a real indication of how hard it is to come back from 20 points down. The trouble is that it's often hard to tell the difference between a meaningful, informative statistic and one that's meaningless or misleading. Just be aware that many such statistics are irrelevant time-fillers. My guess is that sportscasters are instructed to do anything to avoid silence. But is silence worse than nonsense? You be the judge.

Consider both absolute size and relative size. Whenever you hear a report about the size of something, consider whether the important thing is absolute size, relative size, or both. You might see a headline, for example, that reads, "National debt reaches $5.6 trillion!" Now, while that certainly is a lot of money, this number has little meaning until we compare it to the size of the entire economy, the gross domestic product (GDP). If you neglect to consider this, it would be impossible to compare the national debt of $5.6 trillion in 2000 to, say, the national debt of $260 billion in 1945. If

---

[16] There would remain, however, factors like injuries, who's pitching, etc., that may make the odds somewhat more or less than 50%.

[17] Look at it this way. The probability of tossing 10 heads in a row is about 1 in 1000. But if you've already got nine heads, you only need one more, and that's a 50-50 shot. So once you've got nine heads in a row, the probability of achieving 10 consecutive heads becomes 50%. Once you've got nine heads, the initial probability of 1 in 1000 is irrelevant.

over the decades our national debt remained the same in the important sense, that is, as a certain percentage of the total economy, it would nevertheless grow because of at least three things: inflation, an increasing population, and increasing real earnings per capita. These factors made the year 2000 national debt more than twenty times greater than what it was in 1945. But when you consider the only thing that really matters, namely the debt as a percent of the country's total economy, it turns out that the 1945 national debt was a little more than twice as large as the 2000 debt. This is a case where it's the relative size, not the absolute size, that's important.

It's not easy to come up with good examples where the absolute size of something is what matters and the relative size has no importance, but perhaps the following will do. If we learn that five thousand people died in a flood in Bangladesh, that absolute number gives us some idea of the magnitude of the human suffering caused by the flood. It may not be especially important to learn that compared to the deadliest floods in history, five thousand deaths is *relatively* small.

Here's an example where both absolute size and relative size are important. Haiti's poverty rate of about 80% is much higher than Mexico's rate of about 30%. So, *relative* to the total population, Haiti's poverty is worse than Mexico's. This might suggest, among other things, that Haiti has fewer natural resources than Mexico or that Haiti's government has been less effective in fighting poverty than has Mexico's. But if you consider only those relative poverty rates, you would fail to recognize that the number of people living in poverty in Mexico—30% of about 100,000,000, or about 30 million people—is far greater than the number of poor in Haiti—80% of about 6,850,000, or about 5½ million people. Thus, in terms of the extent of human suffering, Mexico's poverty is worse.

Sometimes it's the relative size that's important, sometimes it's the absolute size, and sometimes both are important. It depends on the situation. A two-thousand-pound elephant is a *relatively* small elephant, but if he sits on you, that'll be little consolation. The *absolute* number, two thousand pounds, will be the only thing that matters. As a general rule, however, the relative size of something is more telling than its absolute size. So whenever you see or hear a number reported in the media without a comparison to something else, ask yourself whether that bare number tells you what you need to know or whether the relative size is the thing that should have been reported.

When something increases or decreases, consider both the size of the change and the percent change. This distinction is closely related to the above distinction between absolute size and relative size. When a number increases or decreases, sometimes it's the size of the change that matters, sometimes it's the percent change that matters, and sometimes both are important. Every day in the news, we hear about the Dow Jones average (or the S&P 500 or the NASDAQ) going up or down a certain number of points. But what's really important is the percent change. Now, there's nothing really wrong about reporting the point changes instead of the percent changes, especially if the index isn't changing much. As of this writing, for example, the Dow is hovering around 10,000. So a rise or fall of 100 points is a 1% change, a 200-point rise or fall is a 2% change, etc. And as long as the Dow is between, say, 9000 and 11,000, these point-to-percent conversions will remain roughly correct.

The problem arises when a point increase or decrease on one date is compared to another point change at a time when the Dow was at a very different level. For instance, it makes no sense to view a 300-point increase in the Dow when it's at 10,000 as a greater increase than an earlier 200-point increase when the Dow was at 5000. The 300-point increase is a 3% rise; the earlier increase was a 4% rise. The percent increase is all that matters here; the numerical size of the increase is virtually meaningless. Despite this fact, the media, including even the best financial publications, continues to report things like, "Dow rises record number of points." This is downright silly. If this new "record" is a smaller percent increase than some earlier increase, which it usually is, then it is no record at all. My guess is that the media continues to report such things because its readers or viewers have come to expect them. But since it's the percent change that matters, that's what the media should report. And it shouldn't take long for the public to become accustomed to this more intelligent way of reporting stock market news.

Now for an example where it's the numerical size of the change, rather than the percent change, that matters. Let's say a certain toxic chemical found in water is harmless at levels below 20 parts per billion. If this toxin increases from 1 to 3 parts per billion from one year to the next, that's a 200% increase, but the amount of the increase is so small (2 parts per billion) that there's no reason for alarm unless this increase is evidence of a long-term trend. On the other hand, if the toxin increased from 15 to 30 parts per billion, that's only a 100% increase, but the extra 15 parts per billion poses a health risk. In a nutshell, *a large percent increase from a small number may be less significant than a smaller percent increase from a large number.*

Consider the following murder statistics in two cities. This is a case where both the numerical increase and the percent increase matter. In one city, the number of murders from one year to the next went up from 12 to 24; in another city, the number increased from 200 to 220. Going up from 12 to 24 represents 12 more murders and a 100% increase. The 200 to 220 increase is 20 more murders but only a 10% change. The 100% increase is more alarming because it may be evidence of an increasing crime rate, while the 10% increase may be a statistically insignificant fluctuation as opposed to evidence of a trend. On the other hand, the increase of 20 is more disturbing than the increase of 12 because that represents eight more lives cut short and eight more devastated families.

Not all cases fit into the nice categories I've described above, and it's not always easy to decide to what extent the size of the change matters and to what extent the percentage of the change matters. What's important is that you're aware of the distinction and that you don't blindly accept the media's choice of how to report increases and decreases.

Incidence rates of the general population may not apply to you. We often see reports of things like "one out of every 150 Americans aged 55 to 64 will die this year from cancer." This does *not* mean that if you are 55 to 64 years old *you* have a 1-in-150 chance of dying from cancer this year. Why not? Statistics like this tell us something about the population as a whole, but the population statistic will usually not apply to a specific individual. Now, it is true that if you picked at random a 55- to 64-year-old American and you knew nothing about him or her, and, having a somewhat morbid bent, you wanted to bet on whether this person would die from cancer within a year, a fair bet would be 149-to-1 (against), which corresponds to 1 chance in 150. But this is a fair bet only because you know *nothing* about this person. In contrast, you know a lot about yourself.

There are several reasons why this 1-in-150 number does not apply to *you*. First of all, the risk certainly increases with age, so if you're 62, your risk is higher than the risk for a 57-year-old. The cited statistic lumps all 55- to 64-year-olds together. We can't tell from the 1-in-150 number what the rates would be for specific ages. Second, the statistic lumps males with females. The incidence rate is higher for males than for females, but you can't tell by how much from the rate of 1-in-150. Finally, more important for estimating your chances of dying from cancer within a year is whether you've ever been diagnosed with cancer. I don't know the numbers, but I'm confident that the incidence of death from cancer is much higher among people who've had a diagnosis of cancer than among people who've never had the diagnosis. If you've never had a diagnosis of cancer, the 1-in-150 statistic definitely does not apply to you.

Of course, there's also the matter of cancer risk factors. Cancer rates are affected by, among other things, whether or not a person smokes and his or her diet and exercise habits. If you are 55 to 64 years old, exercise regularly, eat a healthful diet, and don't smoke, your long-term probability of dying from cancer will certainly be lower than the probability for the population as a whole. And, of course, if you do smoke, don't exercise, and don't eat well, your probability will be higher than the rate for the general population. And without more information, it's impossible to know how to adjust the general population rate so that it applies to someone in your specific circumstances.

The same thing is true about statistics like "one in so-and-so many Americans will be involved in at least one serious automobile accident sometime in their lives." Whatever this incidence number is, it includes many people who drive drunk or sleep-deprived or over 90 miles per hour or way more than the average number of miles per year. If you do none of these things, the likelihood of your being involved in a serious accident is lower, maybe much lower, than the above-cited incidence rate.

The organization conducting the study may be biased. Be aware that studies are often conducted or funded by organizations with a political agenda or some other axe to grind. While this doesn't necessarily invalidate the reported results, you should, at a minimum, suspect that the results may be exaggerated or skewed a bit. This is obviously true of political polls conducted by a candidate running for office or by a political party that has a vested interest in putting a certain spin on whatever issues are being polled. Less obvious is bias by groups like the national associations that fight cancer or heart illness or diabetes. These are noble goals that no one can disagree with, but even such groups—which have to compete for their share of government funds—may knowingly or unknowingly exaggerate the incidence of the particular disease they're fighting.

Don't assume a survey is based on a valid sample. You know those TV or radio show surveys where you can call in for fifty cents or a dollar to vote yes or no on some issue? Have you ever called in? I haven't—I've never felt it was worth the time, effort, or money to register my opinion. Now, I have nothing against the people who do call in. But what's clear is that the people who call in are not representative of the whole population because only certain types of people call in. This is not a *random sample* of the population at large, so you can't be sure that the survey result is a true reflection of what everyone thinks or does.

Sex surveys can also be suspect for this reason. Only certain people are willing to respond to questions about their sex lives from total strangers. So you should be skeptical when you read in some magazine that, say, "70% of respondents admit to having done such-and-such at least 10 times." Without knowing whether sound statistical methods were used in the survey, there's really no way of knowing whether the results are accurate or not. One thing you can be sure of is that it is definitely *not* the case that "since they conducted the survey, they must know what they're doing."

I suppose I've created the impression that you can't trust any of the studies and surveys you see in the media. But that's not the point I want to make. There are many sound studies that provide us with important information—information that can even improve our health or save lives when it comes to valid medical or traffic safety studies, for instance. I'm merely advocating a healthy dose of skepticism. If you see a new study that claims that fruits and vegetables are bad for you or that fatty bacon is a cure-all, take it with a grain of salt. If any of the findings look like they might be important, the study will be repeated. There's no need to be alarmed the first time a new finding is reported. You can safely wait until a more substantial and definitive study comes out. And just because a report or survey looks good—perhaps with a fancy chart or graph—don't assume the people responsible for the study knew what they were doing. Be an educated consumer of statistics!

CHAPTER 9

Charts and Graphs

Just as a picture can be worth a thousand words, a good chart or graph can convey a great deal of numerical information very efficiently. But badly designed ones can be confusing and misleading. Those who create the charts and graphs we see in newspapers and magazines sometimes unknowingly create misleading ones and at other times intentionally design a misleading chart or graph in order to put a certain spin on the information.

The best way I can describe how a chart or graph should be designed is to go through the several ways they can be flawed. First of all, charts and graphs can be misleading because of the same errors discussed in the last chapter, such as neglecting to account for inflation, confusing correlation with causation, using the mean when the median is a better indication of what's typical, etc. In addition, there are several design flaws peculiar to charts and graphs.

In a nutshell, a bad chart or graph makes something insignificant look meaningful, or vice versa. This can happen when the design of the graph either exaggerates or diminishes differences between numbers. The culprit is often the way the graph's axes are marked. Consider the following.

KILLER BEES INVADE U.S.!

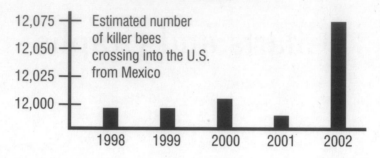

Before you go running to the drugstore for a bee sting antidote, look carefully at the design of this graph. Notice that the vertical axis does not begin at zero. This design flaw makes it look like the incidence of killer bees coming into the United States remained fairly stable from 1998 to 2001 and that following this period there was a dramatic jump in 2002. The obvious implication is that something must be up, something must be changing—and we should be alarmed about it. But if we redraw the graph so that the vertical axis does begin at zero, we see quite a different picture.

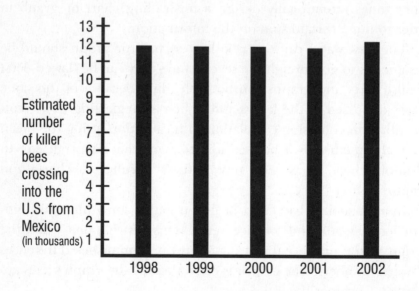

This second graph shows that the increased number of killer bees crossing into the U.S. in 2002 is relatively insignificant as a *percent* increase over the year before. This small percent increase from 2001 to 2002—only about 0.7%—is much more likely to give us a true picture of what's going on than the fact that the increase from 2001 to 2002—85 more bees—was much greater than the changes during the previous years.

The second graph gives us the fairer picture and shows us—at least on the face of it—that there is nothing to be alarmed about. By the way, another reason not to be alarmed is that I made these numbers up. I didn't make up the idea of a killer bee invasion, however. Some of you may recall that there actually was a killer bee scare in Texas and the Southwest in the early 1990s.

Two other things can make a graph misleading. A break in an axis causes the same type of distortion as in the first killer bee graph. Had the killer bee graph been designed as follows,

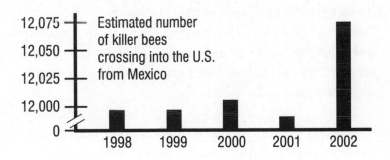

you would see the same exaggerated jump from 2001 to 2002. And if an axis is not marked in equal increments, you also get a distorted picture of things. You've probably seen graphs like the following:

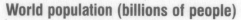

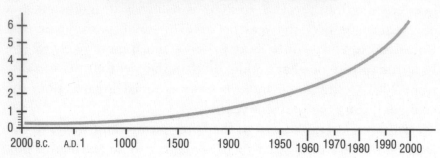

As you move from left to right on the horizontal axis, you can see that the number of years in each increment gets smaller and smaller. On the left, it's about half an inch from 2000 B.C. to A.D. 1; on the far right, half an inch represents only twenty years. This causes the rapid increase in population in the twentieth century to appear *less* dramatic than it would on a graph with equal increments.

This brings us to the following basic principle:

> *When a graph's axes begin at zero, contain no breaks, and are marked in equal increments, the graph gives a fair representation of the data. Such a graph gives an immediate, intuitive sense of* **percent** *increases and* **percent** *decreases—and this is usually what's important.*

Like with every general rule, this one has exceptions, but it's a good basic rule to keep in mind. When you see a graph that doesn't follow the rule, be aware that the increases or decreases you see from one point on the graph to another—the trends you may see—will appear either more or less extreme than they would on a graph that follows the rule.

Sometimes it's impossible or impractical to follow the rule. For instance, in the above population graph, if the person who made the graph wants to present decade-by-decade population numbers for the twentieth century, but also wants to go back as far as 2000 B.C., it's impossible to do this with equal increments on the horizontal axis. The graph either wouldn't fit on the page or the decades in the twentieth century would be so tightly jammed together that the graph would be hard to read. Just be aware of the distortion caused by the unequal increments when you see such a graph.

Here's another exception to the rule. The following graph shows a case where a very small percent change is statistically significant and the only way to show the change is to use a graph like the first killer bee graph.

Concentration of substance XYZ in Great Lakes in parts/billion

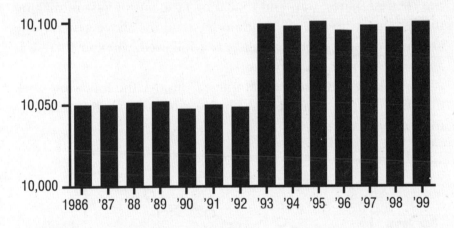

It's conceivable that the jump from about 10,050 in 1992 to about 10,100 in 1993, though only a half of a percent increase, is statistically significant and is therefore evidence of some ecological event sometime in 1992. The math is beyond the scope of this book, but statisticians have ways of determining whether such a change is meaningful or simply a random fluctuation. Let's assume that the jump from 1992 to 1993 was found to be statistically significant. It would be impossible to show this increase with a graph whose vertical axis began at zero and had no breaks. So in this case, breaking the rule is unavoidable.

Well, how do you tell the difference between graphs like the one above that are based on sound statistics, where the only way to show a *meaningful* change is by ignoring the general rule, and graphs like the killer bee graph that are not backed up by sound math or science, where a *meaningless* change is exaggerated simply to create a sensational story? Unfortunately, you can't always tell the difference. It may be impossible to do the statistics yourself, and you can't be sure whether the author of the study or article did the necessary statistical analysis. But you can at least be an educated consumer of statistics: consider the credentials of the author, the type of publication you're reading, and the nature of the report or study; be aware that journalists may not always understand how to present data in the clearest, fairest way, and that they have an interest in making things appear newsworthy; and understand the above general rule and ask yourself, when the rule is not followed, whether there was a good reason for not doing so.

Let's look at two more examples. Consider the following stock market chart (the numbers have little connection to the actual history of the markets):

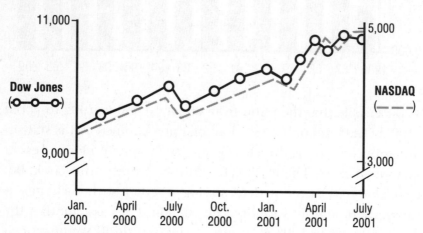

The hypothetical author of this hypothetical chart wanted to show that the ups and downs of the Dow and NASDAQ mirrored each other during this eighteen-month period. This is interesting and something readers might like to know. Thus there is some justification for designing the scales on the left and right axes so that the parallels are apparent. But if the author doesn't explain the distortion here, he's doing his readers a disservice. Did you notice the cause of the distortion (apart from the breaks in the axes)? It's that even though both the left and right axes increase 2000 points, the 9000 to 11,000 increase on the left axis for the Dow is a mere 22% increase, while the 3000 to 5000 increase on the right axis for the NASDAQ is a 67% increase. As a result, the fluctuations in the NASDAQ appear flatter, less dramatic, than they should (or we could say that the Dow fluctuations appear more dramatic than they should—take your pick). To show the true fluctuations in both markets, in terms of percent increases and percent decreases—and percent change is what's important in the stock market—the graph might look something like this:

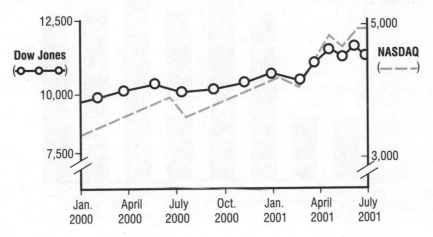

Now we can see that the ups and downs of the NASDAQ were more dramatic than those of the Dow, and that over this eighteen-month period the NASDAQ rose considerably more than the Dow. By the way, putting both the Dow and the NASDAQ on a single graph will be somewhat misleading regardless of how the graph is designed, because there's no agreement on how to equate the two stock indices. In other words, the graph immediately above suggests that

7500 for the Dow is equivalent to 3000 for the NASDAQ and that 12,500 is equivalent to 5000. But there is no such equivalency, or any other, for that matter. No one knows that x for the Dow is equivalent to y for the NASDAQ.

The final example will illustrate how easy it is to lie with statistics. In this hypothetical case, Mr. Smith, mayor of a large city for two terms from 1985 to 1996, runs for mayor again in 2002. His political campaign publishes the following graph about the crime rate during his last two years as mayor and the six-year-term of the current mayor, Mr. Jones:

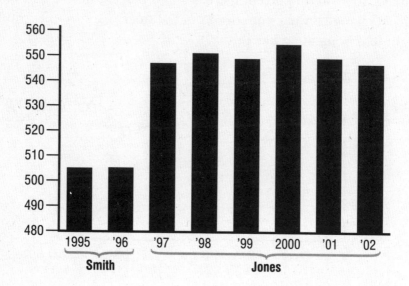

Number of violent crimes reported

This makes Mayor Jones look pretty bad, doesn't it? The crime rate jumped up and stayed up after he took office in 1997. Did you notice that this jump appears larger than it should because the vertical axis starts at 480? If we start the axis at zero, the increase appears quite small:

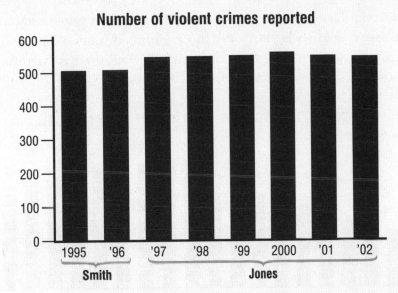

Perhaps you're thinking that while Smith's graph, like all campaign literature, did spin the facts in his favor, the increase in the crime rate is still there and it still looks like Mayor Jones was soft on crime. But consider the next graph, which includes all twelve years of Smith's incumbency:

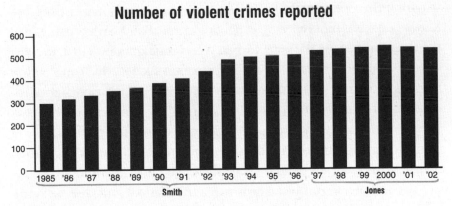

Now the true story begins to unfold. Looking at all eighteen years, we can now see that under Mr. Smith, there was a steady climb in the crime rate, and that it leveled off after Mayor Jones took office.

But wait, it gets worse. It turns out that this city's population has been growing fairly rapidly over these eighteen years. When that's taken into account and the crime rate is measured in reported crimes *per 1000 residents,* we arrive at the following graph:

Number of violent crimes reported per 1000 residents

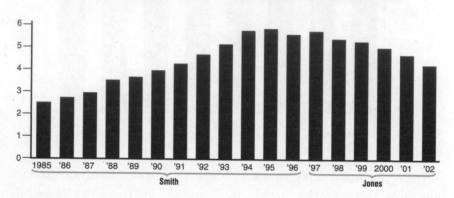

So now it appears that the crime rate rose during Smith's tenure, and began to fall as soon as Jones took over. So who is it who's soft on crime? This last, fair graph, in contrast to the first misleading one, certainly makes it look like Mayor Jones was more effective in fighting crime than Mayor Smith. But at the risk of muddying the waters, when you come right down to it, we can't say for sure, on the basis of this information alone, which mayor was tougher on crime. Maybe Mayor Jones was lucky. Perhaps a long-term federal anti-drug-trafficking program that had no connection to Jones's administration was instituted just as Jones took office. And perhaps this was the major cause of the drop in the city's crime rate. Without more information, we can't draw any definite conclusions. Nothing's ever simple.

Yes, a chart or graph can be worth a thousand words. But be aware of the many ways graphs can distort the facts. Ask yourself whether the author of the article or graph has a political agenda or wants to put a certain spin on the facts. And realize that journalists may unwittingly fail to present data as clearly and objectively as they should.

PART II

Money Matters

CHAPTER 10

Balancing Your Checkbook

For this chapter, you may want to review topics in the following chapter from part I:
• The Fundamentals (chapter 1)

If you're one of the millions of people who don't balance their checkbook but wish they did, read the following straightforward discussion and make up your mind to turn over a new leaf. There's really nothing to balancing your checkbook (with the following method, you don't have to do any arithmetic while standing in the checkout line). And if I can persuade you to make a habit of the following simple procedure, you will have gotten your money's worth out of this book just from this short chapter alone. If adopting this procedure helps you to stop bouncing checks, you will *really* get your money's worth, because the book will have paid for itself as soon as you avoid your first or second overdraft fee.

Before I explain how to do it, I should address the question, "Why bother?" Now, I don't want to discourage you from learning the following procedure—once you get the hang of it, it really is *very easy* and should take you no more than twenty to forty minutes per month—but for some people, not balancing their checkbook is a sensible option. The main advantages of balancing your checkbook are keeping your finances in order and avoiding the cost and embarrassment of bouncing checks. So, if you're the type of person who truly doesn't mind some financial loose ends, and you keep enough money in your account so you're sure you'll never bounce a check, then you can get by fine without balancing your checkbook. (Bank errors are very rare, and when they occur, they're probably just as likely to be in your favor as in the bank's favor. So if finding bank errors is your only reason for reconciling your checkbook, it's probably not worth your time.)

Some people not only don't reconcile their checkbook, they don't even keep a running balance in their register. This can also work as long as you're not bouncing checks, though I can't see why you wouldn't want to spend the twenty minutes per month it takes to keep your balance current. And then there are those who don't even bother to record their transactions in their register—egad! But even such record-keeping-impaired folks are breaking no laws, and this system can also work as long as, again, they're never bouncing checks—but I don't recommend it.

So, if you're truly comfortable with any of those lax systems, they can suffice. But many people wouldn't be happy using any of these somewhat cavalier approaches even if they did work. The fact is that most people who don't balance their checkbooks would probably be happier if they did. And many people can't always afford to keep enough of a cushion in their account to guarantee that they'll never bounce checks, or don't want to worry about whether there's enough in their account to cover their checks. Others feel a natural sense of satisfaction in knowing that their finances are in order. And I suspect that making the decision to bring order to your checking account will tend to make you take more control over all your finances. Well, whatever your reasons for wanting to balance your checkbook, here's how you do it. *It is truly very easy.*

Let's begin by looking at a page from a typical register. The register I use looks like this:

NUMBER	DATE	DESCRIPTION OF TRANSACTION	PAYMENT/DEBT(-)		CODE*	FEE(-)	DEPOSIT/CREDIT(+)		$ 652	14
2439	1/7	Health Club	$ 120	47		$	$			
DC	1/9	Gasoline	12	86						
DC	1/10	Amazon.com	14	35						
DC	1/16	State of Illinois for car	81			·				
2440	1/20	Dr Smith check up	85							
	1/25	Deposit (clients)					675			
	1/25	Phone	35	58						
	1/25	Electric	11	45						
2441	2/1	Parking Ticket	25							
	2/5	Health Insurance	229	62						

*USE THESE CODES WHEN RECORDING NON-CHECKING TRANSACTIONS

D-DEPOSIT   DC-DEBIT CARD   ATM-TELLER MACHINE   AP-AUTOMATIC PAYMENT   TT-TELEPHONE TRANSFER   T-TAX DEDUCTABLE   O-OTHER

The way items are recorded in this register is probably self-evident, but I do want to point out a few things. The most important thing is that you enter any transaction that *reduces* your balance in the "payment/debit" column, then subtract that amount from the balance, and that you enter any transaction that *increases* your balance in the "deposit/credit" column and then add that amount to your balance. That's basically all I ever do. You see the column called "code" and the key on the bottom of the page? Not only have I never used these things, I actually—I'm not exaggerating here—never even *noticed* them until I sat down to write this section of the book. I'm a fairly organized guy, and I always (well, almost always) keep my checkbook in order, including reconciling the balance. So if I got by just fine all these years without bothering about those codes, so can you.

Basically, I just put anything I need to describe a transaction in—can you guess?—the "description" column. And since, for example, I know I pay my electric, phone, gas, and insurance bills with automatic payments, I don't need to add the "AP" code to these entries. (I'm sure once you make a habit of using these codes, it doesn't take any·effort, so if you really want to be thorough, go for it.) I also never use the "fee" column, and there's no need to. This column is for bank fees. My bank doesn't charge for checks written, but even if it did, it seems like a waste of time to put down, say, ten cents in this column every time you write a check. Instead, once a month just note on your statement the total fee for all checks written that month and enter this amount on a separate line in your register. So, there you have it. If you want to keep things simple, just enter items as shown above—and notice that you don't have to bother to compute the new balance for every entry (I'll explain this in a minute).

All right, here we go. By the way, the following seven-step process is for anyone whose checkbook is currently anything from slightly out of order to a total mess and who wants to start fresh and get everything in order. If, on the other hand, you record all transactions meticulously and are confident your current balance is correct *and* you also have been checking off items each month when you get your statement (step 5 below) and you want help only with the reconciliation process, you can skip steps 1 to 5 and go right to step 6.

Step 1: The starting point. This should take you less than two minutes. You need to start fresh. Take your current register out of your checkbook and record on the front of it the dates of the first and last transactions in the register and write "LAST BAD REGISTER." File it away. Then get a new register and write on it "FIRST GOOD REGISTER" and put it in your checkbook. Now take your most recent statement and find the entry called "new balance" or "closing balance" and enter it in the upper right-hand corner of the first page of your new register. (If you can't put your hands on your last statement—I'm shocked!—just wait till you get your next one to begin this process—no big deal.) Your new register should look like this:

NUMBER	DATE	DESCRIPTION OF TRANSACTION	PAYMENT/DEBT(-)	CODE*	FEE(-)	DEPOSIT/CREDIT(+)	$ 852 78
			$		$	$	

As a totally optional step, you may do the following, but if you really want to keep this simple, skip this and go to step 2. (The only reason I'm writing this is that I suspect some readers would be wondering about doing this extra step.) If you've recently recorded in your old register some transactions dated after the closing date of your most recent statement, you can reenter those items in your new register. This will bring your balance more up-to-date. I wouldn't bother looking for any outstanding transactions dated prior to the closing date of the statement—that's just too confusing. Let me repeat—you are free to ignore this optional step.

Step 2: Don't bounce checks. For the first few months—until you're sure everything is in order—make sure you've got enough in your account so you don't bounce any checks. There could be a couple two- or three-month-old checks floating around out there that someone has neglected to cash. Make sure you've got the money in your account to cover these and any other transactions you may have forgotten about. You may want to call your bank occasionally to check on your current balance. If you do bounce a couple checks, don't sweat it.

Step 3: Keep your checkbook in order. To make this system work, you've got to make a habit of entering all your transactions as shown in the figure on page 159. It's no big deal if you forget occasionally—catching such omissions is one of the purposes of reconciling (step 5)—but you should make an effort to keep your checkbook as up-to-date as possible. This shouldn't be very hard to do, especially since you don't have to add or subtract each transaction to your balance unless you want to (see step 4 below).

You can develop your own idiosyncratic system for making sure you record your transactions, but here are a few suggestions. Carry your checkbook with you whenever possible and record checks in the register when you write them. If you carry a couple loose checks in your wallet and don't have your register with you when you write your checks, get a receipt, put a mark on it as a reminder, put it in your wallet, and then record this item in your register the next time you sit down at your desk. (A friend of mine offers this tip: put a Post-it note on each loose check you put in your wallet, and record the amount on the note when you write the check.) The same goes for ATM transactions or debit card transactions that you make when you don't happen to have your checkbook with you. If you use a debit card to order something over the phone or on the World Wide Web, you won't see a receipt for a while, so record the purchase right when you make it if your register is handy, and if not, write down the amount and record it later. If you pay some bills with automatic withdrawals each month, you can enter them on the payment dates if you know the amount, or just wait until you get your statement, but if you do the latter be sure you leave a big enough cushion to cover these items. I'm sure you'll develop your own system, but, obviously, the simplest and best practice is to record transactions in your register right away so you won't have to bother about it later.

Step 4: Figure your current balance occasionally with a calculator. Many people like to compute their balance after each transaction so that they can always see their current balance. Like this:

NUMBER	DATE	DESCRIPTION OF TRANSACTION	PAYMENT/DEBT(-)		CODE*	FEE(-)	DEPOSIT/CREDIT(+)	$ 652	14
2439	1/7	Health Club	$ 120	47		$	$		
								531	67
DC	1/9	Gasoline	12	86					
								518	81
DC	1/10	Amazon.com	14	35					
								504	46
DC	1/16	State of Illinois for car	81						
								423	46
2440	1/20	Dr Smith check up	85						
								338	46
	1/25	Deposit (clients)	11	45			675		
								1013	46
	1/25	Phone	35	58					
								977	88
	1/25	Electric	11	45					
								966	43

If you want to do this, that's fine, but there are a couple advantages in not doing it this way. I recommend that you wait till you have, say, five to ten new transactions, then sit down at your desk, take out your calculator, tally up all the transactions at once, and then record your new balance. Like this:

NUMBER	DATE	DESCRIPTION OF TRANSACTION	PAYMENT/DEBT(-)		CODE*	FEE(-)	DEPOSIT/CREDIT(+)	$ 652	14
2439	1/7	Health Club	$ 120	47		$	$		
DC	1/9	Gasoline	12	86					
DC	1/10	Amazon.com	14	35					
DC	1/16	State of Illinois for car	81						
2440	1/20	Dr Smith check up	85						
	1/25	Deposit (clients)	11	45			675		
	1/25	Phone	35	58					
	1/25	Electric	11	45				966	43

When you do this, do the addition and subtraction twice on your calculator to confirm your answer. And when you do it the second time, do it differently. For example, if the first time you went down the list of transactions in order—adding or subtracting the credits and debits appropriately—the second time you could add all the credits first, then subtract all the debits. Or if you went through the list of transactions top to bottom the first time, go through the list from bottom to top the second time. When you do a computation twice like this, especially if you do something different the second time, and the two answers agree, it's a virtual certainty that you've got the correct answer. If your two answers don't agree, repeat the computation till you get two answers that do agree.

With this method, you don't have to do any math when writing checks or recording other transactions. You just record the transaction and do the math later. You're freed from the annoyance of adding or subtracting, say, while you're standing in line at the grocery store and the people behind you are thinking, "Oh great, I got in line behind a #?@*%! check writer again." The other advantage of this system is that you are *far* less likely to make computation errors. In fact, as mentioned above, it's almost impossible to make a computation error if you do the math twice on your calculator. When you're standing in line somewhere and in a hurry, on the other hand, you might, for example, add when you should have subtracted, etc.

This is an almost effortless way to keep your checkbook up to date. When you just happen to be at your desk paying bills every couple weeks, and you're writing a check, just take out your calculator and tally up your new balance. It shouldn't take more than a minute or two. Of course, with this method you have to watch that your balance doesn't go below zero. But that won't be a problem. You'll know if you're getting close. And, of course, you can figure your balance more frequently whenever you think your balance might be getting low.

Now we reach, in steps 5, 6, and 7, the only real work you'll have to do to keep your checkbook in order. Everything up to this point takes virtually no time or effort once you make it a habit. And even these last three steps shouldn't take you more than fifteen to thirty minutes once a month.

Step 5: Read your monthly statement and compare it to your register. Take your monthly statement and simply go through the listed debits and credits. Check each one against the entries in your checkbook. It's a good idea to do all the debits first, then all the credits. And as you're doing this, make sure that each item is in the proper column in your register. If the debit or credit is in your register, put a checkmark by the item in the register—I use the "code" column for this—and put another checkmark by the item on the statement. If the debit or credit is not in your register, write it in on the first empty line in your register and check it off in the register and on the statement. (Those items that don't appear in your register might include things like bank fees, ATM or debit card transactions you forgot to record, automatic withdrawals, etc.—and, only for the first few months of this new system, checks you've written but not recorded in your new register.) It's important that you do step 5 precisely. When you're done, your register might look like the diagram on the following page.

Step 6: Reconcile your balance. This is very straightforward. After checking off items in your register that appeared on your statement (step 5), there will remain some unchecked items in your register. These items obviously affect the last balance in your register, but since they are not on the bank statement, the statement's closing balance does not reflect them. Thus, you must correct the balance on the statement so that it jibes with the balance in your register. Simply total up all unchecked *credits* in your register and *add* this total to the statement balance. And then from this number *subtract* the total of all unchecked *debits* in your register. This answer should agree with your register balance. And if you've carefully followed the process laid out here, it will. If it does, you're done; if not, on to step 7.

Step 7: What to do if there's a discrepancy. If the corrected statement balance doesn't agree with your register balance, the first thing to do is to compute the amount of the discrepancy

The unchecked items did not appear on your January statement.

The checked items (except for the four at the bottom) had been recorded in your register and also appeared on your January statement.

NUMBER	DATE	DESCRIPTION OF TRANSACTION	PAYMENT/DEBT(-)	CODE*	FEE(-)	DEPOSIT/CREDIT(+)	$ 652	14
2439	1/7	Health Club	$ 120 47	✓	$	$		
DC	1/9	Gasoline	12 86	✓				
DC	1/10	Amazon.com	14 35	✓				
DC	1/16	State of Illinois for car	81	✓				
2440	1/20	Dr Smith check up	85					
	1/25	Deposit (clients)	4 45	✓		675		
	1/25	Phone	35 58	✓				
	1/25	Electric	11 45	✓			966	43
2441	2/1	Parking Ticket	25					
	2/5	Health Insurance	229 62					
2436	12/29	B-day gift for Mom	85 98	✓				
	1/15	ATM withdrawal	200	✓				
DC	1/29	Gasoline	13 12	✓				
	1/31	Bank fees (Jan.)	15 75	✓			396	96

*USE THESE CODES WHEN RECORDING NON-CHECKING TRANSACTIONS

D-DEPOSIT   DC-DEBIT CARD   ATM-TELLER MACHINE   AP-AUTOMATIC PAYMENT   TT-TELEPHONE TRANSFER   T-TAX DEDUCTIBLE   O-OTHER

The last four items were added to your register and checked off only after you saw them on your January statement.

(subtract the smaller number from the larger) and then look for a single item in your register or statement of this same amount—you may have missed one item during steps 5 or 6. If you find such an item, you're done—just make the appropriate correction. If not, redo your computation from step 6. If it works this time, you're done. But if this second attempted reconciliation produces the same wrong answer as the first attempt, then you know (1) that you made a mistake during step 5 while checking off items, or (2) that there's either an error somewhere in your register (very likely) or a bank error (very unlikely). If, by the way, your second run through step 6 produces a *different* wrong answer, you've got to keep redoing the computation until you're sure you're tallying up the numbers correctly. Keep going until you get the same answer twice. This should not be hard to do if you use your calculator carefully. (A calculator with a printout or a screen that displays all your inputted numbers might come in handy. With these calculators, you can check to see that you've input the correct numbers.)

Now that you know there's an error, there are a couple things you can do. My recommendation, as long as the discrepancy is relatively small, is to save yourself the trouble of trying to find the error and just accept the adjusted statement balance. You just write this number on the first empty line of your register, put a note by it, like "fudge," and begin again from there. I realize that this may seem very unmathematical, and if you're the type of person who likes to keep everything in order, ignoring an error like this might be hard to do—I don't blame you, I like things to add up myself. But consider a few things.

First, it is *very* likely that the bank is correct and that the error is yours. In this case, you gain nothing by finding the error—except, perhaps, a little peace of mind. Second, let's assume that the error is the bank's. If the corrected statement balance is *higher* than you expected, just accept this little gift from your bank. (If the error isn't small, it's probably wise to contact your bank.) But even if the corrected statement balance is *lower* than your register balance, it might not be worth the trouble to hunt for an error in your register, find none, double-check your work, still find no error, and then have to go through the hassle of contacting the bank in the hope that they will find an error that they made—what's much more likely is that they'll find an error that *you* made. If your inner parent tells you that not finding such an error is lazy or sloppy, etc., tell him or her to get lost—remind them that they're living in your head rent-free—and then point out that, in fact, it's not lazy or sloppy, it's smart and efficient, and, what's more, accountants do it all the time.

If you want to look for the error, here's what you do. First, *go play with your children.* Then, if you still want to find the error, there are several things you can do. First, check that you didn't make a copying mistake where you had to carry the balance over from one page in your register to the next. Next, redo the comparison process (step 5), making sure that you accurately checked items off in your register and on the statement. During this second runthrough, also double-check that the amount of each check listed in your statement agrees with the amount you record-ed in your register. One common error is reversing digits: for example, you wrote a check for $127.37 but recorded it as $137.27. If you find such an error, look at the canceled check to see whether the error was yours or the bank's. Now do the same thing for all deposits or other credits. If you find an error, check your records to determine whether you recorded your deposit correctly.

If you find one of these errors, take the two numbers—the one that should have been recorded and the one that actually was—and subtract the smaller from the larger. If this difference is the same as the discrepancy you earlier found between the adjusted statement balance and your register balance, congratulations!—you've uncov-ered the culprit. For example, consider the above-mentioned error: you recorded a $127.37 check as $137.27. Subtract $127.37 from $137.27—that's $9.90. If this is the same as the original discrepancy you found, you're done. Simply make the correction on the first empty line of your register. Since the amount of the debit you recorded was $9.90 too much, your register balance ended up too small, so *add* $9.90 to your balance. If this error doesn't explain the full discrepancy, you'll have to keep looking for other errors until you've accounted for the original discrepancy.

It's also conceivable that you made an arithmetic error while tallying up your balance periodically in your register. This is unlikely, however, if you followed my suggestion to use your calculator for this. If you computed your balance by hand each time you wrote a check, you should check all your arithmetic with a calculator. And whether or not you used a calculator, you might also want to do the following. If the original discrepancy you found is an even number, divide it by two. Now look through your register for an item of this amount. If you find such an item, either you or your bank added it when it should have been subtracted or vice versa.

Well, if you've gone through the above and still haven't found the error, just forget about it, it's no big deal—punt. Make the necessary correction on the first empty line of your register and just go from there.

Whether or not everything worked out exactly, you should pat yourself on the back. You've begun a new habit that, over the long run, will help you keep your financial house in order. And even if your first attempt required a fudge correction on your register, your final balance *is* now correct—and that's the whole point. In other words, even when there's a discrepancy and you either can't find the culprit or choose not to look for it, the reconciliation process is nevertheless successful because your register is now balanced. Over time, this whole process will get easier and easier and your register will often reconcile perfectly with your statement. Congrats!

CHAPTER 11

Credit Cards, Loans, and Mortgages

For this chapter, you may want to review topics in the following chapters from part I:
- Fractions, Decimals, and Percents (chapter 2)
- Powers and Roots (chapter 4)

The main thing to understand about borrowing is how much you're paying in interest. It's often more than you think. Below is one of the most important points in the entire book—it applies to many types of loans, but especially to high-interest-rate credit cards. Take it to heart.

Until you do the math, it's very easy to fail to realize how much interest you're paying and the true financial burden of interest payments.

Credit Cards

I hope the following scenario will drive home the perils of carrying a balance due on your credit card month after month or year after year. Let's say the financial circumstances of you and your neighbor are identical in all respects. Both of you have about $2000 per year to spend on nonessentials, fun stuff like clothes you buy but hardly ever wear, DVD players, VCRs, furniture you can do without, etc. Both of you have a credit card with an annual percentage rate (APR) of 19.99% and a $5000 credit limit. And both of your cards are currently maxed out. Both of you have been carrying the $5000 balance year after year, never paying down the balance, but now you're considering turning over a new leaf to gradually pay off the card. If you gradually pay down the balance and your neighbor continues in his errant ways, how will your financial pictures compare? What will happen to the $2000 you and your neighbor each spend annually? Consider the following chart.

KEEPING UP WITH THE JONESES								
	YOU				YOUR NEIGHBOR			
Year	Amount spent on stuff*	Interest paid*	Balance paydown amount*	End-of-year balance	Amount spent on stuff*	Interest paid*	Balance paydown amount*	End-of-year balance
1	$550	$950	$500	$4500	$1000	$1000	$0	$5000
2	$650	$850	$500	$4000	$1000	$1000	$0	$5000
3	$750	$750	$500	$3500	$1000	$1000	$0	$5000
4	$850	$650	$500	$3000	$1000	$1000	$0	$5000
5	$950	$550	$500	$2500	$1000	$1000	$0	$5000
6	$1050	$450	$500	$2000	$1000	$1000	$0	$5000
7	$1150	$350	$500	$1500	$1000	$1000	$0	$5000
8	$1250	$250	$500	$1000	$1000	$1000	$0	$5000
9	$1350	$150	$500	$500	$1000	$1000	$0	$5000
10	$1450	$50	$500	$0	$1000	$1000	$0	$5000
11	$2000	$0	$0	$0	$1000	$1000	$0	$5000
12	$2000	$0	$0	$0	$1000	$1000	$0	$5000

*The total amount that you and your neighbor have to spend each year is $2000, the sum of the amounts in the three columns marked with an asterisk.

Let's look at your neighbor first. Year after year, he keeps his credit card maxed out, buying fun stuff whenever there's available credit on the card. At an APR of about 20%, he pays 0.20 times $5000 or $1000 per year in interest. Since he's got $2000 to spend each year, that leaves $1000 to buy stuff.

Now how about you? Look at the first row of the table. By the end of the first year, you've paid the balance down to $4500. So, $500 of the $2000 you've got to spend goes to paying down the balance. You'll pay $950 in interest, and that leaves only $550 to buy stuff. During this first year, you're going to have to put up with a bit of gloating by your neighbor, who'll have $1000 worth of stuff to show off compared to your modest $550 worth of stuff. When he's showing off his new DVD player, you can smile and say something like, "Boy, you must be having a great year, Joe," and when he asks you why you haven't gotten one yet, just chuckle and tell him not to rub it in.

Each year, you'll pay the balance down another $500. Since the balance will be shrinking, the amount you'll pay each year in interest will gradually decrease, and the amount you'll have left for stuff will gradually increase. In the second year, you'll have $650 to spend on stuff, in the third year, $750, in the fourth year, $850, etc. After biting the bullet a bit for four years, you'll have $950 to spend during the fifth year—if you look for bargains you can get as much for $950 as your neighbor gets for $1000.

Beginning with the sixth year, you'll be outspending your neighbor, and by the end of the tenth year, you'll have spent exactly the same amount on stuff ($10,000) as your neighbor— and your stuff will be newer and better—*and* you'll have paid off the card. Then, from the eleventh year on, you'll have $2000 to spend each year to your neighbor's mere $1000. As you can see, a little frugality for the first few years pays *huge* dividends down the road.

Of course, instead of outspending your neighbor, you could spend $1000 on fun stuff beginning in the sixth year and invest the surplus.[1] Let's say you invest the surplus in a portfolio of stocks that grows at 10% per year. At the end of the thirtieth year, your portfolio would be worth a staggering $73,500!

And after these thirty years, what does your neighbor have to show? He's got $1250 worth of stuff—the amount he outspent you by during the first five years on the chart—stuff that after thirty years is almost certainly worn-out, broken, or outdated. "How can this be?" you may be asking. Is it really possible that by forgoing $1250 in spending you would wind up with $73,500? If you think I'm playing fast and loose with the numbers, I'm not. The above result is not unrealistic. In fact, the above chart shows only one of dozens of possible scenarios, many of which would have even more dramatic results. Imagine, for example, what would happen if you carried a $10,000 balance year after year instead of $5000. What I find so remarkable about this is that you have to reduce your spending only a little bit for three years followed by two years of an almost imperceptible reduction in spending—that's it. Then for the next twenty-five years, you spend exactly like your neighbor, and you wind up with $73,500!

My main point bears repeating. The above scenario accurately shows that

Habitually carrying credit card debt month after month or year after year can have financially devastating long-term effects.

Perhaps one catch in the above story is the difficulty—at least for most people—of having the necessary discipline to pay the balance down as shown in the table. It's so easy to say to yourself something like, "It's

---

[1] Actually, if you're going to spend just $1000 beginning in the sixth year, the first thing you'd want to do with the annual surpluses is pay the card down faster than we've shown in the chart. Then, after the card is paid off, you'd begin investing the surpluses. Doing it this way, the card can be paid off in eight and a half years instead of ten. But, for the sake of simplicity, I did the above math based on paying the card off in ten years, as shown in the chart.

not going to matter much if I put this new sweater on my card; I can always begin paying down the balance next month." One thing you can do to avoid this is to call your credit card company periodically, according to some schedule like the one in the above table, and tell them to reduce your credit limit. This is a relatively painless way to gradually pay down your card.

Oh My God! She's Wearing Her $36,750 Outfit!

$4410 earrings and necklace ($75)

$11,760 coat ($200)

$5880 sweater ($100)

$2940 scarf ($50)

$2940 shirt ($50)

$2940 pants ($50)

$5880 shoes ($100)

total: $36,750 ($625)

In case you're wondering, no, this is not diamond-studded clothing. These are ordinary, department store items—the actual prices are in parentheses. It's a $36,750 outfit because it was purchased on a 20% APR credit card and then the maximum $5000 balance was carried over year after year for about thirty years. To come up with these dollar amounts, I've just used the scenario discussed in the text on pages 172–174. Remember the amount, $1250? That was the amount your neighbor outspent you during the first five years after you started paying down your card. The actual cost of this outfit, $625, is half of that, and thus the long-term cost, $36,750, is half of the long-term cost discussed in the scenario, $73,500.

Determining the True Interest Rate of a Loan or Credit Card

Like the seller of any other product, a person who "sells" you a loan or credit card has an incentive to make it sound better than it is. He or she will thus want to advertise an interest rate lower than the true rate. One way this is done is to advertise the annual percentage rate (APR) instead of the higher, true rate—the effective annual rate. Here's the formula for converting an APR into the effective rate:

$$\text{Effective interest rate} = \left(1 + \frac{APR}{n}\right)^n - 1$$

(Where n is the number of payments or compounding periods per year)

Say you take out a loan with an APR of 10% where your payments are monthly. What's the effective rate?

$$\text{Effective interest rate} = \left(1 + \frac{0.10}{12}\right)^{12} - 1$$

$$= (1.00833)^{12} - 1$$

$$\approx 1.1047 - 1$$

$$\approx 0.1047$$

$$\approx 10.47\%$$

So 10.47% is the true interest rate, not 10%. You would do the same computation to convert a credit card APR into the true, effective interest rate.

Another way lenders are able to advertise an interest rate lower than the true rate is to charge you some sort of loan processing fee, which is, in a sense, a disguised interest payment. I'll show you two ways to determine the true interest rate in this case. First, if you have a financial calculator like Texas Instruments' BA-35 Solar, this computation is a snap. Say you borrow $5000 with an advertised APR of 12%; you pay a processing fee of $75 when you take out the loan, and you'll pay off the loan with 36 monthly payments of $166.07. Notice that while you're technically borrowing $5000, and of course, you must pay back the full $5000, they're giving you $75 less than that—$4925. To figure the true interest rate with the BA-35 Solar,

press: 4925 $\boxed{\text{PV}}$ 36 $\boxed{\text{N}}$ 166.07 $\boxed{\text{PMT}}$ $\boxed{\text{CPT}}$ $\boxed{\text{\%i}}$

The answer, ~ 1.088, is the monthly interest rate. To convert this to the annual effective interest rate, just move the decimal two places to the left—that's 0.01088—then add one—that's 1.01088—and finally raise this number to the 12th power and subtract one:

$$Annual\ effective\ rate = (1 + 0.01088)^{12} - 1$$

$$\approx 1.1387 - 1$$

$$\approx 0.1387$$

$$\approx 13.87\%$$

You're paying almost 14% interest for a loan advertised at only 12%.

Credit Card Annual Fee or Membership Fee

Credit card fees are another type of disguised interest—sort of. I say "sort of" because you can't convert an annual fee into interest in the same direct way we converted the processing fee into interest in the last example. The extra complication here is the fact that your credit card balance may go up and down or you may pay off your card every month and carry a zero balance. And the impact of the annual fee is different depending on the size of your balance. The lower your average balance, the greater the impact of the annual fee. The main thing to remember about an annual fee is that it obviously does add to the amount you pay each year. Don't forget to take this into consideration when comparing two cards. For example, let's say you've got a card with a 15.9% APR with no annual fee, and you're considering getting rid of this card and getting a new card with a 12.9% APR that has a $75 annual membership fee. Is this switch a good idea? It depends on the size of your average balance. If you pay your balance off each month and incur no finance charges, switching cards would be ridiculous. If you tend to carry about a $2000 balance month after month, you're paying about 15.9% of that, or about $318 in finance charges per year. With the new card, you'd instead pay about 12.9% of $2000, or $258 per year, in finance charges, plus the $75 fee, for a total of about $333—so your current credit card is still a better deal. The break-even point occurs at an average balance of $2500. If your average balance is more than that, you'll save by switching cards. It's easy to compute this break-even point:

Step 1) Subtract the interest rates:

15.9% − 12.9% = 3%

Step 2) Divide the annual fee by the result from step 1: $75 ÷ 0.03 = $2500. That's the break-even point.

If you tend to carry a higher average balance than that, get the card with the lower interest rate. (If one of the cards has two or more different fees, use the total of all the fees in step 2. And if both cards have fees, figure the total of all fees for each card separately, and then subtract one total from the other. For example, if one card has an annual fee of $50 and the other has fees totaling $90, subtract $50 from $90 and use the difference, $40, in the computation for step 2.)

CREDIT CARDS WITH A REQUIRED DEPOSIT

If your credit rating is less than perfect, and you haven't been able to qualify for a regular credit card, you may receive offers of credit cards that require you to open a "savings account" with them or make some sort of deposit. Watch out for such deals. The *true* interest rate for such cards—as opposed to the advertised rate—is usually *extremely* high. Let's look at an example. You get a letter from Such-a-Deal Bank telling you that you're already approved for their credit card. Here's the deal. To receive their card with a $5000 credit limit at an APR of 19.9%, you must first deposit $2000 into their "savings account." They emphasize that your $2000 will be working for you because it will earn 3% annual interest. You get a credit card *plus* a savings account! What a deal!

Let's *do the math* to find out what's really going on here. But before I show you what a bad deal this is, I should point out that this type of card can be a sensible option for some people. If you can't qualify for a regular card, and you need a credit card—for hotel reservations, etc.—this type of card could work for you as long as you know that you're disciplined enough to *never* carry a balance and incur finance charges. If you pay off the balance every month, you can enjoy the convenience of a credit card, and the forced savings of $2000 isn't a bad thing either.

But, watch what happens when you start to carry a balance due month after month with such a credit card. Let's say you let the balance creep up to $1000. You're finding it hard to pay down the balance, so you just carry the $1000 balance month after month. In that case, you'd pay about 20% of that, or $200 per year, in finance charges, and you'd earn 3% interest on your $2000 deposit—that's $60 per year—so the net result is that you're out $140 per year *and* *it's you who have actually loaned them $1000!* Are you with me? You gave them $2000, and they "loaned" you $1000 back, so it's really like you just loaned them $1000 in the first place.

If you start to carry a $2000 balance month after month, the net result is that you'd be out about $340 per year. You'd be paying $340 per year for the privilege of having Such-a-Deal Bank loan your own $2000 back to you! Here's one last example. What's the net result if you max out your $5000 credit limit and then carry that balance indefinitely? Here's the math:

Step 1) Figure your annual finance charge:
    19.9% of $5000 is $995.

Step 2) Figure your annual interest earned:
    3% of $2000 is $60.

Step 3) Compute the net result:
    $995 minus $60 is $935. So you pay $935 per year.

Step 4) Calculate the annual interest rate (remember, you've given them $2000, so, in this example, they've only loaned you $3000, not $5000): $935 divided by $3000 is about 0.312 or 31.2%!

Step 5) Convert this to the true, effective rate with the formula from page 176:

$$\text{Effective rate} = \left(1 + \frac{0.312}{12}\right)^{12} - 1$$

$$= (1.026)^{12} - 1$$

$$\approx 1.361 - 1$$

$$\approx 0.361$$

$$\approx 36.1\%!$$

Such a deal!

Determining the Payment Amount for an Installment Loan or Mortgage

Here's the formula for calculating the payment size when you know the loan amount, the interest rate, and the number of installments:

$$PMT = \frac{L \times i \times (1+i)^n}{(1 + i)^n - 1}$$

(Where L is the loan amount, i is the interest rate per installment period, n is the number of payments, and PMT is the payment amount.)

Let's do an example. Say you purchase a home for $200,000 with a down payment of $40,000. The mortgage amount is thus $160,000. If you take out a 30-year, 8% mortgage, how much are your monthly payments?

$$PMT = \frac{\$160,000 \times {}^{0.08}\!/_{12} \times (1 + {}^{0.08}\!/_{12})^{360}}{(1 + {}^{0.08}\!/_{12})^{360} - 1}$$

$$= \frac{\$160,000 \times {}^{0.08}\!/_{12} \times 10.936}{10.936 - 1}$$

$$= \frac{11665.07}{9.936}$$

$$= \$1174.02$$

I suspect that most people would choose to do this computation like we just did it—in several steps. But you can do it in one *very* long, single step with a calculator like the TI-34 II:

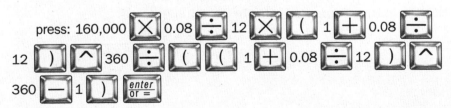

press: 160,000 ⊠ 0.08 ÷ 12 ⊠ (1 + 0.08 ÷ 12) ^ 360 ÷ ((1 + 0.08 ÷ 12) ^ 360 − 1) enter or =

With a financial calculator like Texas Instruments' BA-35 Solar, it's much easier:

press: 160,000 [PV] 8 [2nd] [%i] [%i] 30 [2nd] [N] [N]
[CPT] [PMT]

SHORTCUT METHOD FOR LONG-TERM LOANS

For those who don't have a financial calculator handy, here's a nice shortcut that's a lot easier than the above, offputting formula. Use this shortcut only when you have monthly payments and monthly compounding of interest. Here's what you do. Multiply the annual interest rate by the number of years of the loan and then look up the result on the table below. In the above mortgage problem, for instance, there was a 30-year, 8% mortgage, so you multiply 30 by 8, which equals 240. Look up 240 on the table on page 183.

The multiplier for 240 is 1.10. Now, just multiply the amount of the loan by the *monthly* interest rate (that's the annual interest rate divided by 12) and then multiply the result by the number from the table. This product gives you the approximate monthly payment. Here's the formula:

$$\text{Approximate monthly payment} = L \times \frac{\overline{I}}{12} \times M$$

(Where L is the amount of the loan, I is the annual interest rate, and M is the multiplier from the table.)

In the above example, the loan amount is \$160,000, the annual interest rate is 0.08, and the multiplier from the table is 1.10. Plugging these numbers into the formula gives us:

$$\text{Approximate monthly payment} = \$160{,}000 \times \frac{\overline{0.08}}{12} \times 1.10$$

$$\approx \$1173$$

SHORTCUT FOR FIGURING AMOUNT OF INSTALLMENT PAYMENT

Number of years of loan times annual interest rate	Multiplier
135–137	1.35
137–139	1.34
139–141	1.33
141–144	1.32
144–146	1.31
146–148	1.30
148–151	1.29
151–154	1.28
154–157	1.27
157–160	1.26
160–163	1.25
163–167	1.24
167–170	1.23
170–174	1.22
174–178	1.21
178–182	1.20
182–186	1.19
186–191	1.18
191–196	1.17
196–202	1.16
202–207	1.15
207–214	1.14
214–221	1.13
221–228	1.12
228–236	1.11
236–245	1.10
245–256	1.09
256–267	1.08
267–281	1.07
281–297	1.06
297–316	1.05
316–341	1.04
341–374	1.03
374–424	1.02
424–535	1.01
535 and over	1.00

The exact payment, which we calculated on page 181, is $1174.02. Our shortcut answer is less than a tenth of one percent different from the exact answer. This shortcut will always produce an answer within about half a percent of the exact answer, and it will usually be even more accurate than that.

CHAPTER 12

Insurance

When It Comes to Insurance, *Many* People Have It Backwards.

I can't advise you on how to shop for insurance— except to say that you should shop around—or precisely what type of policies you should buy, or how much coverage you need. You'll have to seek that advice elsewhere. Instead, I want to drive home one *very* important point:

When it comes to insurance, many, many people have it backwards. They insure the little stuff and fail to insure the big stuff.

The proper role of insurance is to protect you against the *unexpected, catastrophic* events that would either bankrupt you or inconvenience you financially to such a degree that it would seriously disrupt your life. You need homeowner's insurance to protect you against a major fire. You need major medical to cover a long-term illness.

You need life insurance to protect your family against your unexpected, premature death. You need disability insurance to protect you and your family against the loss of your income. You need this insurance because you couldn't afford to suffer such losses unprotected. But, *it doesn't make sense to insure against losses you could afford to pay for yourself.* I don't have the numbers, but the amount that people waste on unnecessary insurance is easily in the billions of dollars.

What follow from this are three closely related points. Most people who take the following advice will save loads of money. In general:

- Don't insure small-ticket items like consumer electronics.
- Don't insure against regular, predictable expenses like dental cleanings.
- Buy high-deductible policies.

I'm going to try a couple arguments to persuade you of the above, and, because I know some readers won't be convinced, I'll show you how you can prove to yourself that these ideas make sound financial sense. One way or the other, if I can win you over, you can save hundreds or even thousands of dollars in the long run.

Buying insurance to protect against small losses is just like going to the casino—the longer you "play," the more likely it becomes that the law of averages will catch up to you and you'll end up losing. Sure, some people get lucky and win at the casino, but more lose than win, and for people who play a lot, *far* more lose than win. Insurance is the same. Some people will get "lucky" and collect a lot from their insurance company—when they get reimbursed for having their car towed twice in one year, for example, or when they break their VCR. *But,* it's more likely that you'll come out on the losing end. Casinos always profit in the long run because of the house advantage built into all the games. Insurance companies enjoy the very same "house advantage."

Buying insurance for small-ticket items or buying low-deductible policies is like playing the following game. Let's say you're required to play this game, just like you're "required" to play the game of life. Every Monday morning, you roll a pair of dice. If you roll "snake eyes"—that's a 1 and a 1—you must fork over $100. If you like, you can buy no-deductible insurance for $7.50 per roll, which will cover the $100 if a 1 and a 1 comes up. Does it make sense to buy the coverage? Absolutely not! Now, granted, without the insurance it'll be a bit scary each time you roll, and if you were going to roll the dice just one time, you could make an argument for buying the policy—you won't miss the $7.50, but losing $100 would hurt.

But you've got to consider the long run. What's going to happen if you play for, say, five years (that's 260 rolls)? Each roll, the probability of rolling two 1s is 1 in 36. Thus, in the long run, according to the law of averages, about one thirty-sixth of your tosses will be snake eyes—that's about seven tosses in five years. That'll cost you $700. If you're a bit lucky, maybe you'll lose only $500; if you're unlucky, you might lose $1000. The probability of losing more than $1000 is only 11%; the probability of losing more than $1500 is only 0.3%—one chance in about 350. That's if you don't buy the insurance. If you buy the $7.50 policy each week, it'll cost you $1950 over five years. Now, which should you choose: a likely loss of $700 with a 1-in-350 chance of losing more than $1500, or a guaranteed loss of $1950? I hope I don't have to answer that.

Again, you should buy insurance to protect against losses you could not afford to suffer. So, you'll need some or all of the following:

- Major medical
- Disability insurance
- Life insurance
- Long-term care
- Homeowner's insurance
- Auto insurance (but get high-deductible collision coverage or no collision coverage if your car isn't worth much)

As a general rule, you should *not* buy policies like:

- Extended warranties (except, perhaps, for your car)
- Insurance for things you mail
- Car-rental insurance (if your auto insurance already covers you)
- Add-on riders like towing insurance
- Contact lens or eyewear insurance

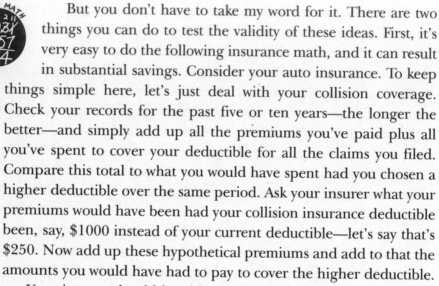 But you don't have to take my word for it. There are two things you can do to test the validity of these ideas. First, it's very easy to do the following insurance math, and it can result in substantial savings. Consider your auto insurance. To keep things simple here, let's just deal with your collision coverage. Check your records for the past five or ten years—the longer the better—and simply add up all the premiums you've paid plus all you've spent to cover your deductible for all the claims you filed. Compare this total to what you would have spent had you chosen a higher deductible over the same period. Ask your insurer what your premiums would have been had your collision insurance deductible been, say, $1000 instead of your current deductible—let's say that's $250. Now add up these hypothetical premiums and add to that the amounts you would have had to pay to cover the higher deductible.

Your insurer should be able to check that you've tallied everything up correctly. But be on guard: your insurer may try very hard to steer you away from this analysis because he knows where it will lead—to your benefit and his loss.

The majority of people who do this analysis find that the higher the deductible, the more they would have saved, and the savings over several years can be substantial. Now, granted, if you choose the higher deductible and then get in a bad wreck and have to shell out $1000, you won't be very happy. Of course, it's possible that you'll get in two bad wrecks. Then you'll *really* wish you had gone for the lower deductible. It's also *possible* that you'll get hit by lightning.

But just as it doesn't make sense to go through life worrying about the extremely unlikely things that might happen to you, it doesn't make sense to run your finances that way either. Look at it another way. Over a ten-year period, the difference between a $250 and a $1000 deductible collision policy could run as high as $1500. So if you're worried about having to take a $750 hit (the difference between the deductibles), what you should really focus on is the *unlikely* possibility of losing $750 (or the *extremely unlikely* possibility of losing $750 twice or more) if you choose the high-deductible policy, as compared with the *certain loss* of $1500 if you choose the low-deductible plan. Switch to a high-deductible policy. You'll come out ahead in the long run. Pick the highest deductible you're comfortable with. As a general rule, pick a deductible where if you had to pay it, you'd be very upset but your finances would not be seriously disrupted. You should do the same analysis with your health insurance. Your insurer will likely have all sorts of persuasive arguments for why you should choose a low-deductible plan, but don't listen to him. Stick to your guns and put the money you save in a sound investment. This last point bears repeating. If you follow my advice to buy high-deductible policies and to buy no insurance for small-ticket items, you should self-insure by putting away the money you save. This is the way to come out ahead. If, instead, you spend the difference, paying for some or your uninsured losses may be difficult.

If the above analysis seems like too much trouble, it might be easier to start today and keep track of what you spend on insurance over the next five or even ten years (I don't suppose that sounds exactly effortless either, but it shouldn't be so hard to do, and it'll pay big dividends). For example, say you're someone who tends to buy insurance like extended warranties and other small-ticket policies. Just keep track of what you spend on such policies and how much you collect from them. Compare the net result to what you would have spent—to replace or repair broken items, for example—had you not bought the insurance. Most people will come out ahead without the insurance. And a little bonus of not insuring this small stuff is avoiding the hassle of filing claims. One more thing: remember, even if you do this comparison test, and you're one of the minority of people who come out ahead because of your insurance, this doesn't necessarily mean that buying the coverage was a good idea. Maybe you just got "lucky." It's like going to the casino. You might win some evening, but that doesn't mean you played well—you just beat the odds that time. In the same way, some of the people who come out ahead by insuring small-ticket items are just getting lucky by beating the odds—this doesn't prove that getting the insurance was the right way to go any more than making a bad move in chess, but then getting away with it means that it was a good move.

This argument works for the majority of people, for the average or typical person. If, on the other hand, you know you're *not* typical—if, for example, you bring your children to the emergency room unusually often and you can qualify for a health plan that covers such expenses—then you might come out ahead with a low-deductible plan. Or, if you know you tend to break things much more than average, it might make sense to insure, say, your cell phone. Or you might find some insurance that you're sure is a good deal (my friend, for instance, is confident that buying towing insurance was the way to go given the age of his car). But such cases are the exception because, remember, when you come out ahead like this, your insurer is losing money on you or making less than they expected. This doesn't happen often because insurers are in the business of studying things like how often kids have to go to the doctor and how often people break their cell phones, and, make no mistake, they've done the math and they've designed their policies to be profitable. If you fall through the cracks of their system, you're the rare recipient of a free lunch. Enjoy it while you can; it may not last.

If You Need Life Insurance, Buy Term Life

Term life insurance is pure insurance. It works like auto or health insurance. You pay your premiums, and, when you die, your beneficiaries collect. As with other insurance, the only time you receive money is when something bad happens—the event you're insuring against. The policy has no other purpose and no other value.

The other type of life insurance, cash value insurance (whole life, universal life, etc.), is life insurance *plus* a built-in savings or investment plan. For most people, cash value insurance is a bad deal because, generally, you get only a mediocre rate of return on this investment. You'd be better off buying term life instead and taking the money you save and investing it elsewhere at a better rate of return. Why invest your money through a life insurance company? Their business is insurance, not investing. And cash value policies are complex and confusing. It's difficult to know exactly what return you're getting for your investment. Keep your investments separate from your life insurance.

One argument insurance salespeople will make in favor of cash value policies is that they force you to save money you might otherwise spend. And, granted, there can be great wisdom in forced saving, because many of us are not as disciplined and organized about our finances as we'd like to be, *but* there are other ways to achieve the same forced savings. You can, for example, have the extra amount you would have spent on whole life automatically withdrawn from your paycheck and put into a retirement account. So, you might ask, "Since I don't need cash value life insurance to achieve forced savings, what else would justify spending so much for it?" Good question. Don't buy it. Of course, your friendly life insurance agent will disagree, and he'll likely sound *very* persuasive—you'd be persuasive too if you spent years making an art out of (and making a living at) selling people things that they don't need.

CHAPTER 13

Three Investment Tables

For this chapter, you may want to review topics in the following chapters from part I:
- Fractions, Decimals, and Percents (chapter 2)
- Powers and Roots (chapter 4)

In a nutshell, the main thing you need to understand about investments is how fast they grow. The growth of an investment is affected by three things: its rate of return, the rate of inflation, and taxes. In chapter 14, we'll go over investment formulas that you can use to compute exact answers, but first, in this chapter, I'll show you how to use a few simple tables to look up approximate answers about the growth of your investments. Just remember, while much of the material in this chapter and the next doesn't look easy, it has, in fact, been oversimplified. It's beyond the scope of this book to do all the math thoroughly. For those whose motto is "the less math, the better," skip to the shortcut on page 209. This shortcut is a simple way to cut to the chase and come up with a rough estimate—taking both inflation and taxes into account—of how your investments will grow and how long you can live on your savings.

The rate of return used in the following tables is the *effective annual interest rate* or just *effective rate*. I'll show you the math for that in the next chapter, but for now all you need to know is that the effective rate tells you how much an investment grows in one year. For example, if you put away $100 in any type of investment and one year later it's worth $106, it's gone up 6%—that's the effective rate. Now, $100 can grow to $106 in different ways. Your investment could earn a flat 6% interest at the end of the year, for instance, or if your investment earns only 5.84% annual interest but the interest is compounded monthly, the $100 will also grow to $106 in one year. Both results are the same, and for you, the investor, there's no difference. And in both cases the effective rate is 6%. Throughout this chapter and the next, I'll always emphasize the effective annual rate because that's the one simple number that tells you how much your investment (or debt) grows each year.

One last comment. For the purpose of using the following tables, the effective rate should include everything that affects the growth of your investment except for inflation and taxes. If you own some stock, for example, and you estimate that it will appreciate 10% per year and that it will also pay you a dividend worth about 2% of the stock's value each year, then you would earn a total of 12% per year, and that's the effective rate. Or if you expect your mutual fund to grow 10% per year, but the fund charges you 1% per year in management fees, then the effective rate would come to 9%.

Let's go through several examples using these three tables. For simplicity's sake, we'll first do examples that ignore the effects of taxes and inflation. In general, this is obviously unrealistic, but such examples can nevertheless have some practical value. With regard to taxes, there are investments that grow tax-free. And with regard to inflation, there are situations where you may want to see what's happening to your investments in future dollars rather than in inflation-adjusted dollars.

In the eight examples that follow, you'll notice a simple pattern: when we know the initial amount of money and want to figure out what will happen to it in the future—in other words, we're going

TABLE I

HOW A $1 INVESTMENT GROWS

(Multiply the size of your investment by the appropriate number.)

Effective rate	Number of years									
	5	10	15	20	25	30	35	40	45	50
1%	1.05	1.10	1.16	1.22	1.28	1.35	1.42	1.49	1.56	1.64
2%	1.10	1.22	1.35	1.49	1.64	1.81	2.00	2.21	2.44	2.69
3%	1.16	1.34	1.56	1.81	2.09	2.43	2.81	3.26	3.78	4.38
4%	1.22	1.48	1.80	2.19	2.67	3.24	3.95	4.80	5.84	7.11
5%	1.28	1.63	2.08	2.65	3.39	4.32	5.52	7.04	8.99	11.47
6%	1.34	1.79	2.40	3.21	4.29	5.74	7.69	10.29	13.76	18.42
7%	1.40	1.97	2.76	3.87	5.43	7.61	10.68	14.97	21.00	29.46
8%	1.47	2.16	3.17	4.66	6.85	10.06	14.79	21.72	31.92	46.90
9%	1.54	2.37	3.64	5.60	8.62	13.27	20.41	31.41	48.33	74.36
10%	1.61	2.59	4.18	6.73	10.83	17.45	28.10	45.26	72.89	117.39
11%	1.69	2.84	4.78	8.06	13.59	22.89	38.57	65.00	109.53	184.56
12%	1.76	3.11	5.47	9.65	17.00	29.96	52.80	93.05	163.99	289.00
13%	1.84	3.39	6.25	11.52	21.23	39.12	72.07	132.78	244.64	450.74
14%	1.93	3.71	7.14	13.74	26.46	50.95	98.10	188.88	363.68	700.23
15%	2.01	4.05	8.14	16.37	32.92	66.21	133.18	267.86	538.77	1083.66
16%	2.10	4.41	9.27	19.46	40.87	85.85	180.31	378.72	795.44	1670.70
17%	2.19	4.81	10.54	23.11	50.66	111.06	243.50	533.87	1170.48	2566.22
18%	2.29	5.23	11.97	27.39	62.67	143.37	328.00	750.38	1716.68	3927.36

TABLE II

HOW YOUR INVESTMENT GROWS
IF YOU INVEST $1 EACH YEAR

(Multiply the size of your annual investment by the appropriate number.

Deposits are made at the beginning of each year;

the final withdrawal is made at the end of the year.)

Effective rate	Number of years									
	5	10	15	20	25	30	35	40	45	50
1%	5.15	10.57	16.26	22.24	28.53	35.13	42.08	49.38	57.05	65.11
2%	5.31	11.17	17.64	24.78	32.67	41.38	50.99	61.61	73.33	86.27
3%	5.47	11.81	19.16	27.68	37.55	49.00	62.28	77.66	95.50	116.18
4%	5.63	12.49	20.82	30.97	43.31	58.33	76.60	98.83	125.87	158.77
5%	5.80	13.21	22.66	34.72	50.11	69.76	94.84	126.84	167.69	219.82
6%	5.98	13.97	24.67	38.99	58.16	83.80	118.12	164.05	225.51	307.76
7%	6.15	14.78	26.89	43.87	67.68	101.07	147.91	213.61	305.75	434.99
8%	6.34	15.65	29.32	49.42	78.95	122.35	186.10	279.78	417.43	619.67
9%	6.52	16.56	32.00	55.76	92.32	148.58	235.12	368.29	573.19	888.44
10%	6.72	17.53	34.95	63.00	108.18	180.94	298.13	486.85	790.80	1280.30
11%	6.91	18.56	38.19	71.27	127.00	220.91	379.16	645.83	1095.17	1852.34
12%	7.12	19.65	41.75	80.70	149.33	270.29	483.46	859.14	1521.22	2688.02
13%	7.32	20.81	45.67	91.47	175.85	331.32	617.75	1145.49	2117.81	3909.24
14%	7.54	22.04	49.98	103.77	207.33	406.74	790.67	1529.91	2953.24	5693.75
15%	7.75	23.35	54.72	117.81	244.71	499.96	1013.35	2045.95	4122.90	8300.37
16%	7.98	24.73	59.93	133.84	289.09	615.16	1300.03	2738.48	5759.72	12,105.35
17%	8.21	26.20	65.65	152.14	341.76	757.50	1668.99	3667.39	8048.77	17,654.72
18%	8.44	27.76	71.94	173.02	404.27	933.32	2143.65	4912.59	11,247.26	25,739.45

TABLE III

HOW MUCH YOU CAN WITHDRAW EACH YEAR
IF YOU BEGIN WITH $1000

(If you begin with $75,000, for example, multiply the appropriate number
by 75, etc. The withdrawals begin one year after the initial deposit.)

Effective rate	\	\	\	\	Number of years	\	\	\	\	\	\
	5	6	7	8	10	12	15	20	25	30	Perpetual
1%	206.04	172.55	148.63	130.69	105.58	88.85	72.12	55.42	45.41	38.75	10.00
2%	212.16	178.53	154.51	136.51	111.33	94.56	77.83	61.16	51.22	44.65	20.00
3%	218.35	184.60	160.51	142.46	117.23	100.46	83.77	67.22	57.43	51.02	30.00
4%	224.63	190.76	166.61	148.53	123.29	106.55	89.94	73.58	64.01	57.83	40.00
5%	230.97	197.02	172.82	154.72	129.50	112.83	96.34	80.24	70.95	65.05	50.00
6%	237.40	203.36	179.14	161.04	135.87	119.28	102.96	87.18	78.23	72.65	60.00
7%	243.89	209.80	185.55	167.47	142.38	125.90	109.79	94.39	85.81	80.59	70.00
8%	250.46	216.32	192.07	174.01	149.03	132.70	116.83	101.85	93.68	88.83	80.00
9%	257.09	222.92	198.69	180.67	155.02	130.66	124.06	109.55	101.81	97.34	90.00
10%	263.80	229.61	205.41	187.44	162.75	146.76	131.47	117.46	110.17	106.08	100.00
11%	270.57	236.38	212.22	194.32	169.80	154.03	139.07	125.58	118.74	115.02	110.00
12%	277.41	243.23	219.12	201.30	176.98	161.44	146.82	133.88	127.50	124.14	120.00
13%	284.31	250.15	226.11	208.39	184.29	168.99	154.74	142.35	136.43	133.41	130.00
14%	291.28	257.16	233.19	215.57	191.71	176.67	162.81	150.99	145.50	142.80	140.00
15%	298.32	264.24	240.36	222.85	199.25	184.48	171.02	159.76	154.70	152.30	150.00

forward in time—we look up a number on one of the tables and then *multiply*. When, on the other hand, we know the future amount we wish to achieve and want to determine what we need at the outset to achieve that result—this time, we're going backwards in time—we look up a number on the appropriate table and then *divide*. You'll see what I mean in a minute. One last point: remember, whenever you're doing investment math, it's okay to simplify the math by approximating and rounding off because no matter how much math you did, you could never get exact results anyway since no one has a crystal ball.[1]

 Example 1 (table I with multiplication). You invest $10,000 in an index fund and hope it will grow about 12% per year (the growth rate of the U.S. stock market since 1926, according to some sources). How much will you have in 15 years?

Solution: Just find 12% on table I, go across to the 15-years column and find the number 5.47. Your investment will grow 5.47 times bigger—$10,000 times 5.47 equals $54,700.

 Example 2 (table I with division). This time you want to determine how much you'd have to invest at a 10% effective rate so that you'd end up with $100,000 after 20 years.

Solution: Go down to the 10% row on table I and across to the 20-years column, where you'll see the number 6.73. Since we know the final amount and want the initial amount, we *divide*—$100,000 divided by 6.73 equals about $14,859. Why not invest $15,000?

---

[1] If you round off, round off in the direction that would make things look slightly worse rather than slightly better. For example, round off in the direction that would make your investments grow less rather than more. This will provide an incentive for you to save slightly more, and it will make it less likely that the future outcome will disappoint you.

Example 3 (table II with multiplication). What do you end up with if you put away $5000 per year for 25 years at an effective rate of 9%?

Solution: The number on table II for 9% and 25 years is 92.32—$5000 times 92.32 equals $461,600.

Example 4 (table II with division). You read that tuition and room and board at your alma mater will come to about $150,000 eighteen years from now. How much do you have to save each year at an 8% effective rate so you can send your newborn there eighteen years from now?

Solution: Look at the 8% row on table II. The number for 15 years is 29.32; for 20 years it's 49.42. We have to estimate the number for 18 years. As 49.42 is about 20 more than 29.32— remember, it's okay to round off—that means as we go up from 15 years to 20 years, the number goes up about 4 each year (because 4 times 5 is 20; by the way, the math isn't really this simple, but this is close enough). Since 18 years is 3 more than 15 years, the number will go up by 4 three times. That gives us 29 + 4 + 4 + 4, or 41. Now, since we know the desired final amount of $150,000, this is a *division* case; $150,000 divided by 41 equals about $3659—the necessary annual deposit. Or, since we're not being exact here, let's round this up and call it $3750; heck, if you can afford to save $3750, why not be safe and put away $4000 each year? By the way, did you notice another way we're being inexact here? You won't need all $150,000 eighteen years from now, only one year's tuition and room and board. But, again, whenever you're doing investment math, it's okay to simplify things and round off if it makes the math easier. Whenever you have a choice, simplify or approximate in the direction that will encourage you to save more.

Example 5 (table III with multiplication). You're retiring and you've got $250,000 in a retirement account earning a 7% effective rate. How much can you withdraw each year if you want the funds to last 25 years?

Solution: The number in table III for 7% and 25 years is 85.81. Since we know the initial amount ($250,000), this is a case where we *multiply*. For table III, we multiply by the number of thousands we start with: 250 times 85.81 is about $21,453—that's what you can withdraw each year.

Example 6 (table III with division). This time you want to determine how much you'd have to start with in an account earning 8% so you could withdraw $20,000 per year for 20 years.

Solution: In table III, the number for 8% and 20 years is 101.85. And $20,000 divided by 101.85 equals 196.367. This is the number of *thousands* you'll need; in other words, you'll need $196,367—why not start with $200,000?

Example 7 (tables II and III with multiplication). You're 35 years old and plan to retire in 30 years, at 65. If you invest $3000 per year at 8% until retirement, how much will you be able to withdraw from the account each year if you want the account to last until you're 90?

Solution: The number in table II for 8% and 30 years is 122.35. Multiply this by your investment amount of $3000. That comes to $367,050, the amount you'll have at retirement. Now look up the 8% and 25 years number in table III, since you want the funds to last for 25 years. That number is 93.68. Multiply this by the number of *thousands* you'll begin with: 93.68 times 367 equals $34,381, your annual withdrawal—just call it $34,000.

Example 8 (tables II and III with division). You want to be
able to draw $50,000 per year for 20 years from your retire-
ment account beginning when you're 70. How much do you
have to deposit each year beginning at age 30? Let's say your
money will grow at 12% per year until retirement—perhaps in
a Standard & Poor's 500 index fund—but that at retirement you'll
transfer your funds into a safer investment earning 6% interest.

> Solution: This time, since you know the final result you want,
> you'll use *division* and you'll start with table III. Look up the
> number for 6% and 20 years in table III—that's 87.18. And
> $50,000 divided by 87.18 equals 573.526; this is the number of
> *thousands* you'll need when you retire at 70—that's $573,526.
> Now go to table II and look up the number for 12% and 40
> years—that's 859.14. Finally, divide $573,526 by 859.14. That's
> about $668, or let's call it $675 or $700—your necessary annual
> deposit.

> Look at the drastically different results of examples 7 and 8.
> "Wait a minute, this can't be right!" you might say. In both exam-
> ples, the funds must last until age 90. But in example 8, the
> investor works five more years (till age 70 instead of 65) and he or
> she begins investing five years earlier (at 30 instead of 35). And in
> example 8, the investor is more aggressive, investing in the stock
> market and hoping for a 12% return, while in example 7, the return
> is only 8%. (After retirement, however, the investor in example 8 is
> more conservative, earning only 6% interest.) Now, it's obvious that,
> given these differences, the investor in example 8 is going to come
> out ahead, but the extent of the difference is truly amazing: in
> example 7, annual deposits of $3000 allow for retirement with-
> drawals of $34,381. In example 8, annual deposits of only $668
> grow into an amount that provides the retiree $50,000 per year!
> Amazing, but true.

Let's Get Real:
Taxes and Inflation

You know what they say about death and taxes; why not make it "death, taxes, and inflation," for while inflation may not be absolutely inevitable, you sure can count on it. Obviously, you've got to include the effects of taxes and inflation if you want to get a complete picture of your investments. Unfortunately, it's beyond the scope of this book to cover the effect of taxes. Different investments are taxed differently and it can get quite complicated, but here are a couple basic points. First, obviously, for tax-free investments, the tables will work perfectly (after you correct for inflation). Second, if your investment is taxed annually, but you won't be making withdrawals from the investment to pay your tax bill, the tables (again, after correcting for inflation) do show how the investment will grow—in other words, if you ignore the taxes you're paying, the tables will certainly overstate the amount of money created by your investment, but as long as you can afford to pay your taxes without touching the investment, your money will grow to the amount shown in the tables. And third, if you have an investment that will be taxed when withdrawn, you can estimate the tax effect by doing the following. Obtain an estimate of what your tax rate will be at the time you plan on making the withdrawal. Then just reduce the amount given in the appropriate table by your estimated tax amount. By the way, if you do this, you must make this tax adjustment to the table amount *before* you correct the amount for inflation. You may want to discuss these matters with a tax expert.

After the following brief comment about taxes, we'll do a couple more problems using the tables, but this time include inflation in the analysis. Say a fond farewell to astronomical returns. If you really want to keep things simple, you can skip the following and go to the shortcut on page 209.

The Taxman:
"There's One for You, Nineteen for Me"

I'll bet you thought the Beatles were exaggerating when they sang in their 1966 hit "Taxman," "There's one for you, nineteen for me." In turns out, however, that the top British income tax rate had been that high, though it had dropped somewhat—to 91.5%—by the time the song was recorded. The top rate during World War II was 95%—nineteen shares for the government, one for the taxpayer!

TAXES

Before we consider inflation, I want to discuss something that's a bit odd about the way that taxes affect an investment. Consider two $1000 investments, both growing at an effective annual rate of 10%. Both investments are after-tax dollars. The first grows without an annual tax liability; the earnings will be taxed at 30% when withdrawn. The earnings from the second investment will be taxed annually, also at a 30% rate. Let's see what happens to both over ten years. Look at the table on the following page.

When we consider the tax bite in both cases, the investment without an annual tax liability grows to about $2116, the other investment grows to only $1967. This illustrates the well-known principle that you come out ahead when you pay taxes in one lump sum at the end rather than a little bit at a time along the way. You come out ahead because you get to use some of Uncle Sam's money for a while to earn interest. So it looks like the first investment is the winner. But while the above numbers are correct, there's more to this than meets the eye.

Consider the second investment. Let's assume that you pay your annual taxes on it, but that you're not taking money out of the account to pay the taxes. In that case, it will grow just like the first investment. After ten years, it will have grown to $2593.74. If you then withdraw the money, you'll have to pay tax on just one year's

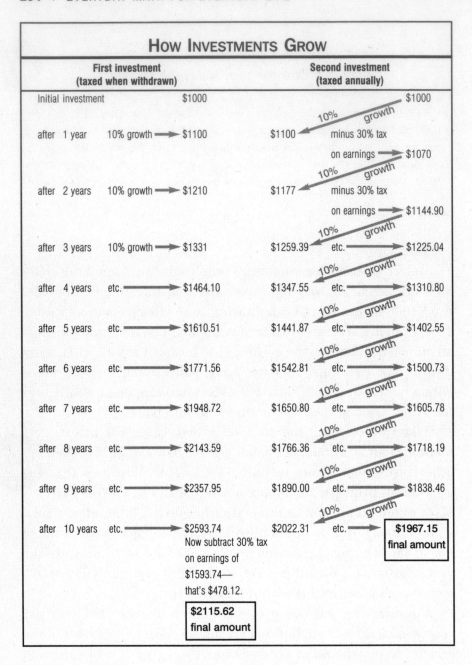

HOW INVESTMENTS GROW

	First investment (taxed when withdrawn)	Second investment (taxed annually)
Initial investment	$1000	$1000
after 1 year	10% growth → $1100	$1100 ← 10% growth / minus 30% tax on earnings → $1070
after 2 years	10% growth → $1210	$1177 ← 10% growth / minus 30% tax on earnings → $1144.90
after 3 years	10% growth → $1331	$1259.39 ← 10% growth / etc. → $1225.04
after 4 years	etc. → $1464.10	$1347.55 ← 10% growth / etc. → $1310.80
after 5 years	etc. → $1610.51	$1441.87 ← 10% growth / etc. → $1402.55
after 6 years	etc. → $1771.56	$1542.81 ← 10% growth / etc. → $1500.73
after 7 years	etc. → $1948.72	$1650.80 ← 10% growth / etc. → $1605.78
after 8 years	etc. → $2143.59	$1766.36 ← 10% growth / etc. → $1718.19
after 9 years	etc. → $2357.95	$1890.00 ← 10% growth / etc. → $1838.46
after 10 years	etc. → $2593.74	$2022.31 ← 10% growth / etc. → **$1967.15 final amount**

First investment (after 10 years):
Now subtract 30% tax on earnings of $1593.74—that's $478.12.

$2115.62 final amount

earnings, and you'd be left with about $2523. The first investment leaves you with only $2116. Now, of course, we're comparing apples and oranges here. You end up with more with the second investment, but you had to pay more taxes every year, and when the taxes are figured in, the first investment wins. But ten years down the road wouldn't you rather have $2523 saved up than only $2116? What's going on here?

With the second investment—again, as long as you're not withdrawing funds to cover the annual tax—paying taxes on it every year is a kind of forced savings. And it's these forced savings that put about $400 more in your pocket in the end—$2523 minus $2116, roughly. Here's the point. The first investor comes out ahead only if he invests the amount he saves each year by not having to pay an annual tax, the amount that the second investor *does* have to pay. Look at year 1 in the above chart. Investor 1 pays no tax; investor 2 pays $30. So investor 1 is temporarily $30 richer. But if he takes this $30 that he didn't pay in taxes and uses it to buy a dinner out—and then does the same thing each year—he'll be $400 behind investor 2 after ten years.

Now, I'm not saying that you should, given a choice, pick the second investment option. The math does show that the first option is better. Just keep the above caveat in mind, and remember that the first option is better only if the investor invests his annual tax savings rather than spending them on something without investment value—and we all know how easy it is to find a way to spend some extra money.

INFLATION

Now let's see how inflation impacts the results given in tables I, II, and III. But first, a brief explanation of how inflation works. Let's say we have an inflation rate of 4%. This means that, on average, goods that cost $100 today will cost 4% more, or $104, one year from now. If the inflation rate is predicted to average 4% over the next five years, here's what happens. The annual 4% increase can be computed by multiplying the previous year's amount by 1.04 (that's 4% expressed as a decimal [0.04] plus 1). Thus, the cost of goods that cost $100 today will grow as follows:

$100.00 × 1.04 = $104.00 (after one year)
$104.00 × 1.04 = $108.16 (after two years)
$108.16 × 1.04 = $112.49 (after three years)
$112.49 × 1.04 = $116.99 (after four years)
$116.99 × 1.04 = $121.67 (after five years)

You can see that we multiplied by 1.04 five times. We can produce the same result in one step by multiplying by 1.04 raised to the 5th power as follows:

$$\$100.00 \times 1.04^5 = \$121.67$$

Note that you will get the wrong result if you simply multiply the inflation rate (4%) by the number of years (5), which equals 20%, and then increase $100 by 20%—that's $120. The error here is small, but over a great number of years it can be *very* substantial.

The above result tells us that what we can buy today for $100 will cost, on average, about $122 five years from now. I keep saying "on average" because the prices of different products and services go up or down at different rates. Four percent inflation means a 4% increase in prices averaged over all goods and services. The prices of some products and services will go up more than 4%, others will go up less, and some things, like computers, will even fall in price.

If we want to do the reverse calculation—backwards in time—we divide instead of multiplying. For example, if we estimate that an investment will grow to $100,000 thirty years from now, what will the purchasing power of that $100,000 be in terms of today's money? Let's use the historic rate of inflation, 3.2%, for this problem. First, express 3.2% as a decimal (0.032), then add 1—that gives us 1.032. Now divide $100,000 by 1.032 raised to the 30th power:

$$\frac{\$100,000}{1.032^{30}} \approx \$38,870$$

A bit depressing, isn't it? The $100,000 will really only be as good as 38,870 of today's dollars. And if we use a slightly higher rate of inflation, 4%, we get an even more deflated result:

$$\frac{\$100,000}{1.04^{30}} \approx \$30,832$$

The Effect of Inflation

If the inflation rate is 4%, something that costs $100 this year will, on average, cost $104 next year, but it does *not* follow that the purchasing power of your dollar will shrink 4%—close, but no cigar. Instead, the key to the answer is the fraction $\frac{100}{104}$, which equals about 0.962, or 96.2%. Your money will shrink to 96.2% of its current value—a loss of 3.8%, not 4%. By the same token, if one of your investments is growing at an effective rate of 10% per year during a period of 4% inflation, the net result is *not* 10% minus 4%, or 6%. This time we compute $\frac{110}{104}$, which is about 1.058, or 105.8%. So, in inflation-adjusted terms, each year your investment will grow to 105.8% of its value the year before—that's a return of 5.8%, not 6%.

Now let's do two examples from tables I, II, and III. For the following examples, we'll use an inflation rate of 3.5%, slightly higher than the historic average.

Example 9 (the completion of example 7). Recall that in example 7, there's a 35-year-old who plans to retire in 30 years. She will invest $3000 per year at 8% until retirement, then she'll withdraw the funds during 25 years of retirement. After inflation is considered, what will this annual withdrawal be worth?

Solution: Refer back to the solution for example 7. We determined that the investor's retirement account would provide her with about $34,000 per year for 25 years. To correct this amount for inflation, divide it by 1.035 raised to the 30th power (because she's retiring in 30 years):

$$\frac{\$34,000}{1.035^{30}} \approx \$12,113$$

Not much to live on, is it? And, wait, it gets worse—$12,113 is how much her first year's withdrawal will be worth in today's dollars. Each subsequent year, the true value of her $34,000 withdrawal will shrink by a factor of 1.035. Her second withdrawal will be worth $12,113 divided by 1.035, or $11,703. The next one will be worth $11,703 divided by 1.035, or $11,307, and so on. The final withdrawal—55 years after her first deposit, when she's 90—will be worth only

$$\frac{\$34,000}{1.035^{55}} \approx \$5126$$

in today's dollars.

Example 10. You buy a five-year, $3000 CD that pays 7% annual interest. What will the CD be worth at the end of the term?

Step 1) The number on table I for 7% and five years is 1.40.

Step 2) Multiply: 1.40 × $3000 = $4200

Step 3) Correct this amount for inflation by dividing it by the inflation rate plus one (we'll use 3.5% again) raised to the 5th power (for five years):

$$\frac{\$4200}{1.035^{5}} \approx \$3536$$

So, in real terms, the $3000 investment grew to only $3536 in five years. That comes to an annual return of about 3.3%.

A Simple Shortcut That Handles Both Taxes and Inflation for Those Who Really Want to Cut to the Chase

No one can predict the future. No one knows what will happen to the stock market or inflation or tax rates in 10, 20, or 30 years. Because of all this uncertainty, it's impossible to be precise about, for example, how your investments will grow in inflation-adjusted terms, or how much annual income your retirement account will provide you with after you factor in taxes and inflation. A ballpark estimate is the best you can do.

A good rule of thumb is that you can expect that in the long run your investments will grow somewhere between 3% and 6% per year *after* factoring in taxes and inflation. The more aggressive your investment strategy, the higher your expected rate of return; the more conservative your strategy, the lower the rate of return. And the higher your taxes, the lower your rate of return, and vice versa. If you're very conservative, for instance, putting all your invest- ments in something with a guaranteed rate of return, like a savings account, a money market account, or CDs, you might eke out only a percent or two of growth after taxes and inflation. But no com- petent financial adviser would recommend this as a long-term strategy.

All you have to do with this shortcut is pick a growth rate from 3% to 6% and then look up the results on tables I, II, or III on pages 195, 196, or 197. That's all there is to it, except for one minor catch. Since one of the main objectives of this shortcut is to give you inflation-adjusted results, we have to tweak the results from the tables a bit. Actually, table I needs no tweaking. Just use 3%, 4%, 5%, or 6% and look up the result. And remember, the results are in inflation-adjusted dollars. For table II, instead of investing the same amount each year, your investment should increase each year to match the inflation rate. For example, if you think you can afford to put away about $1000 per year for 30 years, you should be able to deposit $1000 for the first year then, say, $1050 the second year (to match an inflation rate of 5%), then about $1103 the next year, etc. Since, as a general rule, everything including your salary tends to go up with inflation, investing $1000 today will feel the same to you as putting away $2000 many years down the road when inflation has cut the value of money in half. So, assuming that your deposits will keep pace with inflation, you can just look up the result in table II. Let's use 4% growth for our estimate. After 30 years of annual investments of 1000 of *today's* dollars—that's inflation-adjusted dollars—your investments will have grown to $58,330 in *today's* dollars. ($58,330 is the table entry for 4% and 30 years—that's 58.33—times $1000.) Since this is just an estimate anyway, let's call it $60,000. The nice thing about getting a result in today's dollars is that you know what $60,000 can buy today, and with $60,000 of *today's* dollars 30 years from now, you'll be able to buy just as much.

Let's continue this example with table III. Your account has grown to about $60,000 in 30 years. Now let's say that at the end of these 30 years, you'll stop making deposits and you'll then want to make annual withdrawals from the account for the following 25 years. How much can you take out each year? All you have to do is look up the result in table III. The entry for 4% and 25 years is $64.01. That's the withdrawal amount if you begin with $1000. But in our example, you're beginning with $60,000 so you multiply $64.01 by 60, obtaining a result of about $3840. That's the approximate amount you can withdraw each year for 25 years in constant, inflation-adjusted dollars, and this amount is in *today's* dollars. Let me explain. You're looking ahead 30 years[2] to when you'll begin making 25 annual withdrawals from this account. The result of $3840 means that the amount you'll actually withdraw in each of

---

[2] Actually, your first withdrawal will be 31 years after your first deposit because with table III the withdrawals begin one year after the initial amount begins to earn interest.

those 25 years will have approximately the same buying power as $3840 today. The actual amount you'll take out in 30 years will be more than $3840, and the amount will increase each year for the 25 years to keep pace with inflation, but this retirement account will provide you with 25 years of withdrawals, each of which will have roughly the buying power of $3840 today. This type of inflation-adjusted result is more realistic and helpful than results that don't take inflation into account, because results in *today's* dollars tell you how much your withdrawals will really be worth.

CHAPTER 14

Investment Formulas

(Optional)

(Yeah, right—like the rest of the book is required reading.)

For this chapter, you may want to review topics in the following chapters from part I:

• Fractions, Decimals, and Percents (chapter 2)
• Powers and Roots (chapter 4)

Basic Investment Formulas

SIMPLE INTEREST

With simple interest, the annual interest is calculated as a
flat percentage of the principal, and interest grows by the same
amount each year—you don't earn any interest on interest as
you do with compound interest (see below). Very few investments or
loans are based on simple interest. Here's the formula:

$$Interest = principal \times rate \times time$$

(The *rate* is the annual interest rate expressed as a decimal—for example,
use 0.05 for 5% interest—and the *time* is the number of years.)

COMPOUND INTEREST

Almost all interest is determined with the compound
interest formula. With compound interest, unlike simple
interest, every time you earn interest, you earn interest on the

213

initial principal and also on any interest that has already accumulated. Compound interest on a debt grows the same way. Here's the formula:

$$A = P \times \left(1 + \frac{r}{n}\right)^{n \times t}$$

(Where P is the initial principal, r is the annual interest rate, n is the number of compounding periods per year, t is the number of years, and A is the final value of the investment.)

Say you invest $1000 at 6% annual interest, compounded monthly. What will the investment be worth in ten years? Here, P is $1000, r is 0.06 (for 6%), n is 12 (for 12 months), and t is 10. Plugging these numbers into the formula gives us:

$$A = \$1000 \times \left(1 + \frac{0.06}{12}\right)^{12 \times 10}$$

$$= \$1000 \times (1 + 0.005)^{120}$$

$$= \$1000 \times (1.005)^{120}$$

$$\approx \$1000 \times 1.81940$$

$$\approx \$1819.40$$

With a regular calculator like Texas Instruments' TI-34 II, you can do this in one step:

press: 1000 ⊠ (1 ⊞ 0.06 ÷ 12) ⌃ (12 ⊠ 10) enter or =

With Texas Instruments' BA-35 Solar financial calculator,

press: 1000 PV 0.5 %i 120 N CPT FV

("PV" stands for "present value," 0.5 is the monthly interest rate
[0.06 ÷ 12], 120 is the number of compounding periods,
"CPT" stands for "compute," and "FV" means "future value.")

Now let's examine the above so you see how the formula works. In the first step, we divided the annual interest, 0.06, by 12 to obtain 0.005. That's the monthly interest rate—half of a percent. In the next step, we add 0.005 to 1, obtaining 1.005. This is the growth factor. Each month, the balance gets multiplied by 1.005. Here's how it would grow during the first six months:

At the end of the first month: $1000.00 × 1.005 = $1005.00
At the end of the second month: $1005.00 × 1.005 ≈ $1010.03
At the end of the third month: $1010.03 × 1.005 ≈ $1015.08
At the end of the fourth month: $1015.08 × 1.005 ≈ $1020.16
At the end of the fifth month: $1020.16 × 1.005 ≈ $1025.26
At the end of the sixth month: $1025.26 × 1.005 ≈ $1030.39

We could have reached the same result in one step by multiplying by 1.005 six times like this:

$1000.00 × 1.005 × 1.005 × 1.005 × 1.005 × 1.005 × 1.005 ≈ $1030.39

Multiplying by 1.005 six times is the same as multiplying by 1.005 raised to the 6th power, so the above can be written as:

$$\$1000.00 \times 1.005^6 \approx \$1030.39$$

In our problem, the principal grew once a month for 120 months, so we raised 1.005 to the 120th power:

$$\$1000.00 \times 1.005^{120} \approx \$1819.40$$

Now you see how the formula works: it multiplies the balance by the growth factor once for each compounding period. If we wanted to know how much our investment was worth after a year, or 12 months, we would have multiplied $1000 by 1.005 raised to the 12th power. This brings us to the next topic, the effective annual interest rate.

Effective Annual Interest Rate

The *effective annual interest rate*, or simply *the effective interest rate*, or *effective yield*, tells you how much your money grows in one year. Continuing with the above example, after one year, or 12 compounding periods, your $1000 investment would have grown to:

$$\$1000.00 \times 1.005^{12} \approx \$1061.68$$

Since $1061.68 is 6.168%, or about 6.17% greater than $1000, you would have earned about 6.17% interest for the year. Even though the annual interest rate was only 6%, your money actually grows by more than that because of the compounding of interest. The effective interest rate, 6.17% in this example, not the annual rate of 6%, is the number that matters to you. It tells you what your money is really earning, or, in the case of a debt, what annual interest you're really paying. Here's the formula for effective interest rate:

$$\text{Effective interest rate} = \left(1 + \frac{r}{n}\right)^n - 1$$

Plugging in the numbers from the above example gives us, again, the result of 6.17%:

$$\text{Effective interest rate} = \left(1 + \frac{0.06}{12}\right)^{12} - 1$$

$$= (1.005)^{12} - 1$$

$$\approx 1.0617 - 1$$

$$\approx 0.0617$$

$$\approx 6.17\%$$

The effective interest rate is usually included in the information about investments or loans, or you can compute it with the above formula. Again, it's the true interest rate you're earning or paying, and thus that's the number you should pay attention to. Once you know it, you can use it in simplified versions of financial formulas and in tables based on the effective interest rate like the three tables in chapter 13. For example, the simplified version of the compound interest formula from page 214 is:

$$A = P \times (1 + e)^t$$

(Where P is the initial principal, e is the effective annual rate, t is the number of years, and A is the final value.)

Returning to our original example, we can determine the final value of the $1000 investment after 10 years with the simplified formula and the effective rate of 6.17% that we computed above:

$$A = \$1000 \times (1 + 0.0617)^{10}$$

$$= \$1000 \times (1.0617)^{10}$$

$$\approx \$1000 \times 1.81978$$

$$\approx \$1819.78$$

(The slight discrepancy between this result and the $1819.40 computed above is due to rounding off.)

Present Value and Future Value

When we use the above compound interest formula, we input the principal, the *present value* of our investment, and the formula gives us what it will be worth in a given number of years, its *future value*. If we want to reverse the process, we use the present value formula, which is the compound interest formula solved for P:

$$P = A \div \left(1 + \frac{r}{n}\right)^{n \times t}$$

(Where A is the future value, r is the annual interest rate,
n is the number of compounding periods per year,
t is the number of years, and P is the present value.
Notice that this looks like the compound interest formula except that
P and A have been switched and here we divide instead of multiply.)

Use this formula for a problem like this: What must you deposit today at 6% interest, compounded weekly, to end up with $100,000 in your bank account 20 years from now? Plugging these numbers into the formula gives us:

$$P = \$100{,}000 \div \left(1 + \frac{0.06}{52}\right)^{52 \times 20}$$

$$\approx \$100{,}000 \div (1.001154)^{1040}$$

$$\approx \$100{,}000 \div 3.318$$

$$\approx \$30{,}139$$

With a regular calculator like the TI-34 II,

press: 100,000 [÷] [(] 1 [+] 0.06 [÷] 52 [)] [^] [(]
52 [×] 20 [)] [enter or =]

With TI's BA-35 financial calculator,

press: 100,000 [FV] 6 [÷] 52 [=] [%i] 52 [×] 20 [=] [N] [CPT] [PV]

If you know the effective annual interest rate, you can use the following simplified version of the present value formula:

$$P = A \div (1 + c)^t$$

(Where *A* is the future value, *e* is the effective rate, *t* is the number of years, and *P* is the present value.)

You would also use this formula whenever the compounding period is one year, because in that case the effective rate is the same as the annual interest rate. For example, if you estimate that your stock portfolio will grow at the historic annual growth rate for blue-chip stocks of roughly 11%, what would you have to invest today to end up with $100,000 in 30 years?

$$P = \$100,000 \div (1 + 0.11)^{30}$$

$$\approx \$100,000 \div (1.11)^{30}$$

$$\approx \$100,000 \div 22.892$$

$$\approx \$4368$$

How Long Till Your Money Doubles, Triples, Etc.?

Here's an oh-so-easy formula that will tell you how long it will take for your money to double, triple, quadruple, etc.— depending on the interest rate.

$$t = \frac{\log m}{\log (1 + e)}$$

(Where *m* is the growth multiple—for example, two for doubling your money, three for tripling, etc.—e is the effective annual interest rate, and t is the number of years.)

You estimate that the value of your stock portfolio will grow 10% per year. How long will it take it to grow to 3.5 times its current value? Plug in 3.5 for m and 0.10 for e:

$$t = \frac{\log 3.5}{\log(1 + 0.10)}$$

$$= \frac{\log 3.5}{\log 1.10}$$

$$\approx \frac{0.5441}{0.0414}$$

$$\approx 13.14 \text{ years}$$

With the TI-34 II or similar calculator,

press: [log] 3.5 [÷] [log] 1.10 [enter or =]

If we solve the above equation for e, we get the following formula:

$$e = m^{(1/t)} - 1$$

This will tell you the effective rate you need in order to grow your money by a given multiple in a given amount of time. Say you want your money to triple in 10 years. What effective rate is required?

$$e = 3^{(1/10)} - 1$$

$$\approx 1.116 - 1$$

$$\approx 0.116 \text{ (or about } 11\frac{1}{2}\%)$$

RULE OF 72

If you don't have a calculator handy, here's a shortcut for figuring how long it will take for your investment to double. Just divide the effective annual rate into 72 and the answer tells you how many years till your money doubles.[1] For instance, if the effective rate is 8%, your money will double in about nine years because 8 goes into 72 nine times.

Future Value of Periodic Deposits

Here's the formula for determining the future value of a sequence of equal deposits. Such a sequence of deposits is called an *annuity*.

$$FV = \frac{P \times [(1 + i)^n - 1]}{i}$$

(Where P is the amount of the periodic deposit, i is the annual interest rate divided by the number of compounding periods [in other words, i is the interest rate per compounding period], n is the total number of payments, and FV is the future value of the series of deposits. Note, for this formula, payments are made at the end of each compounding period, and FV is the value of the annuity at the end of the last compounding period.

If, instead, you want to calculate a future value where the payments are made at the beginning of each compounding period, use the same formula and just multiply your answer by $[1 + i]$.)

You deposit $100 each month in an account paying 6% interest, compounded monthly. What will the account be worth in 20 years?

---

[1] Some call this the "rule of 70" and use the number 70 instead of 72. Seventy is better than 72 for low interest rates like 3% and 4%. But 72 is better for interest rates from 5% to 9%. For interest rates of 10% and higher, the number 75 gives the best results. No single number will give accurate results for all interest rates, but if you want to remember just one number, use 72—it works well enough for all interest rates. And, after all, this is supposed to be a simple shortcut.

In this example, P is \$100, i is 6% (0.06) divided by 12, which equals one-half of a percent, or 0.005, and n is 240 because you're making 12 deposits per year for 20 years.

$$FV = \frac{\$100 \times \left[(1.005)^{240} - 1\right]}{0.005}$$

Let's cut to the chase this time

$$= \$46,204.09$$

With Texas Instruments' BA-35 Solar financial calculator,

press: 100 [+/−] [PMT] 0.5 [%i] 240 [N] [CPT] [FV]

(Note: "+/−" changes the 100 to -100—it's a negative amount because you're parting with your money. "PMT" is for "payment," 0.5 is the monthly interest rate [6%/12], "%i" means "percent interest," 240 is the number of payments, "N" is for "number," "CPT" means "compute," and "FV" means "future value.")

If we want to solve the reverse problem—what periodic payment is needed to achieve a desired future value—we solve the above formula for P:

$$P = \frac{FV \times i}{(1 + i)^n - 1}$$

Plug in the future value you desire, the interest rate per compounding period, and the number of payments, and the formula will give you the periodic payment needed to achieve your goal.[2] Let's do one example with a financial calculator. If you want to have

---

[2] This formula gives you the payment amount for payments made at the end of each compounding period. To compute the payment amount for payments made at the beginning of each period use the same formula and then just divide the answer by $(1 + i)$.

$200,000 after 30 years of monthly payments into an account paying 6% annual interest, how much must you deposit each month?

With the BA-35 Solar,

press: 200,000  360 0.5 CPT PMT

The calculator displays the result: *negative* $199.10, which means a *payment* of $199.10 per month. Might as well make it $200.

CHAPTER 15

Economic Terms Explained

For this chapter, you may want to review topics in the following chapters from part I:

- The Fundamentals (chapter 1), topic: Big Numbers
- Fractions, Decimals, and Percents (chapter 2)
- Powers and Roots (chapter 4)

Gross National Product (GNP)

The gross national product is the total value of all goods and services produced by U.S. companies and individuals whether they are operating in the United States or in a foreign country. The GNP in 2000 was about $10 trillion. One way to get a handle on this huge number is to divide it by the number of U.S. workers in 2000, about 135 million. This tells us that the average U.S. worker produced about $75,000 worth of goods and/or services in 2000.

Gross Domestic Product (GDP)

The gross domestic product is the total value of goods and services produced by U.S. or foreign companies or individuals within the borders of the United States. The GDP has recently replaced the

GNP as the primary indicator of the economy's performance. One way to measure how average individual wealth changes over time is to track GDP per capita, which is the GDP divided by the U.S. population. In 2000, the GDP was about $10,000,000,000,000, that's $10 trillion (as you can see from the table below, the GDP is always very close to the GNP), and the U.S. population was about 275 million. Dividing these numbers gives us a GDP per capita in 2000 of about $36,000. The following table gives the GNPs and GDPs for the years 1991 through 2000.

GROSS NATIONAL PRODUCT AND GROSS DOMESTIC PRODUCT (in billions of current dollars*)		
Year	GNP	GDP
1991	$6011	$5986
1992	$6343	$6319
1993	$6667	$6642
1994	$7071	$7054
1995	$7421	$7401
1996	$7831	$7813
1997	$8325	$8318
1998	$8787	$8790
1999	$9288	$9299
2000	$9959	$9963

*"Current dollars" means that the amounts listed are the actual amounts that would have been determined during the given year. In other words, these amounts have *not* been adjusted for inflation. "Current dollars" does not mean "today's dollars."

Federal Budget Deficit

The federal budget deficit is the amount of annual government spending in excess of that year's revenues, which are mainly tax receipts. To make up for the shortfall, the government must borrow by selling Treasury bills, notes, and bonds. In any year when there's a deficit, that deficit adds to the total national debt (see below). The budget deficits (or surpluses) for 1991–2000 are given below.

ANNUAL BUDGET DEFICITS OR SURPLUSES (in billions of current dollars)	
Year	Budget deficit or surplus
1991	-$269
1992	-$290
1993	-$255
1994	-$203
1995	-$164
1996	-$108
1997	-$22
1998	$69
1999	$125
2000	$236

National Debt

In laymen's terms, the national debt is the total amount the federal government is in debt or is in the red. Annual budget deficits and interest on the national debt have caused the debt to grow. The national debt in 2000 was about $5600 billion, which comes to about $20,350 for each of the roughly 275 million U.S. residents.

NATIONAL DEBT	
(in billions of current dollars)	
Year	**National debt**
1991	$3600
1992	$4000
1993	$4400
1994	$4600
1995	$4900
1996	$5200
1997	$5400
1998	$5500
1999	$5600
2000	$5600

Trade Deficit

The trade deficit is the amount that the value of all imports exceeds the value of all exports. The table below lists the U.S. trade deficits for the years 1991–2000. There could also be a trade surplus, but there were none during this period.

ANNUAL TRADE DEFICITS (billions of current dollars)	
Year	**Trade deficit**
1991	-$67
1992	-$85
1993	-$116
1994	-$151
1995	-$159
1996	-$170
1997	-$182
1998	$230
1999	-$329
2000	-$436

Economic Growth

Growth or decline in the economy can be measured in several ways. Two common ways are growth in real GDP (growth in GDP corrected for inflation) and growth in real GDP per capita. Because of increases in business efficiency and advances in technology, among other things, a normal, healthy economy will tend to grow a little each year in terms of real GDP per capita. When economic growth is measured by growth of real GDP, increases in population will also cause growth.[1] For the ten-year period 1991 through 2000, the U.S. economy grew at an average annual rate of 2.3 percent in terms of real GDP per capita. Here are the annual rates of growth (or decline) from 1991 to 2000.

ANNUAL ECONOMIC GROWTH OR DECLINE		
Year	Change in real GDP	Change in real GDP per capita
1991	-0.5%	-1.5%
1992	3.0%	1.9%
1993	2.7%	1.6%
1994	4.0%	3.0%
1995	2.7%	1.7%
1996	3.6%	2.6%
1997	4.4%	3.4%
1998	4.4%	3.4%
1999	4.2%	3.3%
2000	5.0%	4.1%

---

[1] During the 1990s, the U.S. population grew at about 1% per year. This population growth explains the fact that the annual changes in real GDP shown in the table are about 1% larger than the corresponding changes in real GDP per capita.

Recession

A recession is a substantial, widespread fall in general economic activity over an extended period of time. One rule of thumb is two or more consecutive quarters of declining real GDP. The day I sat down to write this section, November 26, 2001, the National Bureau of Economic Research declared that the U.S. had been in a recession since March 2001. Here are the dates of the five most recent U.S. recessions:

Five Most Recent U.S. Recessions
November 1973 through March 1975
January 1980 through July 1980
July 1981 through November 1982
July 1990 through March 1991
March 2001 through ?
(We're still in a recession as I edit this in June 2002.)

Prime Rate

The prime rate is the interest rate charged by the largest banks for short-term loans to their best corporate customers. Some credit card companies and other lenders charge an interest rate of a given number of percentage points above the current prime rate. From January 1, 1991, to January 1, 2001, the prime rate fluctuated between 6.0 percent to 10.0 percent.

Federal Funds Target Rate

When you hear on the news that the "Fed" is raising or lowering the interest rates, they're talking about the federal funds target rate, which is the interest rate charged by banks for overnight loans to other banks.

There is nothing "federal" or governmental about these so-called federal funds—they're private, bank funds. The term "federal" comes from the fact that these funds are transferred electronically through a wire regulated by the Federal Reserve. Lowering the federal funds rate has a ripple effect throughout the banking system so that the interest rates for many other types of loans will also fall. This makes more money available, which tends to increase spending and inflation.

Inflation

Inflation is a rise in prices. If the inflation rate from last year to this year were 10 percent, goods and services that cost you $100 last year would cost, on average, about 10 percent more, or $110, this year. It may surprise you that a 10 percent rate of inflation does *not* mean that the value of your dollar would shrink 10 percent. Instead, the amount of shrinkage is given by the following formula.

$$\textit{Percentage your dollar shrinks} = \frac{\textit{inflation rate}}{100\% + \textit{inflation rate}}$$

With 10 percent inflation we get the following:

$$\textit{Percentage your dollar shrinks} = \frac{10\%}{100\% + 10\%}$$

$$= \frac{10\%}{110\%}$$

$$\approx 0.091$$

$$\approx 9.1\%$$

For single-digit inflation rates, the shrinkage percentage is very close to the inflation rate, so you could just use the inflation rate instead of doing the above computation. But when the inflation rate is very high, the shrinkage rate is considerably less than the inflation rate. For instance, with 50 percent inflation—which some countries have seen in recent years—the value of money shrinks by "only" 33⅓ percent.

Consumer Price Index (CPI)

The most widely recognized gauge of inflation is the consumer price index, which measures the price changes of the items in a representative "basket" of consumer goods and services. Because this basket includes dozens of goods and services used in a typical household, the CPI is a measure of the changes in the cost of living for the average consumer. The operative word here is "average." Inflation affects different goods and services differently. As you probably know, some products, like computers and calculators, actually fall in price even during periods of high inflation. And the inflation rate can differ slightly from region to region in the United States. So the inflation rate and cost of living increases will differ somewhat from household to household, but for most people the rate will be close to the average rate. The table below gives the CPIs from 1950 to 2001.

CONSUMER PRICE INDEXES					
Year	CPI	Year	CPI	Year	CPI
1950	24.1	1968	34.8	1986	109.6
1951	26.0	1969	36.7	1987	113.6
1952	26.5	1970	38.9	1988	118.3
1953	26.7	1971	40.5	1989	124.0
1954	26.9	1972	41.8	1990	130.7
1955	26.8	1973	44.4	1991	136.2
1956	27.2	1974	49.3	1992	140.3
1957	28.1	1975	53.8	1993	144.5
1958	28.9	1976	56.9	1994	148.2
1959	29.1	1977	60.6	1995	152.4
1960	29.6	1978	65.3	1996	156.9
1961	29.9	1979	72.5	1997	160.5
1962	30.2	1980	82.4	1998	163.0
1963	30.6	1981	90.9	1999	166.6
1964	31.0	1982	96.5	2000	172.2
1965	31.5	1983	99.6	2001	177.1
1966	32.4	1984	103.9		
1967	33.4	1985	107.6		

Let's work through a few problems using the consumer price index. Say you're curious about what a gallon of milk cost in 1950. Here's what you do:

Step 1) Look up this year's CPI (you might want to try the World Wide Web) or estimate it. You can estimate it if you have a rough idea of what the inflation rate has been since the year 2001. Let's say you're reading this in 2003, and the inflation rate has been about

3 percent per year since 2001. That's two years of 3 percent inflation, or about 6 percent for both years. (If you want to pick nits,
two years of 3 percent inflation actually comes to this—1.03^2—
which equals 1.0609, which is an inflation rate of 6.09 percent.)
Then increase the 2001 CPI of 177.1 by 6 percent for your estimate of the 2003 CPI. That's 177.1 plus 0.06 times 177.1,
which comes to about 187.7.

Step 2) Divide this year's CPI by the 1950 CPI. Let's use the above estimate for the 2003 CPI. So we divide 187.7 by 24.1, which equals
about 7.79. This tells you that prices have gone up by a factor of
7.79 since 1950.

Step 3) Divide the current price of milk, say $3.09, by the result from step
2: $3.09 divided by 7.79 comes to about 40 cents.

This result assumes that the price of milk has risen at the same rate
as the inflation rate since 1950. Without knowing whether this is
the case, you can use the above result only as a ballpark estimate
of the 1950 milk price.

You would use this three-step process whenever you want to
determine the amount of money in some past year that's equivalent to a given amount today. Now let's do the reverse process. Say
you're reading a novel set in 1958, and some character talks about losing $600 at the races. Ouch! But how badly did that hurt? To get a feel
for this, you've got to convert that $600 into today's dollars. Here's how:

Step 1) This is the same as the first step from above: look up or estimate
the current year's CPI.

Step 2) Also the same as in the problem above: divide this year's CPI by
the CPI for the year in question. Let's use 187.7 again for 2003.
The above table gives 28.9 for the CPI in 1958. So we divide
187.7 by 28.9, which gives us 6.49, the growth factor for the
value of money from 1958 to 2003.

Step 3) Now we *multiply* by the result from step 2, instead of dividing. So
$600 times 6.49 gives us our result, about $3900. OUCH!

For the last problem, let's use the same years from the above problem, 1958 and 2003. What's the annual inflation rate from 1958 to 2003? Like in the above problem, we want to determine the growth factor for the value of money. The first two steps are the same as above, and we obtain, again, a growth factor of 6.49 for the 45-year period from 1958 to 2003. Now, you might think that you would finish this problem by dividing this growth factor of 6.49 by 45 years and then converting that number to a percentage. But this is *not* how you do it, because that would ignore the annual compounding of inflation. By the way, if you do it this way, you get an answer of 14.4 percent annual inflation, which is *way* too high. Instead, after completing the first two steps as above, you finish this problem as follows:

Step 3) Take the 45th root of 6.49 or, equivalently, raise 6.49 to the ¹⁄₄₅th power:

$$6.49^{1/45} \approx 1.042.$$

Step 4) Subtract 1: 1.042 minus 1 equals 0.042.

Step 5) Move the decimal two places to the right: 0.042.

So the annual inflation rate from 1958 to 2003 was about 4.2 percent.

PART III

Around the House

CHAPTER 16

Cooking and Food

For this chapter, you may want to review topics in the following chapters from part I:

- Fractions, Decimals, and Percents (chapter 2)
- Measurement and Conversion (chapter 6)

Units of Measure for the Kitchen

1 drop	= about $\frac{1}{75}$ of a teaspoon		
1 pinch	= about $\frac{1}{4}$ of a teaspoon		
1 teaspoon	= $\frac{1}{3}$ tablespoon	= $\frac{1}{6}$ fluid ounce*	
1 tablespoon	= 3 teaspoons	= $\frac{1}{2}$ fluid ounce	
1 fluid ounce	= 2 tablespoons	= 6 teaspoons	
1 cup	= 8 fluid ounces		
1 pint	= 2 cups	= 16 fluid ounces	
1 quart	= 2 pints	= 4 cups	= 32 fluid ounces
1 gallon	= 4 quarts	= 16 cups	= 128 fluid ounces

*A fluid ounce is different from a weight ounce (16 weight ounces equal 1 pound).

U.S.-to-Metric Conversions for the Kitchen

The following numbers have been rounded off slightly, but they're close enough. This is for the kitchen, after all, not a chemistry lab.

To convert	Multiply by
milliliters to teaspoons	⅕ or 0.2
milliliters to tablespoons	1/15 or 0.068
milliliters to fluid ounces	1/30 or 0.034
liters to cups	4.2
liters to pints	2.1
liters to quarts	1.06
liters to gallons	0.264

To convert from U.S. to metric, which you'll have far less occasion to do, just divide by the numbers in the right-hand column instead of multiplying.

Changing the Size of Recipes for Different Numbers of People

Here are a few simple tips for preparing food for a different number of people from what the recipe calls for. If you want to expand a recipe, the easiest thing to do is to simply double or triple it, etc., and save the leftovers. But you knew that already. And it's easy to reduce a recipe by cutting the amount of each ingredient in half, for instance. But if you want to be exact, here's what you do.

Let's say the recipe is for eight and you'll be serving ten. Just divide the number in your party by the recipe number (you may want to use a calculator): 10 divided by 8 is 1.25. This quotient, 1.25, is now the number you use to *multiply* the amount of each ingredient. If the recipe calls for three tablespoons of oil, use

3 times 1.25, or 3.75 tablespoons (or call it four tablespoons—no one will know). Two sticks of butter become 2 times 1.25, or 2.5 sticks, etc. Here's a chocolate-chip cookie recipe for five dozen cookies:

2 cups flour
1 tsp. baking soda
1 tsp. salt
1 cup butter
¾ cup sugar
¾ cup brown sugar
1 tsp. vanilla
2 cups chocolate chips
1 cup nuts
2 eggs
¼ cup rolled oats

If you want to make eight dozen instead of five, divide 8 by 5, that's 1.6—your multiplier. Use your calculator to multiply each of the above amounts by 1.6, then round off:

Flour	2 × 1.6	= 3.6	Round to 3¼ cups
Baking soda	1 × 1.6	= 1.6	Round to 1½ tsp.
Salt	1 × 1.6	= 1.6	Round to 1½ tsp.
Butter	1 × 1.6	= 1.6	Round to 1½ cups
Sugar	¾ × 1.6	= 1.2	Round to 1¼ cups
Brown sugar	¾ × 1.6	= 1.2	Round to 1¼ cups
Vanilla	1 × 1.6	= 1.6	Round to 1½ tsp.
Chocolate chips	2 × 1.6	= 3.2	Round to 3¼ cups
Nuts	1 × 1.6	= 1.6	Round to 1½ cups
Eggs	2 × 1.6	= 3.2	Round to 3 eggs
Rolled oats	¼ × 1.6	= 0.4	Round to ½ cup

The method for reducing a recipe is identical. If the recipe is for six and you're cooking for four, divide the number of guests by the recipe number: 4 divided by 6 is 0.666 (or ⅔). That's your multiplier. Again, just use that number to multiply the amount of each ingredient. That's all there is to it.

Here's a calculator tip. When you enter 4 ÷ 6 in your calculator, the answer will be displayed as 0.666666. There are three things you can do to avoid having to keep dealing with a decimal like this. First, you can simply use 0.66 or 0.67 for your multiplier—close enough. Second, you can punch the decimal-to-fraction conversion button on your calculator. (If your calculator doesn't have this capability, get yourself a new one like a Texas Instruments' TI-34 II, which goes for about $15.) The calculator will then display the fraction equivalent of 0.666666, namely ⅔, a friendlier-looking number to use for the multiplier. Third, when the calculator gives you the quotient 0.666666, hit the "store" or "memory" button then the "enter" or "=" button. This stores the number 0.666666 into the calculator's memory. Then, for each ingredient in the recipe, enter the amount, hit the "times" (×) button followed by the "memory recall" or "recall" button, and then hit the "enter" or "=" button twice. Once you get used to using the store and recall functions like this, they really come in handy.

You can also use this technique if you have a cookbook in which the recipes always seem to result in portions that are too large or too small—perhaps an old cookbook, written at a time when people were eating larger portions. Let's say you want to reduce the size of the portions by 10%. Subtract 10% from 100%—that's 90%, which equals 0.90—this is the multiplier that will apply to every recipe in the book. Jot it down on the inside front cover of the cookbook where it'll be easy to find.

Now, whenever you use this cookbook, you'll use this portion-reducing multiplier. If a recipe is for six and you're serving six, just use this 0.9 multiplier for each ingredient. If, however, a recipe makes eight servings and you're cooking for ten, first calculate the recipe-expansion number like we did above: $10 \div 8 = 1.25$. Then multiply this by the portion-reducing number: $1.25 \times 0.9 = 1.125$, and round off to 1.1. This product, 1.1, is now a single multiplier that will both adjust the recipe for the size of your party and reduce the overgenerous portions.

If you'd like to increase the size of the portions in a cookbook by, say, 15%, just add 15% to 100%, that's 115%, and move the decimal two places to the left, 1.15. Jot down this portion-increasing multiplier on the inside cover.

Drink Water, Lose Weight!

I'm being totally facetious here—this is *not* a sensible diet plan. However, believe it or not, you do burn about 17.5 calories just drinking 16 ounces of ice water! A calorie is defined as the amount of energy required to raise the temperature of one milliliter of water one degree centigrade. A food "calorie" is actually a kilocalorie, or 1000 ordinary calories. Here's the math: 16 ounces equals about 473 milliliters, ice water is at zero degrees centigrade, and body temperature is about 36.8 degrees centigrade. Your body has to expend energy to raise the temperature of this water up to your body temperature. Raising 473 milliliters of water 36.8 degrees requires 473 times 36.8 or about 17,500 calories of energy—that's 17.5 food calories.

Caffeine

It seems that everyone you talk to has a different opinion on the amount of caffeine in different foods and drinks. Is there more in coffee or tea or Coke or chocolate? Once and for all, here are the correct numbers.

CAFFEINE CONTENT	
Coffees	**Caffeine (in mg.)**
12 oz. fast food coffee	150–300
12 oz. restaurant coffee	180–240
12 oz. instant coffee	160–200
12 oz. Starbucks coffee	about 300
1 shot Starbucks espresso	about 90
12 oz. decaffeinated coffee	6–10
Teas	
12 oz. green tea	about 70
12 oz. black tea	about 140
12 oz. herbal tea	Usually none, but check if you're concerned; some have some.
Soft drinks	
12 oz. regular cola	35–45
12 oz. diet cola	35–45
12 oz. regular Dr Pepper	about 40
12 oz. diet Dr Pepper	about 40
12 oz. Mountain Dew	about 54
12 oz. regular root beer	Some have none; some have about 20.
Chocolate	
2 oz. milk chocolate	about 12
2 oz. semisweet chocolate	25–40
2 oz. white chocolate	none
2 oz. baking chocolate	about 70
8 oz. chocolate ice cream	30–40
12 oz. hot cocoa	20–30

Alcohol

Alcohol content is measured in terms of either percentage or "proof." The proof of a particular liquor is simply twice the alcohol percentage. So 80 proof vodka is 40% alcohol. A handy rule of thumb for alcohol content is that a 12-ounce beer, a 6-ounce glass of wine, and a mixed drink made with one jigger of liquor (about 1½ ounces, as opposed to a "double") all contain roughly the same amount of alcohol.

ALCOHOL CONTENT		
Beverage	**Proof**	**Alcohol %**
beer		4–6%
malt liquor		6%
"lite" beer		4.2%
white wine		11–14%
red wine		12–14%
"blush" wine		9–13%
champagne		10–13%
port		18–20%
sherry		20%
cognac		40%
brandy	80–84	40–42%
gin	80–94	40–47%
vodka	80–110	40–55%
bourbon	80	40%
rum	80	40%
scotch	80–86	40–43%
tequila	80–96	40–48%
Bailey's Irish Cream		17%
Kahlúa		26.5%

Reading FDA Food Labels

Below is a typical FDA-mandated "Nutrition Facts" label. This one is from a gallon of 1% milk.

Nutrition Facts	*Percent Daily Values are based on a 2,000 calorie diet. Your daily values my be higher or lower depending on your calorie needs:

Nutrition Facts	
Serving Size 1 cup (240mL)	
Servings Per Container About 16	
Amount Per Serving	
Calories 110 Calories from Fat 20	
	% Daily Value*
Total Fat 2.5g	**4%**
Saturated Fat 1.5g	8%
Cholesterol 15mg	**4%**
Sodium 125mg	**5%**
Total Carbohydrate 13g	4%
Dietary Fiber 0g	0%
Sugars 13g	
Protein 8g	
Vitamin A 10% • Vitamin C 4%	
Calcium 30% • Iron 0% • Vitamin D 25%	

	Calories:	2,000	2,500
Total Fat	Less than	65g	80g
Sat. Fat	Less than	20g	25g
Cholesterol	Less than	300mg	300mg
Sodium	Less than	2,400mg	2,400mg
Total Carbohydrate		300g	375g
Dietary Fiber		25g	30g

Daily values are based on a 2000-calorie-per-day diet. The daily values for total fat, saturated fat, cholesterol, and sodium set *upper limits* for the amount to eat each day. For total carbohydrates, fiber, vitamins, and minerals, daily values show the *best levels* to aim for each day.

If you know your average daily calorie intake, here's how to adjust the percent-daily-value numbers on an FDA label. Use this method to adjust the percents for total fat, saturated fat, total carbohydrates, dietary fiber, vitamins, and minerals. The cholesterol and sodium percents are not affected by your caloric intake. Let's say you have a 2200-calorie-per-day diet. For the 1% milk, what would your percent-daily-value number be for saturated fat?

Step 1) Divide your daily calorie intake by 2000:

$$2200 \div 2000 = 1.1$$

Step 2) Divide the daily percent given by the FDA label by the result from step 1: $8\% \div 1.1 \approx 7.3\%$. Round this off to about 7%.

What if the number of servings you get from some container of food is different from the number of servings per container listed on the FDA label? Here's how you adjust the FDA numbers. Use the following method for the various numbers of grams per serving on the label as well as the percent-daily-value numbers. If you used the above method to adjust the percent-daily-value numbers for your caloric intake, simply begin with those adjusted percents when you follow the steps below.

Step 1) Divide the number of servings per container listed on the label by the approximate number of servings you'll actually get from the container. *Or,* what amounts to the same thing, divide your serving size by the listed serving size. This quotient is the multiplier you'll use in step 2. The above 1% milk, for example, lists 16 servings per container. If you think you'll actually get 12 servings, you divide 16 by 12—that's 1⅓, your multiplier.

Step 2) Multiply each grams-per-serving number and each percent-daily-value number on the label by the multiplier from step 1. Continuing with the 1% milk example, the label lists 15 mg of saturated fat and a percent daily value for saturated fat of 8%. Multiply those numbers by your multiplier: 15 mg times 1⅓ equals 20 mg and 8% times 1⅓ equals about 11%. If you had first adjusted the label percentages for your 2200-calorie diet, use those adjusted percentages in this step. For example, we determined above that the saturated fat percent-daily-value for a 2200-calorie diet was 7.3%. Multiply this percent by your multiplier: 7.3% times 1⅓ equals about 10%. So a person with a 2200-calorie diet who gets 12 servings from the gallon of 1% milk instead of 16 will get about 10% of her maximum daily allowance of saturated fat from one serving.

CHAPTER 17

Home, Lawn, and Garden

For this chapter, you may want to review topics in the following chapters from part I:
- Fractions, Decimals, and Percents (chapter 2)
- Basic Geometry (chapter 5)
- Measurement and Conversion (chapter 6)

The Cost of Carpeting (an area problem)

To estimate what new carpeting will cost you, you first need to determine the area of the room or rooms you're planning to carpet. If a room is rectangular, the area (in square feet) equals the length times the width. Round the length and width *up* to the nearest half a foot, and if your room is, say, 12 feet 6 inches long, use 12.5 feet when you do your area calculation.

If a room is not rectangular, you can divide the room into two or three rectangular sections and then figure the area of each rectangle separately. Consider the following diagram:

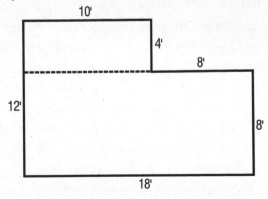

249

This L-shaped room has been divided into two rectangles: the top one is 10' long by 4', or 40 square feet, the bottom one is 18' by 8', or 144 square feet, and the total is thus 40 plus 144, or 184 square feet. You could also calculate the area of this room by figuring the area of an 18'-by-12' rectangle and then subtracting the part that's missing (the 8'-by-4' rectangle). See below:

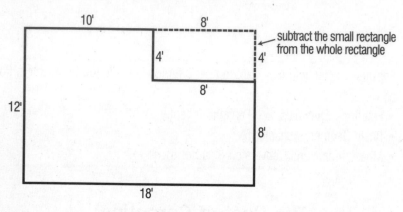

Thus, 18' times 12' is 216 square feet, and from this we subtract 8' times 4', or 32 square feet. And then, 216 square feet minus 32 square feet is 184 square feet, which agrees with our answer above.

The area of a stairway works basically like a rectangle, because if you pulled up the carpeting and laid it out straight, you'd have a long and narrow rectangle. The width of this rectangle is simply the width of the stairway. The length can be determined as follows. Measure the height and the depth of one step (rounding each *up* to the next inch) and then add them together. Use inches for this total; for example, use 14 inches, not 1 foot 2 inches. Now just multiply this number of inches by the number of steps in the stairway and then divide the answer by 12. Now you have the "length" of this "rectangle" in feet. Last, multiply the length by the width for the area in square feet.

The last step is to multiply your total number of square feet by the cost of the carpeting per square foot. If the carpeting is priced by the square yard, first divide this price by 9 to convert it to a price per square foot. You divide by 9 because there are nine square feet in a square yard:

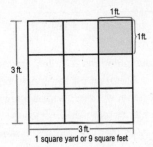

1 square yard or 9 square feet

Let's say your total area is 450 square feet and the carpeting costs $3.50 per square foot. That will come to 450 times $3.50, which equals $1575. But depending on the shape of your rooms and whether seams between carpet sections will bother you, you may have to spend up to 20% more than that total due to wasted carpet. Increasing $1575 by 20% brings your total to $1890. This gives you a rough range of what you can expect to pay. And make sure to ask whether you'll be charged extra for padding, installation, or delivery.

Number of Tiles for a Room (an area problem)

Step 1) Use the rectangular sections method to determine the total area of the room in square feet; let's say this comes to 180 square feet.

Step 2) If the tile happens to be 12 inches by 12 inches, you're done—in our example you'd need 180 tiles (but buy a few extras). Otherwise, figure the area of one tile. Let's say it's a 9"-by-9" tile; 9" times 9" is 81 square inches.

Step 3) Divide 144 (the number of square inches in a square foot) by the result from step 2 (81 in our example). That's about 1.78 tiles per square foot.

Step 4) Multiply the total area from step 1 by the number of tiles per square foot: 180 times 1.78 is about 320 tiles.

Step 5) Add a few tiles for wastage and spares, etc. Pick up about 340 or 350 tiles.

Rounding Off

When doing the computations for tiles (or for bricks for a patio), it's okay to round off, but don't round off too much, and generally it's better to round off in the direction that will give you too many tiles rather than too few. For example, in step 2, it's better to round *down* because that makes the tile smaller, so you'll end up with more of them; in step 3, however, you'd want to round *up* the number of tiles per square foot because, again, that will make the total number of tiles larger. The easiest thing to do, though, is to use a calculator, don't round anything off, and then just add a few tiles to the final number, as we did in step 5.

Number of Boards for a Deck (an area problem)

Step 1) Use the rectangular sections method to determine the total area of the deck in square feet; let's say that's 250 square feet.

Step 2) Figure the area of one board. Say you're using 10-foot-long 2-by-6s. Since a 2-by-6 is actually only 5½ inches wide, take this width and divide it by 12 to convert it to feet. That's about 0.458 feet (use the exact value here or round to three decimal places). Now multiply this by the board's length: 0.458' times 10' equals 4.58 square feet.

Step 3) Divide the total area by the area of one board. In our example, that's 250 divided by 4.58, which equals 54.6. So we need 55 boards. You might want to get a few more, say, 60 boards.

Buying Grass Seed or Lawn Fertilizer, and How Much Is an Acre?
(an area problem)

When buying grass seed or fertilizer for your lawn, you'll need to know your lawn's area. Like most area problems, you determine your lawn's area with the rectangle area formula (*Area = length × width*) and the rectangular sections method (see discussion of the rectangular sections method in chapter 5, "Basic Geometry," or above in "The Cost of Carpeting" section).

If you know the acreage but not the square footage of your property, you may want to use the following conversion equations. Don't forget to subtract from the total acreage the areas taken up by your home, garage, driveway, etc.

$$1 \text{ acre} = 43,560 \text{ square feet}$$

A good way to remember the size of an acre is that it's just a bit smaller than a football field, which is 300' by 160', or 48,000 square feet, not counting the end zones. If you cut off the last ten yards of a football field—in other words, if you go from the goal line at one end of the field to the ten-yard marker at the other end—that's just about exactly an acre. A 200'-by-200' square is also about an acre.

$$\frac{1}{2} \text{ acre} = 21,780 \text{ square feet}$$

A square piece of property 150' by 150' and a rectangular piece of property 100' by 200' are very close to half an acre.

$$\frac{1}{4} \text{ acre} = 10,890 \text{ square feet}$$

A 100'-by-100' square and a 75'-by-150' rectangle are about a quarter acre.

⅛ acre = 5445 square feet

A 75'-by-75' square and a 50'-by-100' rectangle are close to an eighth of an acre.

How Much Water Does an Aquarium Hold and How Much Soil Does a Flower Box Hold? (a volume problem)

 An aquarium and a flower box are both box shapes, so to determine their volumes we use the volume of a box formula:

$$Volume = length \times width \times height$$

Let's say your aquarium measures 2 feet by 10 inches by 1 foot. First, convert the 10 inches into feet by dividing by 12—that's ¹⁰⁄₁₂ or ⅚ of a foot. Now use the formula and your calculator:

$$Volume = 2 \times \frac{5}{6} \times 1$$

$$\approx 1.67 \text{ cubic feet}$$

If you want the volume in gallons, just multiply this number by 7.5 gallons/cubic foot—that's about 12½ gallons of water. And how much would that weigh? Multiply the number of gallons by 8⅓ pounds/gallon: 12½ gallons times 8⅓ pounds/gallon equals about 104 pounds of water.

How Much Soil or Mulch for a Garden? (a volume problem)

It's very easy to quickly estimate how much soil or mulch to buy for your garden or how many bags of wood chips to buy for your landscaping needs. With a good estimate, you'll avoid making a second trip to the lawn and garden shop or making a trip to your doctor when you buy too much and throw out your back.

This is a volume problem because when we buy soil or mulch for a garden, we need to consider the *length* and *width* of the garden and also the *depth* of the soil or mulch. Whenever we have three dimensions (length, width, and depth; or length, width, and height), we're dealing with volume.

To figure the volume, you just multiply the area in question by the desired depth of soil or wood chips or whatever. You compute area with the rectangle area formula (*Area = length × width*) or, if the area in question is not rectangular, you first divide it into rectangles, figure the area of each rectangle, and then add them up (this is the rectangular sections method; see pages 249–251).

Let's say your vegetable garden is 8 feet by 12 feet and you decide to put down 6 inches of new soil. What's the volume?

Step 1) Calculate the garden's area by multiplying the length by the width. 12 times 8 is 96, so the area is 96 square feet.

Step 2) Since the depth is given in inches, we have to convert to feet by dividing by 12. Six divided by 12 is ½, or 0.5, so the depth is half a foot.

Step 3) Multiply the area by the depth: 96 square feet times ½ foot equals 48 *cubic* feet—that's the volume.

Step 4) Since soil is often sold by the cubic yard, you may want to convert this answer: dividing 48 by 27 (the number of cubic feet per cubic yards) equals 1.78 cubic yards.

If your project is this big, you might want to have the soil delivered; 48 cubic feet, or 1.78 cubic yards, of soil will weigh in the neighborhood of a ton, or 2000 pounds.

Weight of a Waterbed
(a volume problem)

If you're contemplating buying a waterbed, make sure your house's structure is strong enough to support the weight.

Step 1) Figure the weight of the water:

a) If the waterbed's capacity is given in gallons, multiply this number by 8⅓ lbs./gallon; if its capacity is given in cubic feet, multiply by 62 lbs./cubic foot. This will give you the weight of the water. Go to step 2.

b) If the capacity is not given, determine the volume of the bed with the volume of a box formula:

Volume = length × width × height

For example, a queen-size waterbed measures about 84" by 60", and let's say the waterbed is 8" high or deep. First, convert each dimension into feet: 84" is 7'; 60" is 5'; and 8" is ⅔'. Now multiply:

$$Volume = 7 \times 5 \times \frac{2}{3} \text{(use your calculator)}$$

$$= 23⅓ \text{ cubic feet}$$

And now multiply this volume by 62 lbs./cubic foot to determine the weight of the water: 23⅓ times 62 is about 1447 pounds.

Step 2) Add the weight of the frame, headboard, etc.

Step 3) Don't forget to add your weight and your spouse's, if appropriate. You now have the total weight. This could amount to close to a ton—2000 pounds—which would come to about 55 pounds per square foot on your floor.

Step 4) Check with an architect or your city's building department to ensure that your structure can support the total weight.

Amount and Cost of Water
for a Circular Pool
(a volume problem)

To determine the volume of a circular backyard pool that's 24 feet across and 4 feet deep, use the formula for the volume of a cylinder:

Volume = area of base × height

Step 1) Since the base of the pool is a circle, use the formula for the area of a circle, Area = π × *radius*². The pool's diameter is 24 feet, so its radius is half of that, 12 feet.

$$Area = \pi \times radius^2$$
$$\approx 3.14 \times 12^2$$
$$\approx 3.14 \times 144$$
$$\approx 452 \text{ square feet}$$

Step 2) Multiply this by the depth (or "height") of the water:

$$Volume \approx 452 \times 4$$
$$\approx 1808 \text{ cubic feet}$$

So you have about 1800 cubic feet of water. Multiply this by 7.5 to convert to gallons—that's about 13,500 gallons. By the way, if you multiply this by 8⅓ lbs./gallon, you get the weight—about 112,500 pounds, or 56 tons, of water! This is about the weight of 35 or 40 average cars and probably more than the weight of your entire house and all of its contents! (If you don't count the foundation, a wood-frame, two-story, four-bedroom house weighs around 10 to 15 tons; a similar brick house weighs about 25 to 30 tons.)

Step 3) Figure the cost. If your water costs $2 per 1000 gallons, it would cost you about $27 to fill this 13,500-gallon pool.

Flipping Your Mattress

This is a sort-of geometry puzzle, in case you're wondering why it's in a math book. First of all, how many different positions can your mattress be in? Did you answer four? Good. There are two ways you can turn your mattress so you run through all four positions:

Method 1) Flip side to side,
Flip head to foot,
Flip side to side,
Flip head to foot.
Repeat.

Method 2) Flip side to side,
Rotate 180°,
Flip side to side,
Rotate 180°.
Repeat.

Lumber Sizes

The actual dimensions of a piece of lumber are generally smaller than the named dimensions. For example, a "2-by-4" (2 inches by 4 inches) is actually only 1½" by 3½". It's called a 2-by-4 because that's the size of the rough piece of lumber that it came from. But then it's "finished" (the rough stuff is cut away), and what remains is a 1½"-by-3½" piece of lumber. Some lumber is sold unfinished. In that case, the named dimensions are the true dimensions. To determine the true size of a piece of lumber, just subtract half an inch from each measurement unless the measurement is 1 inch, in which case it becomes ¾ of an inch. So a 2-by-6 is actually 1½" by 5½", a 4-by-4 is actually 3½" by 4½", and a 1-by-10 is actually ¾" by 9½".

The Cost of Electricity

There are a few things you can do to estimate the cost of running electrical devices. Some appliances come with a rough estimate of the annual cost of running them. Of course, annual costs can vary a great deal from family to family, depending on how much you use the appliance. If there is no annual cost estimate or you want a more accurate number, you'll need to know the appliance's wattage. Look for a wattage rating on the appliance (best) or use the table below (these are only estimates, and, as you can see, there's a wide range depending on the particular model of the appliance). The table also lists the typical energy usage for the appliances. Note that some are given in kilowatt-hours (kWh) per *load,* others in kilowatt-hours per *hour,* and others in kilowatt-hours per *year.* These numbers are also rough, ballpark figures.

Appliance	Wattage rating	Typical energy usage
Kitchen range & oven	7500–12,500	
Range		0.8–1.2 kWh per hour
Oven		2–3 kWh per hour
Clothes dryer	4000–6000	3–5 kWh per load
Water heater	2200–5000	2000–5000 kWh per year
Dishwasher	1000–2000	0.6–1.0 kWh per load
Toaster oven	1200–1700	150–250 kWh per year
Hair dryer	1000–1800	30–60 kWh per year
Iron	1000–1400	35–70 kWh per year
Air conditioner (window unit)	600–1800	500–1500 kWh per year
Microwave oven	800–1500	100–150 kWh per year
Toaster	800–1400	25–50 kWh per year
Drip coffee maker	800–1200	100–300 kWh per year
Washing machine	500–1000	0.3–0.5 kWh per load
Refrigerator	200–700	1500–1800 kWh per year
Color television	150–350	0.08–0.12 kWh per hour
Overhead light	120–180	0.12–0.18 kWh per hour
Lamp	60–150	0.06–0.15 kWh per hour

Once you know the wattage, just divide this number by 1000 to convert it into kilowatts, then multiply by the number of hours of use. This gives you the number of kilowatt-hours of energy. Lastly, multiply this by what your power company charges you per kilowatt-hour. I pay about 12 cents per kilowatt-hour, but it varies from place to place. Some power companies charge different amounts per kilowatt-hour depending on the season, and some use a sliding scale where you pay different amounts depending on how much energy you consume in a given month.

You'll have to check your electric bill to see exactly what you're paying per kilowatt-hour. We'll use 12 cents per kilowatt-hour in the following examples.

Example 1. What does it cost to keep the lights on in your living room for five hours (two 100-watt bulbs and one 150-watt bulb)?

Step 1) Determine the total wattage:

$2 \times 100 + 150 = 350$ watts

Step 2) Divide by 1000:

$350 \div 1000 = 0.35$ kilowatts

Step 3) Multiply by the number of hours of use:

$0.35 \times 5 = 1.75$ kilowatt-hours

Step 4) Multiply by the cost per kilowatt-hour:

$1.75 \times 12¢ = 21¢$

Unfortunately, it's not always this simple. Some appliances are rated in terms of *amps* or *horsepower* instead of watts. In that case, you first have to determine the wattage with one of the following formulas and then continue as above. For the *volts* in the formulas, use 120 for your standard household outlet, 240 for heavy-duty outlets often used for clothes dryers, central air conditioners, electric ranges, and water heaters,[1] and a smaller number if the device uses a power adapter to reduce the voltage.

$$watts = volts \times amps$$
$$watts = 746 \times horsepower$$

Use the first formula if you know the volts and the amps; use the second if you know the horsepower.

Example 2. What does it cost to run my laptop for three hours? The laptop I'm typing this book on uses an adapter that reduces the wall socket voltage to 15 volts. The adapter gives the current—1.9 amps.

Step 1) Use the first formula from above to determine the total wattage since we know the volts and the amps:

$$watts = volts \times amps$$
$$= 15 \times 1.9$$
$$= 28.5$$

Step 2) Divide by 1000:
$$28.5 \div 1000 = 0.0285 \text{ kilowatts}$$

Step 3) Multiply by the number of hours of use:
$$0.0283 \times 3 \approx 0.085 \text{ kilowatt-hours}$$

Step 4) Multiply by the cost per kilowatt-hour:
$$0.085 \times 12¢ = 1.02¢ \text{ (that's 1.02 cents, not \$1.02)}$$

About a penny. What a deal!

Here's yet another complication. For many appliances, the

---

[1] Occasionally, wall outlets will have a voltage other than 120 or 240 (for example, 208 volts). If you really want to be sure what you're using, check with your electrician or building superintendent.

number of watts they use is different from their wattage rating. For example, the above chart gives a range of 7500 to 12,500 watts for the rating of an electric range and oven, but the typical energy usage is only 0.8 to 1.2 kilowatt-hour per hour for the range and 2 to 3 kilowatt-hours per hour for the oven—much less than the 7.5 kilowatt-hours per hour to 12.5 kilowatt-hours per hour that you'd expect from the rating. This is because the rating is based on the maximum current the range and oven would be drawing if all the burners and the oven were on high simultaneously—which is rarely the case. There's a different problem with a refrigerator. Even though it's plugged in all the time, it's not always on. Its thermostat determines when it needs to lower the temperature to the proper level. After it's cooled to a certain temperature, it turns off for a while. A refrigerator draws electricity only a quarter or a third of the time. It's not easy to accurately determine the energy usage for such appliances, but for a rough estimate, you can use the amounts listed in the third column in the above table.

The Cost of Natural Gas

Natural gas is measured in therms. A therm is roughly 100 cubic feet of gas, though this can vary slightly. A therm also converts to 100,000 Btus; a Btu (British thermal unit) is the amount of energy needed to raise the temperature of one pound of water one degree Fahrenheit. The following example will give you a feel for these different units. Let's say you take about three quarts of 50°F tap water and bring it to a boil (212°F) on your gas range. That's about six pounds of water, and you're raising its temperature about 160°F. Six times 160 is about 1000, so boiling that amount of water takes about 1000 Btus of energy. Since there are 100,000 Btus in a therm, 1000 Btus is about $\frac{1}{100}$th of a therm of gas. And since there are about 100 cubic feet of gas in a therm, $\frac{1}{100}$th of a therm is about 1 cubic foot. So the burner on your range uses about 1 cubic foot of gas to boil the three quarts of water (actually it could be up to about twice this much because some of the energy from your range is wasted in heating up the air in your kitchen rather than the water in the pot).

Like with the cost of electricity, the cost of natural gas will vary depending on where you live. Chicagoans, for example, have recently paid anywhere from $0.40 to $1.50 per therm. And if your gas company uses a sliding scale, you'll pay different amounts per therm depending on how much gas you use. Check your gas bill if you want to see exactly what you pay. For the following examples, we'll use $1.00 per therm for the cost. By the way, a therm of natural gas converts to about 30 kilowatt-hours of electricity. Since a kilowatt-hour costs about 10 cents, that's about $3.00 for 30 kilowatt-hours. So you get about three times as much energy for your dollar with natural gas as compared to electricity.

The following table lists the approximate amount of natural gas used by various appliances. These are rough estimates:

Appliance	Typical Usage
Gas clothes dryer	0.2 therms per load
Gas oven (at 350°F)	1.3 therms per hour
Gas range (one burner on high)	0.1 therms per hour
Pilot light for oven/range	15 therms per year
Gas fireplace	70 therms per year
Outdoor gas grill	30 therms per year

You can also determine the cost of running a gas appliance by reading your gas meter. Check the reading on the meter, then run the appliance, say, your clothes dryer, for 30 minutes, and then read the meter again. Subtract the first reading from the second to determine the number of cubic feet of gas used. Divide this by 100 to convert it to therms, and then multiply by your cost per therm.

As you may have realized, this method works only if nothing else in your house is drawing natural gas during the same time period.

The Cost of Water

Like with the cost of electricity and natural gas, the cost of water varies from place to place. In Chicago, where I live, it costs about a dollar per 1000 gallons, which comes to about a tenth of a cent per gallon. Here are some estimates of the amount of water used by various devices or activities. To determine your cost, just multiply the amount of water used by what you pay per gallon.

Device or activity	Water usage	
Washing machine (top loader)	40–60	gallons per load
Dishwasher	7.5–15	gallons per load
Lawn sprinkler	10–20	gallons per minute
Shower	2–8	gallons per minute
Bath	25–60	gallons
Toilet	1.5–7	gallons per flush

If you keep your faucet running while washing dishes or for shaving or brushing your teeth, here's an easy way to determine your water usage. Just turn on the water like you would for the activity, and time how long it takes to fill up something like a gallon milk container. You can then figure the number of gallons used per minute.

You can also use the method discussed above in the natural gas section to determine water cost. Just read your water meter before and after, say, watering your lawn. Subtract the first reading from the second to determine the amount of water used—your water meter may read in gallons or per cubic feet—and then multiply this by the price you pay per gallon or cubic foot. Obviously, make sure that no other water was being used during the same period of time.

CHAPTER 18

Tips for Helping Your Kids with Math

For this chapter, you may want to review topics in the following chapters from part I:
- Fractions, Decimals, and Percents (chapter 2)
- Powers and Roots (chapter 4)

Most of the following tips are from my book *The 10 Habits of Highly Successful Math Students*. These habits or strategies bring math down to earth and promote *understanding* as opposed to rote learning. The first six tips below are for children of all ages. The last three are for students taking algebra or other courses that use algebra—basically most courses from eighth through twelfth grades. All nine tips are easy to learn and easy to teach to your children regardless of your own level of proficiency with math.

Six Tips for Kids of All Ages

1. Make math concrete. Whenever possible, show your children connections between the math concepts they learn in school and the concrete reality of the world around them. Students get a better handle on positive and negative numbers, for example, when they are shown that they're just like temperatures above and below zero on a thermometer. Or you can use ideas about money: assets to represent positive numbers and debt to represent negatives. It's easy to see, for example, that the sum of two negatives must be a bigger negative when you consider that two debts obviously add up to a bigger debt. Using money also helps students with mental arithmetic. For instance, many students who would find it difficult or impossible to multiply 125 by 5 in their head, will have no difficulty once they're shown to do $1.25 times 5 instead: it's just 5 singles plus 5 quarters, which comes to $5.00 plus $1.25, or $6.25—so 125 times 5 is 625. When you're in the grocery store, teach your children about the price per pound or price per ounce of the items you buy. Floor tiles are often one foot by one foot. When they are, the area of a room in square feet is the same as the number of tiles. Show your children this simple relationship. Your children will understand math better and enjoy it more if they're shown that math describes the real world and is not something found only in the classroom.

2. Estimate. Children of all ages should be encouraged to estimate. Estimating flexes their math muscles and helps them develop independence of thought. When children estimate, they are forced to exercise their own independent judgments about the magnitude of things and about what is and is not a reasonable answer to a problem. Estimating thus helps to show students that mathematics is not merely about memorizing foreign, abstract rules and formulas laid down by their teachers. Rather, it is a subject that they can comprehend with their native common sense.

Ask your children to estimate the number of gallons in your aquarium or your local swimming pool, the speed of a bird that flies by, the number of blades of grass in your front yard, or the height of a tree. Answering questions like this will give your children examples of real-world applications of concepts like area and volume, and will give them practice with mental computation and imaginative problem solving.

3. Learn why things are true. Encourage your children to try to understand *why* math concepts work or *why* they are true, rather than just learning the concepts by rote memorization. Here's a simple example. Every student learns the following formulas for the circumference and the area of a circle (circumference is the distance around a circle):

$$C = \pi \times d$$
$$A = \pi \times r^2$$

(*d* is for *diameter,* the distance across the widest part of a circle, that is, through its center; *r* is for *radius,* the distance from the center of a circle to the outside, which equals half of the diameter; and π equals about 3.14.)

Many, perhaps most, students just memorize these formulas like they would memorize words in a foreign language. They don't think about why they work, they just take them on faith. They look upon them as just two more things their teacher wants them to know for a test. When children take this approach to mathematics, the subject remains distant from them—foreign. And when students try to learn math through rote memorization, formulas like the ones above—since students fail to see their *meaning*—are easily forgotten or mixed up.

Let's consider the simple meaning of the circumference formula, $C = \pi \times d$. The Greek letter pi (π) is used for the number that equals about 3.14, which is just a tad more than three. So all this formula says is that the distance around a circle, the *circumference,* is about three times as long as the distance across the circle, the *diameter.* Imagine taking three strings each as long as a circle's diameter and laying them around the outside of the circle. Like this:

This diagram shows the simple meaning of the formula $C = \pi \times d$. Yet for some reason, many students do not make the connection between the formula and its meaning. Students who do see this simple connection will more likely remember the formula and not mix it up with the *area* formula. Encourage your children to learn the logic that underlies mathematical ideas rather than just learning the ideas by rote.

 4. Test your answers. While the study of mathematics is not only about getting correct answers, that obviously is a major objective. Students who want to ensure that their answers are correct should make a habit of testing them. There are several ways to do this; here are a few examples.

To test the answer to the following long-*division* problem,

$$
\begin{array}{r}
23 \\
7\overline{)165} \\
14 \\
\hline
25 \\
21 \\
\hline
4
\end{array}
$$

a student would *multiply* 7 by 23, that's 161, and then add the remainder, 4. Since this total is 165, the answer checks. Similarly, a *subtraction* problem can be tested by *addition*. As you can see, this method of testing an answer involves reversing the solution process to arrive back at the original number.

Another testing method is used to test the answers to problems like the following simple algebra problem:

$$3x + 7 = 19$$

Step 1) Subtract 7 from both sides of the equation:

$$3x + 7 = 19$$
$$\underline{-7 \quad -7}$$
$$3x \quad = 12$$

Step 2) Divide both sides by 3:

$$\frac{3x}{3} = \frac{12}{3}$$

$$x = 4$$

A student would test this answer by plugging the number 4 into the original equation:

$$3x + 7 = 19$$

$$3 \times 4 + 7 = 19\,?$$
$$12 + 7 = 19\,?$$
$$19 = 19$$

The answer checks.

The key to these and other methods of testing answers is that they all involve doing something different from what was done to solve the problem. When the two different processes agree with each other, it's extremely unlikely that the answer is incorrect. This is very different from what often happens when students merely check their work—in other words, when they go over the steps of their solution a second time. While certainly better than nothing, this technique often fails to catch errors, because if a student makes a mistake during the original solution of a problem, he or she will often repeat the mistake when checking the solution.

5. Ask, "Does my answer make sense?" "Does my answer make sense?" is a powerful question. I can't think of anything else that's as simple and as effective in helping your children be more successful in math and science as instilling in them the habit of asking this important question. When a student finishes a problem, he or she should ask whether the answer is reasonable or not. Now, this question isn't always useful, because the solutions to certain types of problems are too complicated or too abstract to be either reasonable or unreasonable. But if a student calculates, say, the number of gallons of water in an aquarium, he or she should reflect on whether the answer is within the ballpark of what is reasonable. Depending on the size of the aquarium, a reasonable answer could be anything from 5 to 30 gallons. An answer of 10,000 gallons would, of course, be ridiculous. You might think that every student would automatically notice that an answer of 10,000 gallons is ridiculous. But, in fact, many students would get such an answer and then blithely go on to the next problem, oblivious to what 10,000 gallons means. It is critical that students learn to pause before going on and, at a minimum, very quickly decide whether the answer is sensible or not. This takes extra effort, and perhaps this is one reason why so many students fail to do it. Make sure your children don't fall into this category. When they tell you that they're done with their homework, remind them that they're not really done unless they have decided that their answers are reasonable. In addition to helping students discover their errors, this strategy has the extra benefit of forcing students to stop operating on autopilot and, instead, to *think*.

6. Do something. It is truly remarkable how often the simple, pedestrian suggestion to *do something . . . anything* will help a student who doesn't know how to proceed on a math problem. If your son or daughter comes to you and says they don't know how to do one of their math problems, try this tip before you actually work through the problem with them. Just tell them to *do something*. When they respond that they have no idea where to begin, say that it doesn't matter, that all they have to do is to put something—any-thing—on paper. They might write down a formula or equation that they think might be relevant, or they could draw a diagram or simply write down some given information about the problem—anything. Insist that they put something down on the paper even if they don't think it's going to help them. You'll be surprised at how often your son or daughter will come back, after following your suggestion, and tell you that they now know what to do. When a student sees some-thing on paper, as opposed to a blank sheet, it somehow triggers a thought process that often leads to the complete solution. When this tip succeeds, not only have you helped your son or daughter solve one more math problem, you've shown them that they didn't really need your help after all, and that will boost their confidence and resource-fulness.

Three Tips for Algebra Students

1. Use numbers to understand variables. This is a powerful tip for helping your kids with algebra, and it's easy to use regardless of how much, if any, algebra you remember. When your son or daughter comes to you with a question like, "does $\sqrt{x^2+y^2} = x+y$?" or "can I cancel the 2s in $\frac{2ab}{2c}$?" or "can I cancel the 2s in $\frac{2a+b}{2c}$?" all you have to say is, "Does it work with num-bers?" If it doesn't work with numbers, it definitely won't work with variables, and if it works with numbers, it will almost certainly work with variables. For some reason, many students fail to understand this basic fact. It follows from one of the most fundamental principles in algebra, namely that

Numbers and variables always behave in the same way.

Variables are really just blank spaces where numbers can be filled in. What's true for variables is true for numbers and vice versa. Let's answer the three questions from above.[1]

Does $\sqrt{x^2 + y^2} = x + y$?

Plug in 3 for x and 4 for y:

$$\sqrt{3^2 + 4^2} = 3 + 4\ ?$$
$$\sqrt{9 + 16} = 7\ ?$$
$$\sqrt{25} = 7\ ?$$
$$5 = 7\ ?$$

No, 5 does not equal 7, and therefore $\sqrt{x^2 + y^2}$ does not equal $x + y$. Here's the next one:

Can I cancel the 2s in $\dfrac{2ab}{2c}$? In other words,

does $\dfrac{2ab}{2c} = \dfrac{ab}{c}$?

Plug in 3 for a, 4 for b, and 5 for c:

---

[1] When using this strategy, students should use small, round numbers that are easy to work with, but they should not use zero, 1, or 2, or numbers that have a lot in common with each other or with other numbers already in the problem.

$$\frac{2 \times 3 \times 4}{2 \times 5} = \frac{3 \times 4}{5}?$$

$$\frac{24}{10} = \frac{12}{5}?$$

$$2.4 = 2.4?$$

Yes, and thus the 2s can be canceled in $\frac{2ab}{2c}$. And here's the last question:

Can I cancel the 2s in $\frac{2a + b}{2c}$? In other words,

does $\frac{2a + b}{2c} = \frac{a + b}{c}?$

Plug in 3 for a, 4 for b, and 5 for c.

$$\frac{2 \times 3 + 4}{2 \times 5} = \frac{3 + 4}{5}?$$

$$\frac{10}{10} = \frac{7}{5}?$$

$$1 = 1.4?$$

No, and therefore you can't cancel the 2s in $\frac{2a + b}{2c}$.

There are other types of algebra problems where students can use a variation of this strategy. Students sometimes won't know what to do with the variables in a problem, for example, when they're asked to do something like add the fractions $\frac{1}{x} + \frac{1}{y}$. But since *numbers and variables always behave in the same way,* you can simply suggest to them that they (1) temporarily replace the variables in the problem with numbers, (2) do the problem with the numbers, observing what steps they perform and exactly what they do with the numbers, and then (3) go back and do the original problem the same way. This tip is effective because all students understand how to deal with concrete numbers better than with abstract variables.

2. Consider a simpler version of the problem. The study of mathematics is cumulative. New topics build incrementally on concepts studied earlier in the curriculum. Students need to be reminded of this; they need to be reminded that the new, complex problems they're currently studying follow the same rules that they've already mastered. Consider the following problem:

$$\text{Multiply: } x^a \cdot x^{a+b}$$

Many students will miss this problem despite the fact that they know everything they need to know to answer it correctly. The only reason they miss it is *math overload:* they blow their math fuse and shut down. They're used to seeing numbers as powers, 3^2 or x^4, for instance, but the variables a and b in the above powers look strange and foreign. This strangeness is frustrating and taxing, and that causes students to lose sight of the simple concepts that are the key to this more advanced problem. If your son or daughter comes to you with a problem like this, suggest to them that they consider a simpler version of the problem. A simple version of the above problem would be:

$$\text{Multiply: } x^2 \cdot x^3$$

When a student considers this simpler problem, she is reminded of the rule she has already mastered, namely, that when multiplying, you add the powers. Thus, the answer is:

$$x^2 \cdot x^3 = x^5$$

Algebra rules like this work the same in advanced problems as they do in basic problems. So all the student has to do in the original problem is add the powers. Every algebra student knows that $a + (a + b) = 2a + b$, and thus:

$$x^a \cdot x^{a+b} = x^{2a+b}$$

You might think that if a student knows the above rule about adding powers and also knows how to add a plus $a + b$, that he or she would never get stuck on a problem like $x^a \cdot x^{a+b}$. But, in fact, this happens all the time. It's "math overload" at work. When this happens to your son or daughter, just tell them (1) that the problem is almost certainly easier than it looks at first, (2) to consider a simpler version of the problem, (3) to do that simpler problem, observing what rules are used, and (4) to then go back and do the original problem the same way.

3. Call in the stunt double. I love this tip and I love the metaphor of the stunt double.[2] Here's how it works. Say your son or daughter is stumped with the following problem:

$$3\sqrt{6} + 4\sqrt{6} = ?$$

Is the answer $7\sqrt{6}$ or $7\sqrt{12}$ or what? Your son or daughter is stuck, so it's time to call in the stunt double: x. The star of the movie, $\sqrt{6}$, takes a break while the stunt double, x, takes his place. So now we have:

$$3x + 4x = ?$$

---

[2] I wish I could take credit for the metaphor, but it was Brian Ficho or Steve Tazalla, former students of mine, who saw that this technique worked just like a stunt double.

Now do the stunt—in other words, do the addition. Every student knows that $3x + 4x = 7x$. And now that the stunt is over, the stunt double sits down and the star comes back on the set, giving us the answer—$7\sqrt{6}$. Here it is again step-by-step.

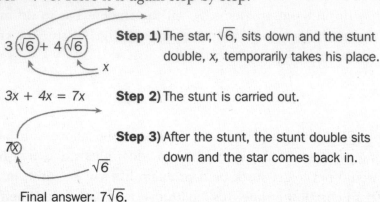

$3\sqrt{6} + 4\sqrt{6}$

Step 1) The star, $\sqrt{6}$, sits down and the stunt double, x, temporarily takes his place.

$3x + 4x = 7x$

Step 2) The stunt is carried out.

$7x$

Step 3) After the stunt, the stunt double sits down and the star comes back in.

$\sqrt{6}$

Final answer: $7\sqrt{6}$.

While this trick will often produce the final solution to a problem, it's also possible that after completing the stunt, more work will need to be done. But this method will always correctly solve at least part of the problem, and it can never produce an error. The fact that it works this way has a lot to do with the very nature of algebra, and using this technique will not only help your son or daughter solve problems, it will help them to learn to think algebraically. So when your son or daughter is stuck on a problem, you can say to them, "What is it in the problem that seems new or strange to you or that makes it difficult for you or that causes the problem to look complicated? Now, just replace each instance of that strange thing with a single x, do this new problem, and then when you're done, make the switch back to the original thing." This technique has no end of applications throughout junior high and high school mathematics.

PART IV

Out and About

CHAPTER 19

Shopping and Tipping

For this chapter, you may want to review topics in the following chapters from part I:
• Decimals and Percents (chapter 2)

How to Figure a Tip

Would you like to be able to figure the tip quickly when you're eating out? There are several methods for doing this. I'll give you two methods to choose from: a fast, shortcut method, and a slightly more difficult but more accurate method. In the examples that follow, I'm assuming that you're satisfied with the food and service. If you're not, or if you're *very* satisfied, you can, of course, adjust the tip accordingly.

SHORTCUT METHOD

For tabs of $30 or more. This method is easy to do and easy to remember. The starting point is the pre-sales-tax dollar amount of the tab—ignore the cents. Let's go through it with an example. Say your pre-sales-tax total for lunch for four is $46.27. What's the tip?

Step 1) Take the dollar amount (46) and drop the ones digit—that leaves 4.
Step 2) Double this number—8. That's the tip: $8—or $2 for each of you.

Here's another one. If your dinner for two comes to $62.74 before tax, drop the 2 in 62 and double—a $12 tip. What could be simpler?

Now, granted, this method isn't precise. In the first example, $8 is a 17.3% tip; in the second example, $12 is a 19.1% tip. But what the method lacks in accuracy it makes up in ease and speed. And who cares about a little imprecision anyway, especially when you're out having fun? An exact 15% tip in the first example is $6.94. Say you round this up to $7. That comes to $1.75 per person, so you'd save a quarter. Is it worth the trouble? If you split the lunch tab, the higher tip would result in each of you paying a total of about $14.25 (after adding in a 6% sales tax). With the lower tip, you'd each pay about $14. Big deal. And consider the waiter's point of view. The relatively insignificant increase from $14 to $14.25 causes the waiter's tip to go up from $7 to $8, which to him or her *is* significant. In the second example, an exact 15% tip is $9.41. If you round this up to $10, the total cost of the dinner (again, after sales tax) would come to about $76.50; with the $12 tip, $78.50. This time, if you pay $78.50 instead of $76.50 (a mere 2½% increase), your waiter's tip goes up from $10 to $12 (a 20% increase!). What's relatively painless to you makes your waiter very happy.

 For tabs less than $30. The shortcut method for small tabs is different. The starting point is again the pre-sales-tax dollar amount without the cents. Round this number up to the nearest $5, double that, then drop a zero and that's the tip. For example, let's figure the tip for a $17.20 tab.

Step 1) Round 17 up to 20.
Step 2) Double 20—that's 40.
Step 3) Drop a zero—the tip's $4.

For both big and small tabs, the shortcut method is fast, easy, and fairly accurate. For tabs over $30, it will always produce a tip between

15 and 20 percent. For small tabs, it will sometimes produce a tip with a high percentage (a 27 percent $3 tip for an $11 tab, for instance), but at these small amounts, the high-percent tip will never cost you more than an extra dollar or dollar and a half. And remember, when this method does produce a high percent tip, it'll make your waiter's day. If you'd like to be a bit less generous for these tabs under $30, just leave a 20% tip. This is also very easy to compute. For example, for the above tab of $17.20, you'd do the following:

Step 1) Round $17.20 up to the next dollar—that's 18.
Step 2) Double 18—that's 36.
Step 3) Move the decimal one place to the left—that's 3.6. The tip is thus $3.60.

If you'd like to be really accurate, just use the accurate method, which we'll go through now.

Accurate Method

This method is a bit more difficult than the shortcut method, but it's really not that bad. Just take the total before the tax, round up to the next *even* dollar amount, then add half of this number to itself and move the decimal one place to the left—that's the tip. For example, what's the tip for a pre-tax tab of $27.45?

Step 1) Round up to $28.
Step 2) Take half of that—$14.
Step 3) Add these two numbers—that comes to $42.
Step 4) Move the decimal one place to the left—the tip is $4.20.

If the pre-tax total is $42.14, round up to the next even dollar amount ($44), then add half of 44 to itself (22 plus 44 is 66), so the tip is $6.60.

TIP AMOUNTS FOR VARIOUS SERVICES

Service	Tip percent or amount
Airport porter	About $1 per bag plus a dollar
Apartment building doorman	Annual tip: $10–$35, depending on service
Apartment building superintendent	Annual tip: $50–$100
Barber, beauty parlor	15%–20%, not less than $1
Bartender or sommelier (wine steward)	15%–20%
Bellman	$1 per bag, not less than $2
Cabdriver	15%–20%, not less than $0.50
Car wash	$1
Cloakroom	$1 per coat; $2 for parcels, umbrellas, briefcases
Facial, waxing, or makeup	15%
Hotel concierge	$5–$10 for special services like getting theater tickets
Hotel doorman	$1–$2 for handling luggage; $1–$3 for hailing a cab, $3 in the rain
Hotel maid	$1–$2 per night
Limo driver	15%–20%
Manicure	$2 for simple manicure; or 15%
Newspaper boy or girl	Annual tip: $5–$15
Pizza delivery	10%, not less than $1
Room service	15%, not less than $2
Ship porter	$1 per bag
Ship steward	$20–$25 per week
Shoeshine	$1
Train porter	About $1 per bag plus a dollar
Valet parking	$1 in small cities; $2 in big ones
Waitress/waiter	15%–20%

Source: Peggy Post, *Emily Post's Etiquette,* 16th ed. (1997), pp. 532–545.

This method will usually produce a tip of between 15 and 16 percent. For very small tabs, the percent will sometimes be higher, but the tip amount for both small and large tabs will never be more than 30 cents above the precise 15 percent amount. If you want to be even more accurate, round up to the next whole dollar amount rather than the next even number. Round an $8.20 tab, for example, up to $9, then add half of $9 to itself: $4.50 plus $9 is $13.50, so the tip is $1.35. This way, your tip will never be more than 15 cents more than exactly 15 percent.

Estimating Discount and Markups

Discounts. When you're shopping and you see an item marked 10% or 20% off, you might like to be able to quickly figure the sale price. Here's what you do.

Step 1) Round off the price of the item to the nearest $5 or $10—this makes all the calculations easier. For example, round $128.95 to $130.00.

Step 2) Figure 10% of the price by moving the decimal one place to the left. In our example, move the decimal in $130.00 one place to the left: 130.00. Thus, 10% of $130.00 is $13.00. If it's a 10% off sale, skip step 3 and go to step 4.

Step 3) *I. Discounts of 20%, 30%, 40%, etc.* Multiply the 10% amount from step 2 by 2, 3, 4, etc., to obtain 20%, 30%, 40%, etc. For example, in step 2, we determined that 10% of $130.00 is $13.00. So 30% of $130.00 would be 3 times $13.00, which equals $39.00

II. Discounts of 15%, 25%, 35%, etc. Figure 5% of the price by cutting the 10% amount in half. In our example, cut $13.00 in half—that's $6.50. Then add this amount to the appropriate percentage from step 3, part I. For a 35% sale, for instance, add the

5% amount ($6.50) to the 30% amount ($39.00). That comes to $45.50.

Step 4) Subtract the sale amount from the original price, but this time round the original price to the nearest dollar instead of the nearest $5 or $10. So the $128.95 item at 35% off would sell for about $129.00 minus $45.50—that's about $83.50. The $128.95 item at 10% off would sell for $129.00 minus $13.00, or about $116.00.

Note: If the discount amount is 25%, you can use the above method or do the following: cut the price in half, cut that amount in half, then subtract. For example, if the $128.95 item was marked down 25%, take $130.00, cut it in half, that's $65.00, then in half again, that's $32.50, and then subtract: $129.00 minus $32.50 gives you the approximate sale price of $96.50.

Markups. Computing a markup is the same as figuring a discount except that in the last step you *add* rather than *subtract*. For example, if a retailer buys an item from a wholesaler for $130.00, then marks it up 35% before selling it to you, the 35% computation would be the same as in the above discount example: 35% of $130.00 is $45.50. This amount is then added to $130.00. The retail price would thus be $175.50.

Rounding Off Numbers

When you round off numbers, there's a tradeoff between ease of computation and accuracy. Since an approximate answer is better than no answer, feel free to round off—your answer will probably be good enough. But the less you round off the more accurate your answer will be, so round off only as much as you need to make the computation easy. And when rounding off two numbers in a problem, round one up and the other down, if possible.

Computing the Sales Tax Amount

Exact method. This is a straightforward percent problem. If the sales tax rate is 6%, just use your calculator, or pen and paper, and multiply the price by 0.06. For example, for a $179 item, multiply $179 by 0.06. The tax is $10.74.

Shortcut method. You can estimate the sales tax quite easily in your head.

Step 1) Round off the price to the nearest $10, then drop a zero. Thus, you would round $179 to $180, then drop a zero—$18.

Step 2) Multiply this amount by the percent. For 6%, multiply 18 by 6. You should be able to do this in your head. Just do 10 times 6, which is 60, and 8 times 6, which is 48. Then 60 plus 48 is 108.

Step 3) Take this number and move the decimal one place to the left. So 108 becomes 10.8. Thus the tax is about $10.80.

Computing the Sales Tax Percent

If you don't know what the local sales tax rate is, there are two simple ways to compute it.

Method I

Step 1) Divide the tax amount by the pre-tax subtotal. For example, say the receipt reads as follows:

> Subtotal: $149.98
> Tax: $ 10.13
> Total: $160.11

Divide 10.13 by 149.98. That's about 0.0675.

Step 2) Move the decimal two places to the right: 0.0675; the tax rate is thus 6.75%, or 6¾%.

METHOD II

Step 1) Divide the total by the pre-tax subtotal. For the above receipt, you'd divide 160.11 by 149.98. That's about 1.0675.

Step 2) Drop the 1 in 1.0675 and move the decimal two places to the right as above: 0.0675. The tax rate, again, is 6.75%, or 6¾%.

CHAPTER 20

Gambling and Games

For this chapter, you may want to review topics in the following chapters from part I:
- Fractions, Decimals, and Percents (chapter 2)
- Probability and Odds (chapter 7)

Luck or Skill?

Some games are pure luck, some are pure skill, and others are a combination of the two. There is no element of chance, for instance, in chess or checkers. Granted, a chess player might be said to be lucky if his or her opponent happens to have a migraine and can't think straight, but that type of luck is external to the game—it has nothing to do with chess itself. Chess and checkers are games of pure skill because they don't involve things like dice or cards that give games an element of randomness.

Most casino games, on the other hand, involve no skill—nada, zilch. These include craps, roulette, keno, and slot machines. State lotteries are also pure luck. There are no winning strategies for these games. Both the casino and the state have built-in advantages in these games, so when you play them, it's like playing against someone with loaded dice. You might win if you get lucky, but it's more likely that you'll lose, and the longer you play, the more likely it is that you'll wind up in the hole.

Many games, including some of the most popular parlor games, involve luck *and* skill. These include most card and dice games, like bridge, hearts, poker, gin rummy, cribbage, and backgammon. One thing that makes these games so entertaining is that while the element of skill makes them a test of wits in which the better player has the edge, the element of luck allows for dramatic reversals of fortune that can give the weaker player many opportunities to win. In such games, the longer you play, the more likely it becomes that the better player will amass the majority of victories.

Casino Games

Perhaps I should make a slight qualification to my above statement that craps, roulette, keno, and slot machines are games of pure luck. They are pure luck in the sense that you can't make a clever move or a brilliant play in any of these games like you can in chess or bridge. And no matter how you play, you can't overcome the house advantage. However, the size of the house advantage differs from game to game and from bet to bet. If you stick to bets with a small house advantage—that is, with a high return—you'll tend to lose less, in the long run, than someone who ignores the size of the house edge. If this constitutes "skill," then I guess you could say that there's some skill in these games. But whatever you call it, the important thing to remember is that there's nothing you can do to outsmart the house, but that you can minimize your losses and increase your odds of winning by making the right bets.

The right bets are the ones with a high return, or, in other words, a low casino advantage. Learn these bets before you go gambling. The size of the house advantage can vary from about 1 percent to 40 percent. If the house edge is 1 percent—that's a return of 99 percent—you should expect to lose, in the long run, about 1 percent of what you bet; if the house edge is 40 percent—a return of 60 percent—you should expect to lose about 40 percent of what you bet. These ideas were discussed in chapter 7, "Probability and Odds." You might want to reread that section before proceeding.

Unlike the above-mentioned games, blackjack does involve some strategy, which will be discussed below. Poker involves a great deal of skill, and talented poker players can win a great deal at casinos. But if you're someone who plays in high-stakes casino poker games, you're probably not reading this book.

SLOT MACHINES

You win!!

Pull the lever or push the button and cross your fingers. That's about all there is to playing the "slots." The house advantage for most slot machines varies from about 2 to 17 percent. All you can do to minimize your losses and maximize your expected return is to pick a "loose" machine (small house edge, high return) rather than a "tight" one (big house edge, low return). Some machines list their return. Pick one with a return of at least 90%.

ROULETTE

As you probably know, American roulette is the game with the beautiful table and spinning wheel. The wheel is spun and the ball whirls around until it falls into one of the 38 slots numbered 1 through 36 plus 0 and 00.[1] Bets are made by placing chips on a table laid out like this:

---

[1] European roulette has a 0 but no 00. This reduces the house advantage.

		0	00	
1-18	1st twelve	1	2	3
		4	5	6
EVEN		7	8	9
		10	11	12
RED	2nd twelve	13	14	15
		16	17	18
BLACK		19	20	21
		22	23	24
ODD	3rd twelve	25	26	27
		28	29	30
19-36		31	32	33
		34	35	36
		2-1	2-1	2-1

The following chart lists each bet that can be made, with its true odds, payoff odds, return, and house advantage. Let's say you bet on 19, 20, 22, and 23 by placing your chip as in the above diagram. The table gives your odds of winning—34-to-4 (against)—and the payoff odds—8-to-1. This means that, in the long run, you'd expect to win 4 times and lose 34 times for every 38 times you placed such a bet. If you bet $1 each time, that would cost you $38. For each of your four wins, you'd get your $1 bet back plus another $8. That comes to 4 times 9 or $36. This nets to a loss of $2 for your betting "investment" of $38. Dividing 36 by 38 gives us the return, about 94.7 percent. Dividing 2 by 38 gives us the house advantage, about 5.3 percent. (Note that the return plus the house advantage always add up to 100 percent, and, thus, that you can subtract either one from 100 percent to get the other.)

Bet	True Odds	Payoff Odds	Return	House Advantage
Red or black	20-to-18	1-to-1	~94.7%	~5.3%
Even or odd	20-to-18	1-to-1	~94.7%	~5.3%
1–18 or 19–36	20-to-18	1-to-1	~94.7%	~5.3%
1–12, 13–24, or 25–36	26–12	2-to-1	~94.7%	~5.3%
Any column	26-to-12	2-to-1	~94.7%	~5.3%
Two adjacont rows	32-to-6	5-to-1	~94.7%	~5.3%
0, 00, 1, 2, and 3	33-to-5	6-to-1	**~92.1%**	**~7.9%**
Any 4-number square	34-to-4	8-to-1	~94.7%	~5.3%
Any row	35-to-3	11-to-1	~94.7%	~5.3%
Two adjacent numbers	36-to-2	17-to-1	~94.7%	~5.3%
Any single number	37-to-1	35-to-1	~94.7%	~5.3%

As you can see from the above table, all roulette bets have the same return of about 95 percent, with one exception—never bet the five-number bet (0, 00, 1, 2, 3); it's the only bet with a lower return. As long as you don't make that bet, you should expect to lose about 5 percent of the amount you bet—or about $5 for each $100 you bet. If you play for an hour and make 20 $10 bets, for example, that's a total of $200 in bets. You should "expect" to lose about 5 percent of that, or $10. That's "expect" in the mathematical sense—which means that if you did the above for a hundred nights, you would probably lose, on average, about $10 per night. On any given night, however, there's no telling how well or poorly you'd do—though it's more likely that you'll lose than win.

KENO

Keno is another game of pure chance. It's a simple game of matching numbers on your card with the numbers drawn at random by the casino. It's a lot like playing the lottery. The cards contain the numbers 1 through 80, and, depending on which version you're playing, you pick anywhere from one to fifteen numbers. Then twenty numbers are drawn at random, and you win if your numbers match the house numbers. The more matches, the more you win.

You'd be much better off spending your time at the roulette table, because the house advantage in keno is about *four!* times as much as roulette. For all fifteen types of keno cards—the 1-spot card through the 15-spot card—the house percentage is about 22 percent. If you placed twenty $10 keno bets over the course of an evening—for a total of $200 like in the roulette example above—you would expect to lose, on average, about 22 percent of that, or $44.

CRAPS

There is no such thing as a "good" craps player. Craps is a game of luck, not skill. If someone tells you he has a winning strategy for craps, don't believe him. And if you think you know how to win at craps, well, to be perfectly frank, you're deluding yourself. Of course, if you can find a sucker willing to make a bad side bet with you, you can win at this or any game, but this doesn't change the fact that craps itself is a game of chance played against the house, and regardless of how you bet, the odds are in the house's favor.

Let me back up a bit and give you the rules of the game. At the craps table (see diagram below), the roller, or "shooter," throws two dice. If he rolls 7 or 11 on the first roll, he wins. If his first roll is 2, 3, or 12, he loses (he "craps out"). Any other number on the first roll establishes his "point." The roller then keeps rolling until he either matches his point and wins ("passes") or throws a 7 and loses.

The following are some of the more common bets that can be made at various times during the shooter's turn:

- *Pass.* Betting that the shooter will win. This bet is made on the first roll.
- *Don't pass.* Betting that the shooter will lose. (If he loses by rolling a 12 on his first roll, it's a standoff and the bettor takes his bet back.) This bet is also made on the first roll.
- *Come.* This bet is identical to betting "pass," except that it's made anytime after the first roll. The roll immediately following the bet is treated like the first roll with a pass bet.
- *Don't come.* This is identical to "don't pass," except that it's made anytime after the first roll.
- *Field.* Betting that the next roll is a 2, 3, 4, 9, 10, 11, or 12. A roll of 2 or 12 pays double.
- *Big 6.* Betting that the next 6 comes up before the next 7.
- *Big 8.* Betting that the next 8 comes up before the next 7.
- *The hard way.* Rolling a number with doubles, say, rolling an 8 with double 4s is called rolling it the hard way or a 7 comes up. Rolling the number any other way is the easy way. Betting on 4, 6, 8, or 10 the hard way wins if the number comes up the hard way before it comes up the easy way.
- *Craps.* Betting that 2, 3, or 12 comes up on the next roll.
- *Numbers.* Betting that a specific number will come up on the next roll.
- *Place bets.* Betting that a specific number will come up before a 7 comes up.

Perhaps the only "skill" involved in craps is in learning the size of the house advantage for different types of bets (see table below). But all you need to remember is that if you want to lose as slowly as possible, and maximize your long-term return, you should always bet "pass," "don't pass," "come," or "don't come." (Actually, you might want to stay away from betting "don't pass" and "don't come," because craps players don't like it when someone bets against the shooter.) If you know this, you're as "good" at craps as you can be. And if you make only these bets, you'll do better, on a typical night, than others who make other types of bets. Yes, you'll probably do better, but you'll probably still lose. Here are the probability of winning, the payoff odds, the return, and the house advantage of the different bets that can be placed.

Bet	Probability of win	Payoff Odds	Return	House Advantage
Pass	~49.3%	1-to-1	~98.6%	~1.4%
Don't pass	~49.3%	1-to-1	~98.6%	~1.4%
Come	~49.3%	1-to-1	~98.6%	~1.4%
Don't come	~49.3%	1-to-1	~98.6%	~1.4%
Field	≈ 44.4%	1-to-1 on 3, 4, 9, 10, or 11 / 2-to-1 on 2 and 12	~94.4%	~5.6%
Big 6 or big 8	~45.5%	1-to-1	~90.9%	~9.1%
6 or 8 the hard way	~9.1%	9-to-1	~90.9%	~9.1%
4 or 10 the hard way	~11.1%	7-to-1	~88.9%	~11.1%
Craps	~11.1%	7-to-1	~88.9%	~11.1%
3 or 11	~5.6%	15-to-1	~88.9%	~11.1%
2 or 12	~2.8%	30-to-1	~86.1%	~13.9%
7	~16.7%	4-to-1	~83.3%	~16.7%

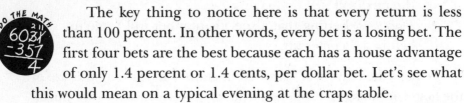 The key thing to notice here is that every return is less than 100 percent. In other words, every bet is a losing bet. The first four bets are the best because each has a house advantage of only 1.4 percent or 1.4 cents, per dollar bet. Let's see what this would mean on a typical evening at the craps table.

Craps is a fast-paced game. If you placed a bet on every roll, you might be able to place over 100 bets in an hour. Or you can watch a lot and bet as little as you want. But let's say you place only one bet for each turn with the dice. In other words, you place a bet, then don't place your next bet until the roller wins or craps out. At this rate, you might make about 30 bets in an hour. If you're playing with $5 chips, that's 30 times

$5, or $150 in bets placed per hour. If you make only the best bets described above, you should expect to lose 1.4 cents per dollar bet. So that's 1.4 cents times 150, or roughly $2 per hour. You might win, of course, if you have a lucky night. But, *on average*, you will lose about $2 an hour. If, instead, you make a lot of the other types of bets, which are *much* worse than the four best bets, you should expect to lose (again, with $5 chips) anywhere from about $7.50 to $25 per hour.

Do I sound like a killjoy? Well, I'm not telling you not to play craps (or other casino games). Craps is fun. Casinos are fun. If you lose a bit, who cares? You can look at it as the price of good entertainment. My point is simply that you should know the true odds before you decide to play. It may be exciting to follow your hunch that the next roll will be box cars (6, 6). And if you're right, the payoff is great—30-to-1. But just know that this is one of the worst bets you can make: your expected loss is about 14 cents per dollar bet—that comes to a loss of about $70, on average, for every hundred $5 bets you make.

BLACKJACK
(THIS DISCUSSION ASSUMES YOU KNOW HOW TO PLAY.)

Unlike the above four casino games, blackjack involves some skill and strategy—in other words, it's possible to play blackjack well or poorly. The same cannot be said about the other casino games discussed in this section. Unlike chess or backgammon or hearts, however, it's a limited type of skill where once you've memorized the strategies, the plays you make are automatic. If you memorize the following strategies, the house advantage can be reduced to something between half a percent and one percent, making blackjack the best deal (it's a pun!) at the casino.

Drawing and Standing
1) Draw with a hard hand of 11 or less.
2) Draw if you have a hard hand with a score between 12 and 16 and the dealer's up card is 7 or higher, including ace.
3) Draw if you have 12 and dealer has a 2 or a 3 up.
4) Draw if you have a soft hand of 17 or less.

5) Draw if you have a soft 18 and the dealer's up card is a 9, 10, or ace.

6) Stand if none of these conditions are met.

Doubling Down: Takes Precedence over Drawing

1) Double down if your total is 11.

2) Double down if your total is 10 and the dealer's up card is 9 or less.

3) Double down if your total is 9 and the dealer's up card is 3 through 6.

4) (a) Double down if your first two cards are a 6 or a 7 and the dealer shows 3, 4, 5, or 6 up.

(b) Double down if your first cards are a 4 or a 5 and the dealer shows 4, 5, or 6 up.

(c) Double down if your first two cards are a 2 or a 3 and the dealer shows 5 or 6 up.

Splitting Pairs: Splitting Pairs Takes Precedence over Drawing

1) Always split a pair of 8s or aces.

2) Don't split a pair of 4s, 5s, or 10s.

3) (a) If you have a pair of 2s or 3s, split if the dealer's up card is 4, 5, 6, or 7.

(b) If you have a pair of 6s, split if the dealer's up card is 3, 4, 5, or 6.

(c) If you have a pair of 7s, split if the dealer's up card is 2, 3, 4, 5, 6, or 7.

4) Split a pair of 9s if the dealer shows a 2 through 6, 8, or 9.

Insurance

Don't buy insurance unless more than a third of the deck is 10-value cards. Since the only way you can make this determination is by counting cards, never buy insurance, including "even money," if you're not counting cards.

You can do better than the above and actually obtain up to about a one percent *edge* over the house if you use a system called counting cards. Basically, this involves keeping track mentally of whether more high cards (10, jack, queen, king, and ace) or low cards (2, 3, 4, 5, and 6) have been dealt. If more low cards have been dealt, you bet a lot; if more high cards have been dealt, you bet a little.

Yes, you can actually beat the casino if you learn this system well. What's the catch? The catch is that if they *catch* you, they'll kick you out—and they're very good at catching card counters. It's not illegal to count cards, but do you really want to spend your holiday looking over your shoulder?

Strategies for Losing Least at the Casino

- Don't go.
- If you go, watch, don't play.
- If you play, make small bets, and the fewer bets you place, the better.
- Okay, all kidding aside now. Let's assume you want to enjoy a long evening at the casino and you want to gamble a lot. What can you do to minimize your losses? If you follow a few simple suggestions, you can gamble a great deal and leave with some money in your pocket—you might even come out ahead.
   1) First of all, establish a limit for your losses. Before you set foot in the casino, decide on the maximum amount you could lose without ruining your evening—an amount you could live with. You must make this an absolute rule and promise yourself that you'll stop as soon as you hit your number, *and not one dollar more.* Without such a system in place, what often happens is that your losses gradually build, and you keep saying to yourself, "What harm could there be in just one more $5 bet? I might recoup

some of my losses." Then, just one more bet, and just one more, and just one last one . . . then just one more . . . Before you know it, the night's over, you're *way* in the hole and *very* unhappy.

2) Make small bets. Okay, if you want to feel the thrill of a possible huge jackpot, make a couple of larger bets, but for the most part, stick to small bets for the whole evening. And remember two things. First, if you start to win a lot, *do not* raise your bet amount because you think you're hot. You've been lucky, not hot. When you're in the black, the best way to stay up and walk away a winner at the end of the evening is to *reduce* your bet amount. And second, if you start to lose a lot, *do not* raise your bet amount because you think your luck's bound to change and you can recoup your losses. In fact, the best thing to do if you're, say, halfway to your limit, is to reduce your bet amount. That's the best way, short of not betting, to ensure that you don't reach your limit and that you'll be able to continue gambling for the entire evening.

3) Learn the above blackjack system and spend a good amount of time at the blackjack table.

4) Play a lot of craps and make the following types of bets: "pass," "don't pass," "come," and "don't come."

5) Play some roulette; it doesn't matter what types of bets you make, with one exception: never make the five-number bet (0, 00, 1, 2, 3).

6) Don't play the slot machines unless you know the house percentage is 10% or less, or play a few times just to try it out.

7) Don't play keno.

8) Stick to this system. Let your friends follow their hunches. At the end of the evening, you can enjoy a little gloating.

Parlor Games

POKER

The table below tells you how likely it is to get a pat hand when you're dealt five cards.

PROBABILITIES OF PAT HANDS IN POKER		
Hand	**Probability**	**Average frequency**
Pair	~42.3%	About 3 in 7
Two pair	~4.8%	About 1 in 20
Three of a kind	~2.1%	About 1 in 50
Straight	~0.4%	About 1 in 250
Flush	~0.2%	About 1 in 500
Full house	~0.14%	About 1 in 700
Four of a kind	~0.024%	About 1 in 4,000
Straight flush	~0.0014%	About 1 in 72,000
Royal flush	~0.00015%	About 1 in 650,000
None of the above	~50.1%	About 1 in 2

Poker Probabilities

Let's say you're playing five-card stud with three other players and your first four cards are spades. What's the probability that your fifth card will be a spade, giving you a flush? Here's the formula for such a problem:

$$\text{Probability of getting a card you want} = \frac{\text{number of unseen winners}}{\text{number of unseen cards}}$$

"Number of unseen winners" is the number of different cards that would complete the hand you're hoping for, not counting any of those cards that are face up on the table. And "number of unseen cards" is simply the total number of cards in the deck (52) minus any you can see because they're face up or in your hand. Let's return to our example. As I said above, four cards have been dealt in the game of five-card stud—that would be one "down" card and three "up" cards for each player. How many "winners" are there—in other words, how many different cards would complete your flush? Well, there are thirteen spades and you have four, so that leaves nine. But you then have to subtract from this any of those nine "winners" that you can see. If you can see two spades among your opponents' "up" cards, that leaves seven cards as the number of unseen winners. For the number of unseen cards, subtract from 52 the total number of cards you can see—that's the twelve "up" cards plus your one "down" card, for a total of thirteen cards you can see. That gives us 52 minus 13, which equals 39 unseen cards.[2] Plugging those numbers into the formula gives us:

$$\text{Probability of completing your flush} = \frac{\text{number of unseen winners}}{\text{number of unseen cards}}$$

$$= \frac{7}{39}$$

$$\approx 0.179$$

$$\approx 18\%$$

---

[2] You might think you should also subtract your opponents' "down" cards because, since they've already been dealt, you certainly can't get them. But, take my word for it, it doesn't work that way.

BRIDGE HANDS

DISTRIBUTION OF BRIDGE HANDS					
Distribution of suits	**Longest suit**	**Frequency in 10,000 hands**	**Distribution of suits**	**Longest suit**	**Frequency in 10,000 hands**
4441		299	7600		1
4432		2,155	7510		11
4333		1,054	7420		36
			7411		39
	4	3,508	7330		27
			7321		188
5530		89	7222		51
5521		317			
5440		124		7	353
5431		1,293			
5422		1,058	8500		0
5332		1,551	8410		5
			8320		11
	5	4,432	8311		12
			8221		19
6610		7			
6520		65		8	47
6511		71			
6430		133			
6421		470	9400		0
6331		345	9310		1
6322		565	9220		1
			9211		2
	6	1,656		9	4

From Howard C. Levinson, *Chance, Luck, and Statistics* (Dover, 1963), 187.

One or more	Probability
Four-card suits	0.67
Five-card suits	0.46
Six-card suits	0.17
Seven-card suits	0.035
Eight-card suits	0.005

From Levinson, *Chance, Luck, and Statistics*, 188.

	Probability on deal
Number of four-card suits	
1	0.409
2	0.228
3	0.030
Number of five-card suits	
1	0.417
2	0.041
Number of six-card suits	
1	0.165
2	0.001
Number of seven-card suits	
1	0.035
Number of eight-card suits	
1	0.005

From Levinson, *Chance, Luck, and Statistics*, 194–195.

DICE ODDS

If you're playing a dice game where you roll two dice, you may want to learn the following table of dice odds. Since each die can land six different ways, there are 6 times 6 or 36 different outcomes for two dice. Here they are:

When calculating the probability of rolling a particular number, the denominator is always 36. The numerator is the number of ways a particular number can come up. For example, a total of 2 can come up just one way, a 1 with a 1 (called "snake eyes"). Thus, the probability of throwing a 2 is $\frac{1}{36}$. A 7, on the other hand, can come up six different ways (1, 6; 2, 5; 3, 4; 4, 3; 5, 2; 6, 1). So the probability of rolling a seven is $\frac{6}{36}$. Here's the complete list:

PROBABILITIES FOR TWO DICE			
Number	Ways you can roll it	Probability (fraction)	Probability (percentage)
2	1, 1 ("snake eyes")	$\frac{1}{36}$	≈ 2.8%
3	1, 2; 2, 1	$\frac{2}{36}$	≈ 5.6%
4	1, 3; 2, 2; 3, 1	$\frac{3}{36}$	≈ 8.3%
5	1,4; 2, 3; 3, 2; 4, 1	$\frac{4}{36}$	≈ 11.1%
6	1, 5; 2, 4; 3, 3; 4, 2; 5, 1	$\frac{5}{36}$	≈ 13.9%
7	1, 6; 2, 5; 3, 4; 4, 3; 5, 2; 6, 1	$\frac{6}{36}$	≈ 16.7%
8	2, 6; 3, 5; 4, 4; 5, 3; 6, 2	$\frac{5}{36}$	≈ 13.9%
9	3, 6; 4, 5; 5, 4; 6, 3	$\frac{4}{36}$	≈ 11.1%
10	4, 6; 5, 5; 6, 4	$\frac{3}{36}$	≈ 8.3%
11	5, 6; 6, 5	$\frac{2}{36}$	≈ 5.6%
12	6, 6 ("box cars")	$\frac{1}{36}$	≈ 2.8%

Did you notice the symmetry in the above table? Seven, the middle number, is the easiest number to roll—it comes up $\frac{6}{36}$ or $\frac{1}{6}$ or 16.7% of the time. Then, as you move away from 7 in either direction, the probabilities decrease in a symmetric pattern. Six and 8 are each one away from 7, and each has a probability of $\frac{5}{36}$; 5 and 9 are each two away from 7, and each has a probability of $\frac{4}{36}$, etc.

BACKGAMMON
(THIS DISCUSSION ASSUMES THAT YOU KNOW THE RULES OF BACKGAMMON.)

The following tables list the dice probabilities for frequently encountered situations in backgammon. Some of the entries follow directly from the above diagram of the 36 possible outcomes of tossing two dice. For example, let's say you're trying to come in from the bar and the only open points in your opponent's board are his 1 and 2 points. So to come in, you need a 1 or a 2 to appear on either die. If you refer to the figure on page 303, you can count twenty different rolls that contain a 1 or a 2. Thus, the probability is $\frac{20}{36}$. Some entries are a bit more complicated. Say, for example, you want to hit your opponent's blot that's eight pips away. How many ways can you roll an 8? The table on page 303 lists five ways of rolling an 8. But there's one more roll—double 2s—that will also hit your opponent. That brings the total to six rolls, or a probability of $\frac{6}{36}$, which reduces to $\frac{1}{6}$.

PROBABILITY OF ENTERING FROM THE BAR	
Number of open points in home board	Probability of entering from the bar
0	$\frac{0}{36}$ or 0%
1	$\frac{11}{36}$ or about 31%
2	$\frac{20}{36}$ or about 56%
3	$\frac{27}{36}$ or 75%
4	$\frac{32}{36}$ or about 89%
5	$\frac{35}{36}$ or about 97%
6	$\frac{36}{36}$ or 100%

PROBABILITY OF HITTING OPPONENT'S BLOT

(This assumes that none of
the possible dice rolls is blocked.)

Distance from your checker to opponent's blot	Probability of hitting blot	
1	$^{11}/_{36}$ or about 31%	
2	$^{12}/_{36}$ or about 33%	
3	$^{14}/_{36}$ or about 39%	Increasing
4	$^{15}/_{36}$ or about 42%	(mostly)
5	$^{15}/_{36}$ or about 42%	
6	$^{17}/_{36}$ or about 47%	
7	$^{6}/_{36}$ or about 17%	
8	$^{6}/_{36}$ or about 17%	
9	$^{5}/_{36}$ or about 14%	
10	$^{3}/_{36}$ or about 8%	
11	$^{2}/_{36}$ or about 6%	Decreasing
12	$^{3}/_{36}$ or about 8%	(mostly)
15	$^{1}/_{36}$ or about 3%	
16	$^{1}/_{36}$ or about 3%	
18	$^{1}/_{36}$ or about 3%	
20	$^{1}/_{36}$ or about 3%	
24	$^{1}/_{36}$ or about 3%	

CHAPTER 21

Baseball Statistics

For this chapter, you may want to review topics in the following chapters from part I:
- Fractions, Decimals, and Percents (chapter 2)

Hitting

BATTING AVERAGE

A batting average is just a percentage. If a hitter gets a hit 28.5 percent of the time, his batting average is .285. If someone is hitting .333, he's getting hits 33.3 percent of the time, or one hit for every three at-bats. That's all there is to it. Note that batting averages are read as three-digit numbers. For instance, you would say, "He's hitting 342," not "He's hitting .342," and not, "His average is 34.2 percent." Computing a batting average is the same as figuring any other percentage, except that you always round off to three decimal places. You just divide the number of hits by the total number of attempts, or "at-bats." Walks and getting hit by a pitch do not count as at-bats. Nor does a "sacrifice," which is when a hitter makes an out but in the process advances a runner closer to home. If a hitter has 16 hits in 55 at-bats, for example, his average would be 16 divided by 55, or .291.

The record batting average for a whole season is Rogers Hornsby's .424 in 1924. No one has hit .400 since Ted Williams did it in 1941. In 2001, the average batting average was .264, including pitchers, who are usually terrible hitters. If you don't count pitchers, the average would probably be somewhere around .270.

ON-BASE PERCENTAGE

Unlike a batting average, which does not take walks into consideration, a ballplayer's on-base percentage reflects his ability to get on base by any means, including walks. Getting on base is obviously important, because if you can get on base, you might later score a run. Hits are often better than walks, because, unlike walks, they almost always advance the runners on base, and any hit, even a single, will usually advance the runners on base farther than a walk will. But a walk can be as good as a hit. If no one is on base, for instance, a walk is exactly the same as a single. And a walk will advance the runners on base if runners are on first, or first and second, or first and third (only the runner on first advances), or when the bases are loaded. The ability to draw a walk is especially valuable for a leadoff batter who needs to get on base in any way possible so that the good hitters behind him can advance him around to home. Because it factors in walks, a batter's on-base percentage is thus another good measure of his value to the team.

Computing an on-base percentage is simple. Just divide the total number of times the hitter gets on base—except when it's due to an error or a fielder's choice—by the total number of times he came up to bat (called "plate appearances"). Then, as with a batting average, round to three decimal places. The record on-base percentage is Ted Williams's .551 in 1941. The average on-base percentage in 2001 was .328, including pitchers.

SLUGGING PERCENTAGE

A third measure of a hitter's ability and value to the team is his slugging percentage, which is determined by dividing his "total bases" (a single counts as one base, a double counts as two, a triple three, and a home run is four) by his number of at-bats and then rounding to three decimal places. In 2001, Barry Bonds slugged .863, smashing the record of .847 set by Babe Ruth in 1920. In 2001, the average slugging percentage was .426, including pitchers.

Let's work through an example and compute a hitter's batting average, on-base percentage, and slugging percentage. Let's say he has come to the plate 50 times, has 9 singles, 3 doubles, 2 home runs, 5 walks, and was hit by a pitch once. (Do the math and you'll see that he made an out 30 times— he got on base $9 + 3 + 2 + 5 + 1$ or 20 times, so the rest of the time he made outs: 50 minus 20 equals 30.) Since walks and getting hit by a pitch don't count for at-bats, he has 50 minus 6, which equals 44 at-bats. To compute his batting average, we divide his number of hits (14) by his number of at-bats (44), which equals .3181818 . . . , or .318 rounded off. To calculate his on-base percentage, we note that he got on base 20 times—14 hits plus 5 walks plus getting hit once—out of 50 plate appearances, so we divide 20 by 50, which gives us .400. To figure his slugging percentage, we first tally his total bases: 9 singles is 9 bases, 3 doubles is 6 bases, and 2 home runs is 8 bases—that's a total of 23 bases. Now we divide his total bases (23) by his at-bats (44), which equals about .523.

Runs Batted In

A fourth measure of hitting performance is total runs batted in, or RBIs. A batter gets credited with an RBI when he gets a hit or sacrifice fly that advances a base runner to home plate, scoring a run. Since the team that scores more runs wins the game, RBIs are of obvious importance. The record for the most RBIs in a season is held by Hack Wilson, who had 191 in 1930.

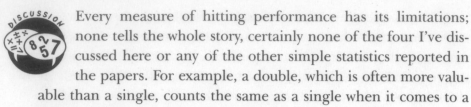

Every measure of hitting performance has its limitations; none tells the whole story, certainly none of the four I've discussed here or any of the other simple statistics reported in the papers. For example, a double, which is often more valuable than a single, counts the same as a single when it comes to a hitter's batting average. For slugging percentage, on the other hand, a double counts as much as two singles, but it's rarely worth that much. So a batting average undervalues a double, while a slugging percentage overvalues a double. To really get a true measure of a hitter's offensive value to a team, one would have to perform a very complex numerical analysis taking many factors into account. "Sabermetricians" use computers to do such analyses. Among the factors you would want to consider are things like how often a batter contributes to a run. Say, for instance, there's a runner on first, a batter gets a single advancing the runner to third, and then the next batter drives the runner home with another single. Both singles were needed to produce the run, but only the batter who drives the run home is awarded an RBI. Any formula that truly measures a hitter's value to the team would give some weight to the run-producing contribution of the first single. Another factor to consider is

The Amazing Babe Ruth

There will always be disagreement among baseball fans about who's the greatest player to ever play the game. But it's easy to make the case for Babe Ruth. Here are a couple of my favorite Babe Ruth stats. First, guess who's the only *pitcher* to pitch at least ten seasons and have a winning record in every season he pitched. Give up? It's Babe Ruth. Second, there's a stat that's the sum of a player's on-base percentage and his slugging percentage. Until 2001, Babe Ruth had six of the top eight seasons for this stat, including the record for best season, 1.379. In 2001, Barry Bonds tied this record. And here, in my view, is the pièce de résistance: in 1920, Ruth hit more home runs than the rest of his teammates combined and more than any other *team* in baseball!

whether the runs a hitter produces or contributes to are important runs, that is, runs that were needed to win the game or come close to winning, as opposed to runs produced after there's an insurmountable lead. Obviously, better ballplayers will usually have better stats, but because of the limitations of the above commonly reported statistics, there is a less than perfect correlation between a player's statistics and his value to his team.

Pitching

EARNED RUN AVERAGE (ERA)

When a run is scored, the pitcher is charged with an "earned run" unless the run is due to an error.[1] The basic idea behind this distinction is that if a run scores because of an error, it isn't the pitcher's fault. A pitcher's earned run average is calculated as follows:

$$ERA = \frac{\text{total number of earned runs}}{\text{total number of innings pitched}} \times 9$$

This computation gives a pitcher's average number of earned runs per nine-inning game. An ERA of 3.50, for instance, means that, on average, if the pitcher pitched an entire nine-inning game, the other team would score 3.50 runs. Note that an ERA is always printed, and read, to two decimal places.

The record for lowest ERA for a whole season is held by Dutch Leonard, who in 1914 had an amazing ERA of 0.96. (This was, however, during the "dead-ball" era). Bob Gibson had an ERA of 1.12 in 1968. In 2001, the average ERA for all major league pitchers was about 4.41.

---

[1] If a relief pitcher comes in with men already on base, and they later score, the original pitcher, not the relief pitcher, is charged with those earned runs.

WIN-LOSS RECORD

A second measure of pitching performance is the win-loss record. A starting pitcher is credited with a win when his team wins the game, and

1) He pitches the whole game, or
2) He pitches at least five full innings—unless he leaves the game due to an injury, in which case there is no minimum number of innings, and
3) If he leaves the game, his team must be ahead when he leaves and stay ahead for the rest of the game.[2]

A starting pitcher gets a loss when his team loses and

1) He pitches the whole game, or
2) He leaves the game when his team is behind or it falls behind as a result of runners he left on base, and his team stays behind for the rest of the game.[3]

Jack Chesbro won 41 games in 1904—the most wins ever in a single season. No one has won 30 or more games since Denny McClain won 31 in 1968. The record for best win-loss percentage is held by Elroy Face, who went 18–1 in 1959 for a winning percentage of .947.

PITCHING BATTING AVERAGE

A third measure of pitching performance is how successful hitters are against a pitcher. This pitching "batting average" is calculated exactly like a hitter's batting average. You divide the total number of hits given up by a pitcher by the total number of at-bats—remember that walks, hit batters, and sacrifices don't count as at-bats. Let's say a pitcher has a pitching

---

[2] Actually, it's a bit more complicated, but this gives you the basic idea.
[3] Ditto.

batting average of .257. This would mean that on average (not counting walks, hit batters, and sacrifices) a hitter facing this pitcher would have a 25.7 percent chance of getting a hit. The record pitching batting average for a whole season is Pedro Martinez's .167 in 2000—this of course is the record *low* average.

PITCHING ON-BASE PERCENTAGE

A fourth measure of a pitcher's performance is his on-base percentage, which is calculated by dividing the total number of hits, walks, and hit batters he's responsible for by the total number of batters he faces. Intentional walks aren't counted in either of the two numbers. A pitcher's on-base percentage simply tells you, on average, the probability that a batter he faces will reach base safely (not counting intentional walks). In 2000, Pedro Martinez also set the record for the best (that's the lowest) pitching on-base percentage: .214.

Fielding

FIELDING AVERAGE

The most common measure of fielding performance is a ballplayer's fielding average. It's given by the following quotient:

$$\text{Fielding average} = \frac{putouts + assists}{putouts + assists + errors}$$

This stat tends to overrate a player with minimal range but good hands, who may be less valuable to his team than a fielder who handles more chances but occasionally makes an error.

Like with the measures of hitting ability, the above pitching and fielding statistics don't tell the whole story. Nonetheless, the best pitchers and fielders generally do compile the best stats.

Games Ahead or Behind

You'll often hear about a team being some number of games ahead or behind another team. Here's what it means. Say, sometime in August, the Cubs' win-loss record is 82–50 and the Mets' is 75–56. The Cubs have seven more wins and six fewer losses than the Mets. Both of these facts obviously contribute to the Cubs' advantage, so you add them—that's thirteen—and then divide by two because each win or loss counts for only half a game. Thirteen divided by two is 6½, so the Cubs are 6½ games ahead. Here's another example. Say the Yankees' record is 35–20 and the White Sox are 34–18. Unlike in the first example, the Yankees have more wins *and* losses. When this happens you subtract instead of add. The Yankees have two more losses and one more win, so you subtract one from two, which equals one. And then, like above, you divide this result by two: one divided by two is one-half. Your common sense should tell you that the Yankees are worse off than the White Sox since they have two more losses and only one more win. The Yankees are thus half a game *behind* the White Sox.

Magic Number

Toward the end of the season, when a team gets close to clinching its division, sports pages may list the team's magic number. Say the Diamondbacks are leading their division with a win-loss record of 95–60 with 7 games to play, and the second-place Dodgers have a record of 90–64 with 8 games remaining. In this scenario, the Diamondbacks would have a magic number of 4, which means that any combination of Diamondback wins and Dodger losses that total 4 or more will give the Diamondbacks a lock on the division title.

Here's how you determine a team's magic number. Consider the example above. The Dodgers' record is 90–64 with 8 games still to play. If they were to win all their remaining games, they'd end the season with 98 wins. The Diamondbacks would thus need 99 wins to beat them, and they've got 95 wins now, so they'd need 4 more wins–that's their magic number, 4.

CHAPTER 22

Weather

For this chapter, you may want to review topics in the following chapters from part I:
- Fractions, Decimals, and Percents (chapter 2)
- Basic Geometry (chapter 5)

Heat/Humidity Index and Windchill

In some parts of the United States, weather forecasters report not only the temperature in the summertime but also the heat/humidity index; in other places, in the wintertime, people want to know the windchill in addition to the temperature. People who live, as I do, in places like Chicago have to put up with both unbearably hot and humid days and dangerously cold and windy days. Here are the numbers:

		70	75	80	85	90	95	100	105	110	115	120
	0%	64	69	73	78	83	87	91	95	99	103	107
	10%	65	70	75	80	85	90	95	100	105	111	116
	20%	66	72	77	82	87	93	99	105	112	120	130
	30%	67	73	78	84	90	96	104	113	123	135	148
	40%	68	74	79	86	93	101	110	123	137	151	
	50%	69	75	81	88	96	107	120	135	150		
	60%	70	76	82	90	100	114	132	149			
	70%	70	77	85	93	106	124	144				
	80%	71	78	86	97	113	136					
	90%	71	79	88	102	122						
	100%	72	80	91	108							

The table above is titled **HEAT INDEX** with a subheading **Actual temperature (°F)** across the top, and the left axis labeled **Relative Humidity**.

For the most part, this table just tells you what you already know: that when it's hot *and* humid, it feels especially hot. A few observations. Notice that if the humidity is low enough—how low it has to be depends on the temperature—it actually feels *cooler* than the actual temperature (see the top two rows in the table). Also observe that when the temperature is only 70°F, increased humidity has little effect on how warm it feels. This is understandable in light of the fact that when it's cool out, say 50°F, damp air feels *colder* than dry air. As the temperature increases, the effect of high humidity is increasingly severe. Look at the third from the last line, for example: 80 percent humidity makes 70°F air feel only one degree warmer than it actually is; if it's 75°F out, it feels three degrees warmer; if it's 80°F, six degrees warmer; at 85°F, twelve degrees warmer; at 90°F, twenty-three degrees warmer; and when it's 95°F, the 80 percent humidity makes it feel forty-one degrees warmer—that's 136°! If the forecast predicts 95°F with 80 percent humidity, don't plan on moving a lot of heavy furniture.

At the opposite end of the comfort spectrum are cold and windy days:

NEW WINDCHILL CHART

Frostbite occurs in 15 minutes or less

Wind (mph)	Temperature (°F)											
	30	25	20	15	10	5	0	-5	-10	-15	-20	-25
5	25	19	13	7	1	-5	-11	-16	-22	-28	-34	-40
10	21	15	9	3	-4	-10	-16	-22	-28	-35	-41	-47
15	19	13	6	0	-7	-13	-19	-26	-32	-39	-45	-51
20	17	11	4	-2	-9	-15	-22	-29	-35	-42	-48	-55
25	16	9	3	-4	-11	-17	-24	-31	-37	-44	-51	-58
30	15	8	1	-5	-12	-19	-26	-33	-39	-46	-53	-60
35	14	7	0	-7	-14	-21	-27	-34	-41	-48	-55	-62
40	13	6	-1	-8	-15	-22	-29	-36	-43	-50	-57	-64
45	12	5	-2	-9	-16	-23	-30	-37	-44	-51	-58	-65
50	12	4	-3	-10	-17	-24	-31	-38	-45	-52	-60	-67
55	11	4	-3	-11	-18	-25	-32	-39	-46	-54	-61	-68
60	10	3	-4	-11	-19	-26	-33	-40	-48	-55	-62	-69

From usatoday.com/weather.

The windchill factor tells us how cold it feels when wind speed is taken into consideration.[1] It also tells us what effect the cold has on exposed skin. If it's 5°F with a wind speed of 20 mph, for example, the windchill factor is 15° below zero. That tells us that exposed skin is, roughly, at the same risk of getting frostbitten as on a windless day when it's 15° below. Our risk of suffering hypothermia (overexposure to the cold) would also be roughly equal on those two days.

Wind makes it feel colder because the stronger the wind, the faster heat is drawn away from the body. The wind has a similar effect on other things as well. Higher wind speeds make water freeze faster. However, water cannot freeze unless the air temperature is below 32°F even if the wind chill factor is below 32°F. Since the windchill factor is a good indicator of how cold it feels, you should use it, rather than the temperature, in deciding what to wear on a cold day.

In case you're curious about how they calculate windchill or you want to compute some windchill numbers that aren't on the chart, here's the formula. Isn't it a beauty?

$$\textit{Windchill temperature} = 35.74 + 0.6215 \times T - 35.75 \times V^{0.16} + 0.4275 \times T \times V^{0.16}$$

(Where T is the Fahrenheit temperature and
V is the wind speed in miles per hour.)

---

[1] The U.S. National Weather Service began using these new windchill numbers in the fall of 2001. The data is based on new research on how cold and wind affects *people*—seems logical, doesn't it? The old windchill numbers we had been using since 1945 were based on how cold and wind affects *water*—go figure. The new, accurate windchill numbers are less severe than the old numbers. For example, on a day that's 10° above zero with a 25 mph wind, the old windchill number was 29° below, but according to the new numbers, it feels like only minus 11°F, etc.

Fahrenheit-Centigrade Conversions

Let's go over the formulas for converting from Fahrenheit to centi-grade and vice versa. Then I'll give you some shortcuts so you can figure, in your head, a quick estimate of the converted tempera-ture.

Centigrade to Fahrenheit (exact). To convert from centigrade to Fahrenheit, use the following formula:

$$F = \frac{9}{5}C + 32$$

Say it's 25°C and you want the Fahrenheit temperature. Plug the 25 into *C* and then multiply 25 by ⁹⁄₅ (if you read chapter 2, you should be able to do this without a calculator):

$$\frac{9}{5} \times 25$$

$$= \frac{9}{5} \times \frac{25}{1}$$

$$= \frac{9}{\cancel{5}_1} \times \frac{\cancel{25}^5}{1}$$ (Cancel a 5 from the 25 and the 5, and then multiply straight across the numerator and straight across the denominator)

$$= \frac{45}{1}$$

$$= 45$$

Now add 32 for the final answer: 77°F.

Fahrenheit to centigrade (exact). Here's the formula for convert-ing from Fahrenheit to centigrade:

$$C = \frac{5}{9}(F - 32)$$

If it's 70°F, for example, plug the 70 into the "F," subtract 32 from 70—that's 38—then take out your calculator and multiply 38 by $\frac{5}{9}$; the approximate answer is 21°C.

Memorizing the Formulas

If you have trouble memorizing these formulas or think you might mix them up, here's a way to make sure you're using the proper formula. You probably know that water boils at 212°F. In centigrade, water boils at 100°—what number could be easier to remember? So, if you're not sure whether you've got the right formula, just make sure that it converts 212°F to 100°C, or vice versa. If it does, the formula is correct. (After reading part I, you should be able to do this quite easily on paper or in your head.) Let's do it. To test the Fahrenheit-to-centigrade formula, you first subtract 32 from 212, which equals 180. Then you should be able to do $\frac{5}{9}$ times 180 in your head: $\frac{5}{9}$ times 180 means the same thing as $\frac{5}{9}$ of 180, which is 5 times as much as $\frac{1}{9}$ of 180, and since $\frac{1}{9}$ of 18 is 2, $\frac{1}{9}$ of 180 is 20, and, finally, 5 times 20 is 100. Since we were supposed to get an answer of 100, the formula checks. To test the centigrade-to-Fahrenheit formula, you'd first do $\frac{9}{5}$ times 100: $\frac{9}{5}$ of 100 is 9 times as much as $\frac{1}{5}$ of 100, and since $\frac{1}{5}$ of 100 is 20, $\frac{9}{5}$ of 100 is 9 times 20, or 180. Then, since 32 plus 180 is 212, the formula checks.

Centigrade to Fahrenheit (shortcut). Since you probably don't need to determine precise conversions, here's a shortcut for doing approximate conversions quickly, in your head. Let's first do the centigrade-to-Fahrenheit conversion—which you're much more likely to need. Say you're traveling in Italy in July, and the forecast calls for partly cloudy skies with a high of 17°C to 20°C. What should you wear? Let's do the shortcut conversion for both of those temperatures. Here's how to convert 17°C into Fahrenheit:

Step 1) Double the temperature: $17 \times 2 = 34$.

Step 2) 34 is in the 30s, so subtract 3 (if the number is in the 40s, subtract 4; in the 50s, subtract 5, etc.): $34 - 3 = 31$.

Step 3) Add 32—the number 32 should be easy to remember because it's the freezing point for water: $31 + 32 = 63°F$.

Now let's convert 20°C into Fahrenheit:

Step 1) Double 20: that's 40.

Step 2) 40 is in the 40s, so subtract 4: that's 36.

Step 3) Add 32 to 36: 68°F.

So the forecast calls for a high of 63°F to 68°F—take a light jacket.

This shortcut produces either the exact answer or an answer off by one degree. And, with a little practice, you should be able to do it quickly in your head. There's one catch, however. If the number you use in step 2 is negative, you have to *add* rather than subtract.

Fahrenheit to centigrade (shortcut). Now for the reverse conversion, Fahrenheit to centigrade. You'll notice that this is simply the centigrade-to-Fahrenheit shortcut reversed: the order of the steps is reversed, and within each step the math is "reversed"—addition becomes subtraction, etc. Let's convert 80°F to centigrade.

Step 1) *Subtract* 32: $80 - 32 = 48$.

Step 2) 48 is in the 40s, so *add* 4: $48 + 4 = 52$.

Step 3) Cut in half: $52 \div 2 = 26$.

Like the centigrade-to-Fahrenheit shortcut, this method will always give you an answer within one degree of the actual temperature. And there's the same catch as above: if the number you use in step 2 is negative, you have to *subtract* rather than add.

Centigrade to Fahrenheit (shorter shortcut). At the risk of confusing you, here's a shorter shortcut to use if you're really in a hurry or if your motto is "the less math, the better."

Step 1) Double.
Step 2) Add 30.

This method will usually give you an answer within one, two, or three degrees Fahrenheit of the exact answer, but it can be off by as much as four or five degrees. However, since the larger errors occur only for very cold and very hot temperatures—you'll think it's 0°F when it's really 5°F or you'll think it's 100°F when it's really 95°F—the error won't affect your decisions about what to do or what to wear. In short, it's good enough.

Fahrenheit to centigrade (shorter shortcut). And here's the shorter shortcut for converting Fahrenheit to centigrade.

Step 1) Subtract 30.
Step 2) Cut in half.

Let's convert 80°F again with this shortcut.

Step 1) Subtract 30: 80 − 30 = 50.
Step 2) Cut in half: 50 ÷ 2 = 25°C.

Piece of cake, right?

Centigrade to Fahrenheit (yet another shortcut!). Now I'll give you a third shortcut method that's shorter than the first longer shortcut, but longer than the second shorter shortcut—just kidding! Actually, I do have one last shortcut method. But let's just do the centigrade-to-Fahrenheit conversion for this one. This method is about as fast as the first shortcut, is slightly more accurate, and has the advantage that if you use it enough, it will help you to start thinking in centigrade—you know, like dreaming in French.

First, you have to remember two simple conversions: 0°C equals 32°F (water's freezing point) and 22°C equals 72°F (room temperature). The first should be easy to remember. For the second, here are a couple possible mnemonics: for 22°C, think of "Catch-22" for C22; or think about the conversions we're doing, Fahrenheit *to* centigrade and centigrade *to* Fahrenheit, *to-to* or 22. On days at or below 10°C (that's 50°F), you'll use the freezing numbers, 0°C and 32°F; on days at or above 50°F, you'll use the room temperature numbers, 22°C and 72°F.

Now, to convert from centigrade to Fahrenheit, all you have to do is notice how far away the actual centigrade temperature is from the centigrade key number (0 or 22), double that, and the Fahrenheit temperature will then be that distance from the Fahrenheit key number (32 or 72). For example, 25°C is three degrees above 22°C—that's three degrees above room temperature. Now double 3, which is 6. So the Fahrenheit temperature is 78° because 78° is six degrees above 72°F or six degrees above room temperature. Here's another one. If the temperature is 18°C, it's four degrees below 22°C, or four degrees below room temperature. Now, since twice 4 is 8, it's 64°F because 64°F is eight degrees below 72°F or eight degrees below room temperature. On a cold day, say −10°C, we notice that −10° is ten degrees below the key number of 0°C—that's ten degrees below freezing. Next, we double 10°—that's 20°. So the Fahrenheit temperature is twenty degrees below the key number of 32°; that's 12°F (20° below freezing).

Relative Humidity

The relative humidity is a measure of how much moisture is in the air. It is given as a percentage of the maximum moisture possible at a given temperature. For example, if it's 75°F with a relative humidity of 80 percent, that means that the air contains 80 percent of the maximum moisture it could hold at that temperature. Here's the formula:

$$\text{Relative humidity} = \frac{\text{amount of water vapor in the air}}{\text{amount of water vapor the air can hold}}$$

Since warm air can hold more moisture than cool air, 75°F air at 80 percent humidity contains more moisture than 50°F air at 80 percent humidity. This last principle is what explains the dew point.

Dew Point and Frost Point

The dew point is the temperature to which air must be cooled so that moisture from the air will condense on an object or form dew on the ground. The best way to understand this is through an example. When it's 85°F with 75 percent relative humidity, the dew point is 76°F. So if there were, say, a glass of milk at or below 76°F, moisture from the air would condense on the sides of the glass. Here's how it works. Recall that warm air can hold more moisture than cool air. The 76°F air in the above example can hold only 75 percent of the moisture that the 85°F air can hold. So when the 85°F air comes in contact with the 76°F glass of milk, the air is cooled to 76°F and its relative humidity goes up from 75 percent to 100 percent. The same amount of moisture is in the air, but the amount of moisture that constitutes 75 percent capacity for 85°F air totally saturates the 76°F air. Since the 76°F air is now at 100 percent humidity, it can't hold any more water. So if it's cooled any more, the water would condense out of the air and onto the glass.

The frost point works the same way, except that the moisture that condenses out of the air forms ice instead of water. This happens when the air comes in contact with an object or the ground that's at a temperature below freezing. Another way of looking at this is that if you're given the air temperature and the relative humidity and you then determine the condensation point and your answer is at freezing (32°F) or above, then this temperature is a dew point, but if your answer is below freezing, then this temperature is a frost point.

The Distance to Lightning

Lightning is basically an enormous electrical shock—like the little flash of light you see shoot from your finger to a metal object when you get a shock, only *many, many* times stronger. Thunder is the sound made by the lightning—just like we hear a little click or snap when we get a shock. So thunder and lightning occur simultaneously. We see the lightning before we hear the thunder, however, because light travels so much faster than sound. Regardless of how far away the lightning occurs, we see it virtually instantaneously, because light travels at the amazing speed of 186,000 miles per *second!* Sound travels *much* slower, about 750 miles per *hour,* or one mile in about five seconds. You can use this fact to estimate the distance to a bolt of lightning. Try the following the next time you're in a thunderstorm. This works especially well when you're lying in bed listening to a storm. When lightning flashes, count the number of seconds until you hear the thunder. Every five seconds represents a mile, so if you counted to ten, the lightning struck two miles away, fifteen seconds means it struck three miles away, etc.

Barometric Pressure

Barometric pressure is the measure of the air pressure caused by the weight of our atmosphere. As sea level, barometric pressure is about 14.7 pounds per square inch, but it varies a bit depending on factors described below. This 14.7 pounds is the weight of the air in a one-inch-by-one-inch column reaching from the ground to the top of the atmosphere, about 400 miles (see diagram below).

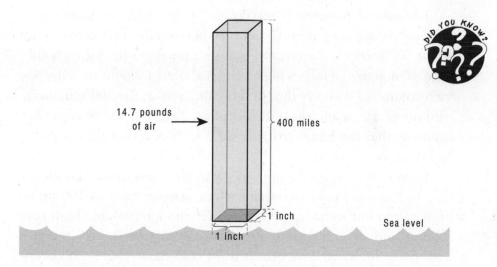

14.7 pounds of air → 400 miles

1 inch

1 inch

Sea level

(Air gets thinner and thinner the higher you go. In fact, about 90 percent of the air in the column shown above—and 90 percent of the weight—is in the lowest layer of the atmosphere, the troposphere—up to about seven and a half miles.)

The greater your altitude above sea level, the less the barometric pressure, because as you go higher and higher, the column of air gets shorter and shorter.

Gravity is of course pulling down on this column of air—that's what gives it its weight—but the air pressure is not only downward.

The atmospheric pressure of 14.7 pounds per square inch presses on everything from every direction. It's this pressure that makes one of those little suction-cup thingamajobs stick to your refrigerator or window. It seems that it's the suction that *pulls* the suction cup to the refrigerator, but, in fact, with this and other types of suction, what seems like a pull is really a push from the other side. Air pressure pushes on the outside of the suction cup, and since there's no air on the inside of it to push back, it gets pushed hard to the surface and then friction makes it stick.

Barometric pressure is usually given in inches of mercury. A barometric pressure of 14.7 pounds per square inch converts to about 30 "inches" of mercury because a one-inch-by-one-inch column of mercury 30 inches high weighs about 14.7 pounds. This 30-inch column of mercury thus weighs the same as the 400-mile-high column of air in the diagram on page 327. You might hear, for instance, that the barometric pressure is 29.32. That means 29.32 inches of mercury.

Heat makes things expand, so warm air is less dense and therefore lighter than cold air—that's why warm air rises. A 100-mile-high column of warm air is thus lighter than a 100-mile-high column of cold air, and therefore the barometric pressure is generally a bit lower on warm days than it is on cold days. That's a bit oversimplified, though, and other factors such as humidity affect the barometric pressure. Weather systems also affect the barometric pressure, and, as a general rule, falling barometric pressure foretells stormy weather, while rising barometric pressure is a sign of calm, clear weather.

Flattened Like a Pancake!

We've all seen cartoon characters flattened by a steamroller. Well, you might wonder why this doesn't happen to all of us from the atmospheric pressure squeezing us on every side. An average-size adult has somewhere in the neighborhood of 2000 square inches of skin. Multiplying this by the atmospheric pressure of 14.7 pounds per square inch comes to about 30,000 pounds! That's 15 tons! Why don't we feel this enormous pressure? I wish I knew.

The Seasons

I used to get fooled every year by a short warm spell in February or early March and I'd think, "Oh, beautiful springtime weather must be just around the corner." Nope. Wrong again. (If you're wondering how I could get fooled like this not once, not twice, but year after year after year, that makes two of us.) Well, I got tired of this and finally sat down and figured out the following simple rule of thumb. Just about no matter where you are in the Northern Hemisphere, the coldest day of the year is about January 20. The warmest day is half a year later, roughly July 20. (It's vice versa in the Southern Hemisphere). Since January 20 is closer to February than December, a typical February is slightly colder than a typical December. This pattern continues as you go further away from the dead of winter. So, on average, you'll find that

February is slightly colder than December,
March is slightly colder than November,
April is slightly colder than October.

If this coming April disappoints you, because you think it "should" be filled with warm spring days, just remember that normal temperatures for the first week of April (about eleven weeks after the dead of winter) are the same as normal temperatures for the first week of *November* (about eleven weeks before the dead of winter).

CHAPTER 23

Travel and the Globe

For this chapter, you may want to review topics in the following chapters from part I:
- Fractions, Decimals, and Percents (chapter 2)
- Basic Geometry (chapter 5)

Converting between U.S. and Foreign Currency

Currency conversions are listed in two ways: the number of the foreign currency in one U.S. dollar, and the number of U.S. dollars in one of the foreign currency. For example, the day I wrote this, May 1, 2002, the *New York Times* gave the following conversions:

Euros in 1 dollar	Dollars in 1 euro
1.1107	0.9003

Yen in 1 dollar	Dollars in 1 yen
128.57	0.007778

Dollars are worth more than most foreign currencies, so for most conversions, there'll be more than one of the foreign currency in a dollar and less than a dollar in one of the foreign currency—like with the euro and yen above. (Note that for all currencies, one of the two conversion numbers is less than the number 1 and the other is greater than 1. Also, the two conversion numbers are always *reciprocals*—that is, if you divide the number 1 by either one of them, you get the other.) It's the other way around with the British pound, for example:

Pounds in 1 dollar	Dollars in 1 pound
0.6863	1.4571

Now, here's a nifty way to do currency conversions with a calculator. You can do this with any $5 credit-card-size calculator. When you're traveling and you get some foreign currency, note the exchange rate. Regardless of whether there's more or less than one of the foreign currency in a dollar, you always want to use the larger of the two conversion numbers. If, for some reason, you have only the smaller number—this is always less than 1—just divide 1 by this number to obtain the larger conversion number. Now, just enter this number into your calculator and press the "store" or "memory" button.

Say you're in Japan. Enter 128.57 into your calculator's memory. Then, when you're out shopping and you see a coat for sale for 31,500 yen, you just take out your pocket calculator and

press: 31,500

The answer is $245. If you want to convert $80 into yen, just

press: 80

That's about 10,285 yen.

Notice that when we converted a larger number of yen into the smaller number of dollars, we *divided,* and when we converted a smaller number of dollars into the larger number of yen, we *multiplied.* Here's the rule:

*Always **divide** when you want to make an amount **smaller**.*
*Always **multiply** when you want to make an amount **larger**.*

If you're in England, you'll *multiply* to convert from pounds to dollars because you'll be converting, say, 50 pounds into the *larger* number of U.S. dollars, about $73. Wherever you are, it will always be obvious to you whether you need to make the amount in question larger or smaller, so all you have to remember is to

press: to make smaller

press: to make larger

The great thing about this system is that when you go to a different country, you just enter the new conversion number, and then forget about it. No matter what country you're in, the simple calculator steps are always the same.

Here are four more tips:

- Memorize a few benchmarks in round amounts of U.S. money, and round off the conversion to make it easy to remember. For instance, for yen, memorize that $10 equals about 1300 yen or that $50 equals about 6500 yen.

- For each country you go to, make up a little card with a list of round amounts of the foreign currency. Here's what your card might look like for British pounds:

Pounds	U.S.	Pounds	U.S.	Pounds	U.S.
1	$1.50	40	$60	150	$220
5	$7	50	$73	200	$290
10	$15	60	$87	250	$365
15	$22	70	$100	300	$435
20	$30	80	$115	400	$580
25	$35	90	$130	500	$730
30	$45	100	$145	750	$1090
35	$50	125	$180	1000	$1450

- You can fit this on the back of a business card that you can discreetly hide in your hand. When you're out shopping, simply locate the price of an item between two entries on your card to estimate the price in dollars.

- When you get foreign cash, always take out the same amount, say, $100 worth, then, as you spend your wad, you'll have a rough sense of what fraction of your $100 you're spending. Another thing you could do is to take out the equivalent of $100, and separate the foreign currency into four packs worth $25 each. Keep the four packs separated in your wallet.

- You could keep a set of the common currency denominations in your wallet, paper-clipped together with a Post-it note on each bill with its dollar amount on it. In Britain, for example, the commonly used bills are 5, 10, 20, and 50 pounds. Clip the four bills together and keep them in your wallet as a handy reference.

Distance = Rate × Time

You use the above formula whenever you know two of the above three quantities and you want to determine the third. If you want to determine the *distance,* you multiply the *rate* by the *time.* If you want to determine the *time,* you divide the *distance* by the *rate.* And if you want to determine the *rate,* you divide the *distance* by the *time.* Here's a nice mnemonic device for remembering these three alternatives:

$$\frac{D}{RT}$$

To help you remember this, notice that D, R, and T are in alphabetical order. This single diagram expresses all three computations. To compute distance, cover up the D and what's left, namely RT, tells you what to do: you calculate RT, which means the same thing as $R \times T$, so you multiply rate by time. When you cover up the R, you see $\frac{D}{T}$, so to determine rate, you divide distance by time. And when you cover up the T, you see $\frac{D}{R}$, which tells you that time equals distance divided by rate.

Let's do some examples. Say you've been driving at 60 mph for 3 hours and you want to calculate the distance traveled. D equals $R \times T$, so you multiply the rate (60) by the time (3) to obtain the distance: $60 \times 3 = 180$ miles. If you're planning a 700-mile trip and you estimate you can average 50 mph, how long will the drive take? Since T equals $\frac{D}{R}$, you divide the distance (700) by the rate (50) to obtain the time: $700 \div 50 = 14$ hours. If you flew the 3000 miles from Chicago to London in 6 hours, what was the plane's average speed or rate? Since R equals $\frac{D}{T}$, divide the distance by the time to determine the rate: $3000 \div 6 = 500$ mph.

Whenever you use these formulas, make sure you're using the correct units. Consider the unit for rate in the above examples. Since we used *miles* per *hour* for the rate, we must use miles for the distance and hours for the time. As long as the units follow this pattern, you're okay. You could use, for example, *meters* per *second* for the rate if you use meters for the distance and seconds for the time. If the units you're using don't fit this pattern, you have to do a conversion. If you've been driving for 45 minutes at 55 mph, for example, and you want to determine the distance, you first have to convert from minutes into hours. You do that by dividing 45 by 60, which equals ¾ of an hour, or 0.75 hours—you may have known that, of course, without doing the division. Now you can multiply the rate (55) by the time (0.75) to obtain the distance: $55 \times 0.75 = 41.25$ miles, or 41¼ miles. Lastly, when you convert times like 3 hours and 15 minutes into hours, remember that 3 hours and 15 minutes is 3¼ hours, or 3.25 hours; it's *not* equal to 3.15 hours.

Latitude and Longitude

Every point on the earth's surface has a location given by degrees of latitude and degrees of longitude. For example, Chicago is at about 42° N latitude, 88° W longitude, Los Angeles is at 34° N latitude, 118° W longitude, and London is at 51½° N latitude, 0° longitude (neither east nor west). Here's what these numbers mean.

LATITUDE

The latitude of a point on earth tells you how far north or south it is. The latitude number is the measure of the angle formed like in the diagram below.

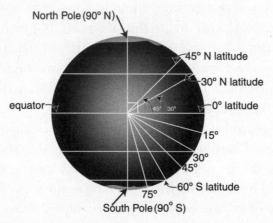

You can see the right angle (90°) made by the horizontal and vertical lines in the diagram. So straight up—the North Pole—is at 90° N latitude. Since 45° is half of 90°, a location at 45° N latitude would be halfway up from the equator to the North Pole; 30° is a third of 90°, so 30° N latitude is a third of the way from the equator to the North Pole, etc. The Southern Hemisphere works the same way.

Degrees are divided into minutes and seconds just like hours are: there are 60 seconds in a minute and 60 minutes in a degree. So if you want to be really precise, you can give a location in degrees, minutes, and seconds of latitude and longitude. This gives the north-south position and the east-west position to within about 100 feet. If you want to be *really* precise, carrying the seconds out to two decimal places will give your location to within one foot! The distance between lines of latitude are roughly:

$$1 \text{ degree} \approx 70 \text{ miles}$$
$$1 \text{ minute} \approx 1 \text{ mile}$$
$$1 \text{ second} \approx 100 \text{ feet}$$

You can use this conversion table to estimate how far north or south one location is from another. For example, since Chicago is at 41° 50' N latitude and Los Angeles is at 34° 07' N latitude, Chicago is 7° 43' north of Los Angeles. Now just multiply 7° by 70 miles and 43' by 1 mile and add the two products together: 7 × 70 + 43 × 1 = 490 + 43, or 533. So Chicago is about 530 miles north of L.A.

LONGITUDE

The longitude of a point on earth tells you how far east or west it is. The lines of longitude, or meridians, are semicircles that go from the North Pole to the South Pole—like this:

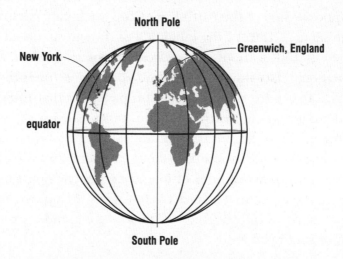

The meridian passing through Greenwich, England—the so-called *prime meridian*—was chosen to be the zero point. Everywhere else is located in terms of degrees east or west of Greenwich. Imagine looking down on the earth from above the North Pole. Like this:

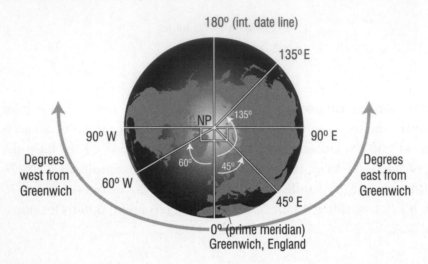

The longitude number of a meridian is the measure of the angle between that meridian and the prime meridian. The numbers go from 0° to 179° E and from 0° to 179° W. If you go 180° either east or west from Greenwich, you get to the international date line on the opposite side of the earth from Greenwich. Since 180° E would be the same as 180° W, the longitude of the international date line is given as 180° without east or west designation. More about the international date line in the section about time zones (below).

You can see from the diagram on page 337 that the closer the meridians get to the North and South poles, the less distance there is between them. So, unlike latitude numbers, where one degree always equals a north-south distance of about 70 miles, the east-west distance between lines of longitude depends on how far you are from the equator. The chart below gives the approximate east-west distance of one degree of longitude depending on how far north or south you are.

DISTANCE BETWEEN LINES OF LONGITUDE

Latitude (north or south)	One degree of longitude equals about
0°	69 miles
5°	69 miles
10°	68 miles
15°	67 miles
20°	65 miles
25°	63 miles
30°	60 miles
35°	57 miles
40°	53 miles
45°	49 miles
50°	44 miles
55°	40 miles
60°	35 miles
65°	29 miles
70°	24 miles
75°	18 miles
80°	12 miles
85°	6 miles
90°	0 miles

Some Hemispheres Have All the Luck

For some odd reason, about 70 percent of the world's land is in the Northern Hemisphere (that is, north of the equator). If you don't count Antarctica, the number becomes about 75 percent. And about 87 percent of the world's population—that's seven out of every eight people—lives in the Northern Hemisphere.

Time Zones

The globe is divided into time zones basically so that the middle of the day will be roughly at the same time—noon— no matter where you live. Without time zones, things would be really weird—the sun would set somewhere at noon and somewhere else at midnight, and your ordinary nine-to-five job would become a four-to-twelve job or a one-to-nine job.

The need for time zones is related to the earth's rotation. The earth spins from west to east. This is what makes the sun rise in the east, move across the sky, and set in the west. Say the sun is setting in New York at 7 P.M. At that moment, in Chicago, it would be an hour before sunset. An hour later, because of the earth's rotation to the east, Chicago would be about where New York was an hour earlier and the sun would thus set on Chicago. In order for the sun to set at 7 P.M. Chicago time, Chicago time has to be one hour behind New York time. This is how the time zones work—the distance from one time zone to the next corresponds roughly to the amount the earth spins in an hour.

The earth rotates one time around—that's 360 degrees—in 24 hours. If we divide 360 by 24 we get 15 degrees, the amount the earth spins each hour. Since each time zone represents one hour of the earth's rotation, each zone spans about 15 degrees of longitude. Refer again to the table on page 339. This shows the distance represented by each degree of longitude at various latitudes. If we multiply each number in the table by 15, we get the distance represented by 15 degrees of longitude, which is roughly the distance between the east and west borders of each time zone.

Approximate East-West Distance Spanned by Each Time Zone

Latitude (north or south)	Distance Spanned by Time Zone
0°	1040 miles
5°	1030 miles
10°	1020 miles
15°	1000 miles
20°	970 miles
25°	940 miles
30°	900 miles
35°	850 miles
40°	790 miles
45°	730 miles
50°	670 miles
55°	600 miles
60°	520 miles
65°	440 miles
70°	350 miles
75°	270 miles
80°	180 miles
85°	90 miles
90°	0 miles

These distances are pretty good approximations in most cases, but in some places around the world the actual distance from the eastern to the western edge of a time zone can be quite different from what's given in the table, because time zone lines often wind their way irregularly along the borders of a state or country or along a river or mountain range. By the way, did you know that there are a few weird time zones that are squeezed between two normal time zones and that differ from neighboring zones by half an hour? And some zones are even stranger. Katmandu, Nepal, for instance, is fifteen minutes ahead of Calcutta, India.

Since the earth spins at the rate of one time zone per hour, the above table also tells you how fast you're moving due to the earth's rotation. I live in Chicago at 42° N latitude—since this is about halfway between 40° and 45° in the table, the answer is about halfway between 790 and 730—so I'm moving toward the east at about 760 mph. (Sure, that's pretty fast, but it's nothing compared to the 67,000 miles per hour or 19 miles per second that we're moving due to the earth's revolution around the sun.)

The International Date Line

For each time zone you cross going east, you add an hour; for each one you cross going west, you subtract an hour. This rule holds unless you cross the international date line. The international date line runs from the North Pole to the South Pole mostly through the Pacific Ocean—it's about 1400 miles west of Hawaii. When you cross the international date line going west, you jump ahead one day; when you cross it going east, you go back one day. Here's why we need it. Let's say it's noon in New York on a Monday. What time is it in Tokyo? Tokyo is 14 time zones east of New York, so it's 14 hours ahead of New York. Fourteen hours ahead of noon on Monday is 2 A.M. on Tuesday. But what if we had figured Tokyo's time by going west instead of east? Tokyo is 10 time zones west of New York, so it should be 10 hours behind New York. Ten hours earlier than noon on Monday is 2 A.M. *Monday.*

We get different results going east and west. But this can't be—we should be able to determine the correct time in Tokyo or anywhere else going east or west. The international date line makes this possible. Going west from New York to Tokyo, you cross the international date line and must move your calendar ahead one day. Thus, going west you subtract 10 hours *and* add a day. Subtracting 10 from noon on Monday brings you to 2 A.M. Monday; then adding a day makes it 2 A.M. on Tuesday. Going east from New York to Tokyo, you don't cross the international date line, so you figure the time change the regular way as we did above—for a result, again, of 2 A.M. Tuesday.

The international date line has some bizarre travel consequences. If you fly from Tokyo to Honolulu, for instance—about a six-and-a-half-hour flight—you could leave at 9 A.M. and arrive at 8:30 P.M. the day before!

Do You Know Your Geography?

Here are three geography fun facts or trivia questions that are guaranteed to stump your friends. First, which is farther east, Atlanta or Detroit? Believe it or not, the answer is Detroit. Actually, this problem won't stump anyone, because of course they'll know it's a trick question. Here's the next one: what's the largest U.S. city east of Reno, Nevada, and west of the Mississippi? The answer is Los Angeles! And here's my favorite: if you were to go straight south from Atlanta all the way to the South Pole, which countries in South America would you pass through? Many people will guess Brazil; some won't remember South American countries so they'll answer, "Somewhere in eastern South America," and others will say that you'd miss all of South America and pass by it to the east, in the Atlantic Ocean. But the correct answer—hold on to your hat—is that you'd miss all of South America to the west! You pass by it in the Pacific Ocean. Check a map if you don't believe me. Try this one on a dozen friends. I'd be amazed if even one gets it right.

Great Circle Routes

A "great circle" on any ball or sphere, including the earth, is a circle that goes around the middle of the sphere, where the sphere is widest. The earth's equator is a great circle, as are all the longitude lines (see the diagram on page 337), and there are others that go in every possible direction. Pick any two points on the earth and there's a great circle that goes through those two points. In fact, the shortest path between any two points on earth is along a great circle. Since airlines obviously want to get you to your destination as quickly as possible, they often take such great circle routes or a route close to a great circle. Wind direction and air traffic may cause them to deviate somewhat, however.

With a globe and a piece of string, you can get a handle on how great circles work. First, take some string and wrap it around your globe at the equator. Cut the string so that it fits around the equator exactly once—the ends should just barely touch. Now, let's say you're flying from Los Angeles to London, and you're wondering how far that is as the crow flies and where that shortest path is. Grab the string a couple of inches from one end, place the string on Los Angeles, holding it tight there, then with your other hand pull the rest of the string so that it stretches from Los Angeles to London. Pull it taut so that the string is snug against the globe running from Los Angeles to London. The string now shows you where the great circle route from Los Angeles to London is. Again, this is the shortest path between the two cities, and if you're flying direct, your flight will probably take a route close to this great circle path. This route may surprise you. Perhaps you expected to fly close to Chicago or New York on your way to London. This is what you might expect from looking at the straight-line path from Los Angeles to London on a regular flat world map. But in fact, the shortest path takes you way north of Chicago and New York, over Montana, Hudson Bay in Canada, and Greenland. As a matter of fact, as you leave L.A. for London, you'd fly more north than east. If you trace this great circle route on a flat map, it will curve way up then back down and will appear much longer than the straight-line path. This is one of the distortions caused by a flat map. Using the string and the globe, you can find other surprising results, like the fact that Maine is closer to Africa than Florida is.

Now let's calculate the distance from Los Angeles to London along this great circle route:

Step 1) Holding the string taut, with your two hands as described above, pinch the string with your fingers, marking precisely with your fingernails where the string meets Los Angles and London.

Step 2) Lift the string from the globe, gripping it at the two positions, and then measure the length along a ruler or yardstick. On my globe, this length is 8⅜ inches.

Step 3) Measure the length of the whole string. This length represents the circumference of the earth. On my globe this length is 38 inches.

Step 4) Divide the length from step 2 by the length of the whole string. With my numbers, I divide 8⅜ by 38, obtaining a result of about 0.22. This tells us that the great circle route from Los Angeles to London is 22 percent of the earth's circumference. By the way, your first two numbers will differ from mine if your globe is a different size, but your percentage result should be the same as mine or very close to it.

Step 5) Multiply the result from step 4 by the earth's circumference, about 25,000 miles: 0.22 times 25,000 gives us our answer, about 5500 miles.

The Earth's Curvature

How much and how rapidly does the earth curve? You may be surprised to learn how fast the earth curves away from you as you stand on the shore and look out at the horizon. Here's a simple rule of thumb. It's not exact, but it's close enough.

The horizon is half your height away in miles.

This rule only works for heights between about four to seven feet. Say you're six feet tall. Half of that is three, so, for you, standing at the water's edge, the horizon is three miles away. If you could watch a Ping-Pong ball floating out to sea on a still day (you'd need

Newswire, Madrid, 1492:
Columbus Discovers Earth Is Round!

Nonsense, I say. How often have you heard about this so-called discovery? Let's set the record straight. First of all, Eratosthenes (c. 276–c. 194 B.C.), chief of the library at Alexandria, not only knew that the earth was spherical, he measured the earth's circumference. He used a clever experiment involving how shadows cast by the sun differ in cities 500 miles apart. His result, 25,000 miles, was off by only half of a percent! And Aristotle—and I suspect others as well—observed the circular shadow cast by the earth on the moon during a lunar eclipse.

Of course, it's very possible that this knowledge was lost or forgotten by the fifteenth century, and there probably were vast numbers of people at that time who thought that the earth was flat. The earth certainly seems flat as we look about and move around on it. So the view that it's flat isn't so unreasonable—particularly for the uneducated masses, especially if they lived inland. *But,* and here's my main point, anyone with a lick of sense living on or near the Mediterranean or the Atlantic or any other large body of water couldn't possibly have thought that the earth was flat, because whenever they watched ships sailing off they would see them gradually drop below the horizon. The ships would eventually disappear completely and then later return safely, proving that they hadn't fallen off the edge of the earth. By the way, some ships in Columbus's day just ten miles offshore would have gone so far below the horizon that only the top half of their sails would be visible. This can't happen on a flat surface. Granted, this wouldn't prove that the earth is a sphere, but it does show that it's curved, not flat.

a telescope), it would begin to disappear over the horizon when it was three miles away. Because of the earth's curvature, only the top half of an eighteen-inch diameter beach ball would be visible once it was four miles offshore. At four and a half miles, it would disappear completely. Here's the precise (almost) formula for computing how far off the horizon is. This formula works for any height.

$$\textit{distance to horizon} \approx \sqrt{1.5 \times \textit{height}}$$

(Where "height" is the height of the observation point in feet.)

Another surprising fact about the earth's curvature is how much it causes a small lake to bulge up in the middle. Here's the formula:

$$\textit{Bulge} = \frac{\textit{Diameter}^2}{6}$$

(Where *Diameter* is the diameter of the lake in miles,
and the size of the bulge is given in feet.)

The size of the bulge grows rapidly as the lake's diameter increases. A lake that's one mile across has only a two-inch bulge in the middle ($\frac{1}{6}$ equals $\frac{1}{6}$ foot or 2 inches). But a three-mile-wide lake has a one-and-a-half foot bulge ($\frac{3^2}{6}$ equals $\frac{9}{6}$ foot or 1.5 feet), and a five-mile-wide lake has about a four-foot bulge ($\frac{5^2}{6}$ equals $\frac{25}{6}$ foot or 4$\frac{1}{6}$ feet or 4 feet 2 inches). I get a thrill out of the fact that you can actually see the earth's curvature. Here's how. The next time you're vacationing near a lake that's two and a half to five miles across, go out on a very still day and lie down near the shore so your eyes are only about a foot above the water's surface—or do this while you're in the water. If you look at the opposite shore, you'll notice that you can't see the shoreline. The shore will be below the horizon, obscured by the bulge of water in the center of the lake. Binoculars will make this clearer, but if your eyes are good, you won't need them. You will actually see, with your own eyes, the curvature of the earth![1]

---

[1] At least I think this works. I'm pretty sure I saw this while vacationing on Indian Lake in the Adirondacks, though I suppose there's some likelihood that it was an optical illusion or an instance of wishful thinking.

Taking a Cruise

When you book a cruise, you may have to decide among several cabin sizes. How does 172 square feet sound? Is it worth it to pay more for 190 square feet? Or if you want to save money, would you be happy with only 160 square feet? These sizes are difficult to picture, and you can be sure that the brochures make the cabins look bigger than they are. So before you buy your tickets, figure out what the cabin sizes are like in comparison to a room in your home. First, remember that the square footage listed by the cruise line includes the closets and bathroom. So try to obtain the actual size of the cabin (excluding closets and the bathroom) from the cruise line or your travel agent. Or, if they don't have this figure, subtract about 50 square feet from the number of square feet listed. Next, measure one of your bedrooms to get a feel for what the different cabin sizes are like. Or, alternatively, mark off the perimeter of the cabin on your living room floor. Typical cabins range from 140 to 220 square feet unless you're lucky enough to be able to afford a multiple-room suite. The table below gives the approximate dimensions of different-size cabins excluding the closets and bathrooms.

DIMENSIONS OF CRUISE SHIP CABINS (EXCLUDING CLOSETS AND BATHROOMS)	
Cabin size	Approximate dimensions
140 square feet	9' by 10'
160 square feet	10' by 11'
180 square feet	10' by 13'
200 square feet	10' by 15'
220 square feet	12' by 14'

Appendix

U.S./Metric Conversions

LENGTH

25.4 millimeters	= 1 inch
2.54 centimeters	= 1 inch
30.5 centimeters	≈ 1 foot
39.4 inches	≈ 1 meter
3.3 feet	≈ 1 meter
3280 feet	≈ 1 kilometer (easy to remember if you know that there are 5280 feet in a mile)
1.1 yards	≈ 1 meter
1094 yards	≈ 1 kilometer
1609 meters	≈ 1 mile (thus the 1600-meter run is almost exactly a mile, and the 400-meter run is almost exactly a quarter mile.)
1.6 kilometers	≈ 1 mile

AREA

6.45 square centimeters	≈ 1 square inch
1550 square inches	≈ 1 square meter
10.8 square feet	≈ 1 square meter
108,000 square feet	≈ 1 hectare

1.2 square yards	≈	1 square meter
11,960 square yards	≈	1 hectare
4047 square meters	≈	1 acre
2.47 acres	≈	1 hectare
247 acres	≈	1 square kilometer
259 hectares	≈	1 square mile
2.59 square kilometers	≈	1 square mile

VOLUME

(1 milliliter is the same as 1 cubic centimeter)

4.9 milliliters	≈	1 teaspoon
14.8 milliliters	≈	1 tablespoon
16.4 milliliters	≈	1 cubic inch
29.6 milliliters	≈	1 ounce
61 cubic inches	≈	1 liter
33.8 ounces	≈	1 liter
4.2 cups	≈	1 liter
2.1 pints	≈	1 liter
1.06 quarts	≈	1 liter
3.79 liters	≈	1 gallon
28.3 liters	≈	1 cubic foot
264 gallons	≈	1 cubic meter
35.3 cubic feet	≈	1 cubic meter

WEIGHT

28.3 grams	≈	1 ounce
454 grams	≈	1 pound
35.3 ounces	≈	1 kilogram
2.2 pounds	≈	1 kilogram
2200 pounds	≈	1 metric ton
907 kilograms	≈	1 ton
1.1 ton	≈	1 metric ton

SPEED

1.1 kilometers/hour	≈	1 foot/second
1.6 kilometers/hour	≈	1 mile/hour
1.85 kilometers/hour	≈	1 knot
3.28 feet/second	≈	1 meter/second
2.24 miles/hour	≈	1 meter/second

MASTER CONVERSION TABLE

(Simply look up the desired conversion alphabetically and
multiply by the number given.)

To convert from	into	multiply by	To convert from	into	multiply by
Acres	Square feet	43,560	Cubic inches	Cubic cm	16.3871
	Square kilometers	.0040469		Cubic feet	0.000579
	Square meters	4046.9		Gallons	0.00433
	Square miles	.0015625		Liters	0.01639
	Square yards	4840		Ounces	0.55411
Btu	Cal(g)	252.00	Cubic meters	Cubic feet	35.3147
	Cal(kg)	.252			
	Joules	1054.4	Cubic yards	Cubic feet	27
	kW-hours	.00029288		Cubic meters	0.76455
Byte	Bit	8	Cup	Gallon	0.0625
				Pint	0.5
Calories, g	Btu	.0039683		Milliliter	236.588
	Joules	4.184		Ounce	8
	kW-hours	.000001162		Quart	0.25
				Tablespoon	16
Calories, kg	Btu	3.9683		Teaspoon	48
	Cal(g)	1000			
	Joules	4184	Fathom	Feet	6
	kW-hours	.001162			
			Feet	Centimeters	30.48
Centimeters	Feet	0.03281		Meters	0.3048
	Inches	0.3937		Inches	12
	Meters	0.01		Miles (statute)	0.000189
	Millimeters	10			
			Feet/second	Kilometers/hr	1.09728
Carats	Milligrams/gram	41.666		Miles/hr	0.681818
Cu Centimeters	Cubic inches	0.06102	Furlongs	Feet	660
	Liters	0.001		Meters	201.17
	Ounces (U.S. liquid)	0.03381		Miles	0.125
	Quarts (U.S. liquid)	0.00106			
			Gallons (Brit.)	Gallons (U.S. liquid)	1.2009
Cu feet	Cubic centimeters	28316.8			
	Cubic inches	1728.0	Gallons (U.S. dry)	Gallons (U.S. liquid)	1.163647
	Cubic meters	0.02832			
	Cubic yards	0.03704	Gallons (U.S. liquid)	Cubic feet	0.13368
	Gallons (U.S. liquid)	7.48052		Gallons (Brit.)	0.83267
	Liters	28.31687		Gallons (U.S. dry)	0.85937
	Ounces (U.S. fluid)	957.506		Liters	3.7854
	Pints (U.S. liquid)	59.8442		Ounces (U.S. fluid)	128
				Pints (U.S. liquid)	8
				Quarts (U.S. liquid)	4

To convert from	into	multiply by	To convert from	into	multiply by
Grams	Kilograms	0.001	Miles/hr	Feet/minute	88
	Milligrams	1000		Feet/second	1.4667
				Kilometers/hr	1.6093
Hands	Centimeters	10.16			
	Inches	4	Milliliters	Liters	0.001
	Feet	0.3333		Ounces (U.S. fluid)	0.0338
Hours	Days	0.04167	Millimeters	Centimeters	0.1
	Minutes	60		Inches	0.03937
	Seconds	3600		Microns	1000
Inches	Centimeters	2.54	Minutes	Days	0.000694
	Feet	0.08333		Hours	0.016667
	Meters	0.0254			
	Millimeters	25.40	Months		
			(mean calendar)	Days	30.4167
Leagues	Fathoms	2640		Weeks	4.34524
	Feet	15840		Years (calendar)	0.08328
	Kilometers	4.828			
	Miles (statute)	3	Ounces	Cubic cm	29.5735
				Cubic inches	1.80469
Liters	Cubic cm	1000		Cups	0.125
	Cubic feet	0.03531		Gallons (U.S. liquid)	0.00781
	Cubic inches	61.0237		Liters	0.02957
	Cubic meters	0.001		Pints (U.S. liquid)	0.0625
	Gallons (U.S. liquid)	0.26417		Shots	1.0
	Milliliters	1000		Teaspoons	6.0
	Ounces (U.S. fluid)	33.81402		Tablespoons	2.0
	Pints (U.S. fluid)	2.1134			
			Pints	Cubic feet	0.01671
Megabyte	Byte	1048576		Cubic inches	28.875
				Cubic yards	0.000619
Meter	Centimeters	100		Cups	2
	Fathoms	0.54681		Gallons (U.S. liquid)	0.125
	Feet	3.28084		Liters	0.473176
	Furlongs	0.00497		Ounces (U.S. fluid)	16
	Inches	39.3701		Quarts (U.S. liquid)	0.5
	Kilometers	0.001		Shots	16
	Miles (statute)	0.000621			
	Millimeters	1000	Pounds	Kilograms	0.4536
	Yards	1.0936		Ounces	16
Microns	Centimeters	0.0001	Pounds of water (0°C)	Cubic feet	0.01602
	Millimeters	0.001		Gallons (U.S.)	0.1198
Miles (nautical)	Miles (statute)	1.15078	Quarts	Cubic feet	0.0334
				Cubic inches	57.75
Miles (statute)	Feet	5280		Gallons (U.S.)	0.25
	Kilometers	1.609344		Liters	0.94635
	Meters	1609.344		Ounces (U.S. fluid)	32
	Miles (nautical)	0.86898		Pints (U.S. liquid)	2

To convert from	into	multiply by
Seconds		
(mean solar)	Hours	0.0002778
	Minutes	0.0166667
Shots	Ounces (U.S. fluid)	1
	Pints	0.0625
Square feet	Square meters	0.0929
	Square yards	0.1111
Square inches	Square centimeters	6.4516
	Square feet	0.00694
	Square yards	0.000772
Square kilometers	Acres	247.1054
	Square miles	0.3861
Square meters	Square centimeters	10000
	Square feet	10.7639
	Square inches	1550.003
Square miles	Acres	640
	Square kilometers	2.58999
Square yards	Square feet	9
	Square inches	1296
	Square meters	0.8361
Tablespoons	Cups	0.0625
	Ounces (U.S. fluid)	0.5
	Teaspoons	3

To convert from	into	multiply by
Teaspoons	Ounces (U.S. fluid)	0.16667
	Tablespoons	0.3333
Tons (short)	Kilograms	907.185
	Pounds	2000
	Tons (long)	0.89286
Townships	Acres	23040
	Square miles	36
Watts	Btu/hr	3.41214
	Kilowatts	0.001
Watt-hours	Btu	3.4144
	Cal(g)	860.42
Weeks (mean calendar)	Days	7
	Hours	168
	Minutes	10080
	Months	0.230137
	Years	0.019178
Yards	Fathoms	0.5
	Feet	3
	Furlongs	0.004545
	Inches	36
	Meters	0.9144
Years (calendar)	Days	365
	Hours	8760
	Minutes	525600
	Months	12

Common object <small>(THESE SIZES ARE EITHER EXACT OR VERY CLOSE TO EXACT.)</small>	Size
Dollar bill	2⅝ inches by 6⅛ inches
Standard credit card	2⅛ inches by 3⅜ inches
Standard business card	2 inches by 3½ inches
Quarter	15/16 inches wide
Dime	9/16 inches wide
Penny	¾ inches wide
Piece of paper	8½ by 11 inches
Legal pad	8½ by 14 inches
Business envelope (#10)	4⅜ by 9½ inches
Unsharpened pencil	7½ inches long
CD box	4⅞ by 5⅝ inches
CD	4⅝ inches in diameter
Pint of water	about a pound or 16 ounces
Cup of water	about half a pound or 8 ounces
Full can of soda	12⅔ ounces
Roll of fifty pennies	4⅓ ounces
Videotape in box	about half a pound

Index